PORTLAND OREGON 97211

bite-size desserts

WEST SLOPE COMMUNITY LIBRARY
3678 SW 78TH AVE
PORTLAND OREGON 97225

bite-size desserts

CREATING MINI SWEET TREATS, FROM CUPCAKES
AND COBBLERS TO CUSTARDS AND COOKIES

CAROLE BLOOM, CCP

WILEY

JOHN WILEY & SONS, INC.

This book is printed on acid-free paper. ∞

Copyright © 2009 by Carole Bloom. All rights reserved.

Photography copyright © 2009 by Glenn Cormier

Published by John Wiley & Sons, Inc., Hoboken, New Jersey

Published simultaneously in Canada

No part of this publication may be reproduced, stored in a retrieval system, or transmitted in any form or by any means, electronic, mechanical, photocopying, recording, scanning, or otherwise, except as permitted under Section 107 or 108 of the 1976 United States Copyright Act, without either the prior written permission of the publisher, or authorization through payment of the appropriate per-copy fee to the Copyright Clearance Center, Inc., 222 Rosewood Drive, Danvers, MA 01923, (978) 750-8400, fax (978) 646-8600, or on the Web at www.copyright.com. Requests to the publisher for permission should be addressed to the Permissions Department, John Wiley & Sons, Inc., 111 River Street, Hoboken, NJ 07030, (201) 748-6011, fax (201) 748-6008, or online at http://www.wiley.com/go/permissions.

Limit of Liability/Disclaimer of Warranty: While the publisher and author have used their best efforts in preparing this book, they make no representations or warranties with respect to the accuracy or completeness of the contents of this book and specifically disclaim any implied warranties of merchantability or fitness for a particular purpose. No warranty may be created or extended by sales representatives or written sales materials. The advice and strategies contained herein may not be suitable for your situation. You should consult with a professional where appropriate. Neither the publisher nor author shall be liable for any loss of profit or any other commercial damages, including but not limited to special, incidental, consequential, or other damages.

For general information on our other products and services or for technical support, please contact our Customer Care Department within the United States at (800) 762-2974, outside the United States at (317) 572-3993 or fax (317) 572-4002.

Wiley also publishes its books in a variety of electronic formats. Some content that appears in print may not be available in electronic books. For more information about Wiley products, visit our Web site at www.wiley.com.

DESIGN BY Vertigo Design, NYC

FOOD STYLING BY Carole Bloom

PROP STYLING BY Carole Bloom, Glenn Cormier, and Jerry Olivas

LIBRARY OF CONGRESS CATALOGING-IN-PUBLICATION DATA:

Bloom, Carole.

Bite-size desserts / Carole Bloom.

    p. cm.

Includes index.

ISBN 978-0-470-22697-1 (cloth : alk. paper)

1. Desserts. I. Title.

TX773.B6145 2010

641.8'6—dc22

                2008019011

PRINTED IN CHINA

10 9 8 7 6 5 4 3 2 1

With love to:

MY MOTHER, FLORENCE

MY SWEETIE BOYS, TIGER AND CASANOVA

MY NIECE, ANNA, WHO IS AN AMAZING YOUNG WOMAN

AND MY HUSBAND, JERRY, WHO ALWAYS INSPIRES ME TO DO MY BEST.

contents

ACKNOWLEDGMENTS viii

INTRODUCTION ix

chapter one

MAKING BITE-SIZE DESSERTS: INGREDIENTS, EQUIPMENT, AND TECHNIQUES

Ingredients 2 | Equipment 5 | Techniques 8

chapter two

CAKES, CUPCAKES, AND BROWNIES

Brown Sugar and Cornmeal Bundt Cakes with Honey Whipped Cream 12 | Mixed Spice and Walnut Bundt Cakes 15 | Spiced Chocolate-Pecan Bundt Cakes 17 | Dried Cherry, Toasted Pecan, and Sour Cream Pound Cakes 18 | Cinnamon–Sour Cream Cupcakes 21 | Peanut Butter Cupcakes with Bittersweet Chocolate Ganache Frosting 23 | Bittersweet Chocolate Five-Spice Cupcakes 26 | Wicked Brownie Bites 29 | Gingerbread Bites 31 | Apricot-Orange Loaf Cakes 34 | Petite Cheesecakes with Raspberry Sauce 36 | Walnut and Lemon Tea Cakes 38 | Maple Walnut Tea Cakes 39 | Mini Pistachio Tea Cakes 40 | Almond-Cornmeal Cakes 41 | Triple Lemon Pound Cakes 43

chapter three

SCONES, SHORTCAKES, MUFFINS, AND PASTRIES

Cornmeal–Dried Cherry Scones 47 | Raisin and Walnut Scones 49 | Macadamia Nut and Toasted Coconut Scones 51 | Lemon-Cornmeal Shortcakes 53 | Raspberry, Ginger, and Honey Shortcakes 55 | Apricot, Almond, and Toasted Coconut Muffins 58 | Coconut–Macadamia Nut Muffins 59 | Spiced Buttermilk Doughnut Holes 60 | Caramelized Pear and Dried Cherry Strudel 61

chapter four

TARTLETS, COBBLERS, CRISPS, TURNOVERS, AND GALETTES

Double Lemon Meringue Tartlets 65 | Bittersweet Chocolate and Hazelnut Tartlets 67 | Cacao Nib–Walnut Ganache Tartlets 69 | Caramelized Walnut Tartlets 72 | Venetian Almond Tartlets 75 | Almond, Lemon, and Berry Tartlets 77 | Pavlovas with Passion Fruit Sauce 79 | Mixed Berry Cobblers 82 | Peachy Cobblers 84 | Pear and Triple Ginger Cobblers 86 | Raspberry-Blueberry Crisps 89 | Apple-Walnut Crisps 92 | Blueberry Turnovers 94 | Nectarine and Walnut Galettes 97 | Pear and Pecan Galettes 99

chapter five
MOUSSES, CUSTARDS, AND PUDDINGS

Creamy Caramel Mousse 103 | Mocha Mousse 104 | Cardamom Pots de Crème 106 | Chocolate-Espresso Pots de Crème 108 | Maple Pots de Crème 109 | Raspberry and Lemon Cream Martinis 110 | Mocha Soufflés with Cacao Nib Whipped Cream 113 | Mascarpone-Raspberry Parfaits 115 | Lemon Crème Brûlée 118 | Coconut Crème Brûlée 119 | Butterscotch Crème Brûlée 120 | Toasted Pecan Crème Caramel 123 | Toasted Coconut–Chocolate Pudding 125 | Rice Pudding 126

chapter six
COOKIES

Walnut Fingerprint Cookies 129 | Fudgy Chocolate-Hazelnut Bites 131 | Hazelnut and Cacao Nib Madeleines 132 | Devilish Dark Chocolate Madeleines 134 | Crackly Ginger Chips 136 | Peek-a-Boo Hazelnut Sandwich Cookies 138 | Walnut Filo Triangles 140 | Almond and Mocha Macaroon Sandwich Cookies 142 | Toasted Pecan Shortbread Bites 145 | Lemon-Lime-Coconut Squares 146 | Cardamom Butter Cookies 148 | Pecan-Ginger Biscotti 151 | Cantuccini di Prato 152 | Toasty Oatmeal Cookies 153 | Man-in-the-Moon Cookies 154 | Tuile Cookie Cups 155

chapter seven
SORBETS AND ICE CREAMS

Raspberry Sorbet Shots 158 | Cantaloupe Sorbet 160 | Toasted Coconut Ice Cream 161 | Double Ginger Ice Cream 163 | Mocha Ice Cream 164 | Buttermilk and Nutmeg Ice Cream 165 | Peanut Butter Ice Cream 166 | Chocolate and Coffee Ice Cream Sandwiches 167

chapter eight
CANDIES

Almond Buttercrunch Toffee 170 | Gianduia Truffle Cups 173 | Salted Caramel–Bittersweet Chocolate Truffles 174 | Bittersweet Chocolate–Mint Truffle Squares 177 | Green Tea Truffles 178 | White Chocolate–Coconut Mounds 179 | Bittersweet Chocolate–Peppermint Candy Bark 180 | Sea Salted Peanut Brittle 183 | Malted Milk Chocolate Balls 184

APPENDICES

Sources for Ingredients and Equipment 185 | Measurement Equivalents 186 | Metric Conversions 188

INDEX 190

acknowledgments

ALTHOUGH WRITING A BOOK IS A SOLITARY VENTURE, IT TAKES A TEAM TO BRING IT TO FRUITION.
WITH GRATEFUL THANKS TO:

Susan Ginsburg, my terrific agent, who is always there when I need her and always follows through.

Pam Chirls, my immensely talented editor, for the opportunity to work together again and for her excitement about this book.

Ava Wilder, senior production editor, for her enthusiasm for this book and so skillfully guiding it through the publishing process.

Rochelle Palermo Torres, copyeditor, for her great attention to detail, helping to make this book read so consistently. And Deborah Weiss Geline, proofreader, for her eagle eye.

Alison Lew of Vertigo Design for the exciting book design, and Jeff Faust for the cover design.

The entire team at John Wiley & Sons, Inc., for supporting this book and bringing it to the public.

Florence Bloom, my mother, who takes great pride in my work and is always supportive.

Kitty Morse, good friend and colleague, who is a great sounding board and great support.

Lesa Heebner, good friend and fashionista, who is a big source of encouragement. I always look forward to Lesa's e-mails and our "show and tell" dates.

Bonnie Manion, another good friend, who is always very interested in and supportive of my work, and for bringing me the occasional terrific eggs from her chickens, "the girls."

My neighbors and friends for cheerfully eating my experiments and giving me feedback.

Land O'Lakes for providing me with plenty of delicious butter for developing and testing the recipes.

Scharffen Berger Chocolate Maker and Valrhona Chocolate for supplying me with superior-quality chocolate to use.

Patricia Rain, The Vanilla Queen, for superb vanilla products.

Photographer Glenn Cormier for his incredible talent that makes my desserts look so luscious. Glenn and I have a great collaboration, and working together is a true pleasure. This is our third book, and I look forward to more in the future.

Ben Carufel, Glenn's assistant, who makes our photo sessions go as smooth as butter and greatly enjoys tasting what we photograph.

Tiger and Casanova, my feline boys, who are a constant source of amusement and bring so much love and joy to my life.

Jerry Olivas, my husband, for his unstinting assistance with everything, including tasting all the recipes (often more than once), providing ideas, editing, food and prop styling, being the general gofer, making me laugh a lot, and making my life sweet.

introduction

HAVE YOU EVER WANTED JUST A BITE OR TWO OF A SCRUMPTIOUS DESSERT? DO YOU SOMETIMES ORDER ONE NORMAL-SIZE DESSERT WITH SEVERAL FORKS OR SPOONS SO EVERYONE CAN SHARE? AND, HOW ABOUT WHEN YOU ASK FOR A TAKE-OUT CONTAINER TO TAKE HOME THE DESSERT THAT YOU HAVEN'T FINISHED?

More and more, people want smaller-size desserts, but they don't want to sacrifice great flavor, texture, and sensory experiences. *Bite-Size Desserts* offers 87 recipes for small-size desserts that are easy to prepare, look beautiful, and are every bit as delicious as their full-size cousins.

With portion control becoming more prevalent in our health- and weight-conscious society, the desserts in this book are right in line with what people desire. Smaller-size desserts are eaten with only a few bites, so less is consumed. Also, bite-size desserts allow flexibility for people to choose to have one, or two, or maybe three. Bite-size desserts are a great option for a group of people at a dinner party or other gathering who have different dessert likes as well as different appetites. And you will not hear guests saying, "Make mine small," because bite-size desserts are just that—small portions.

One great benefit of bite-size desserts that's exciting to me is that a variety can be offered. Everyone doesn't have to eat the same dessert, and those who like a certain one are free to eat just that. And because of their small size, you don't feel compelled to eat a large serving at one time. It's fine to have one, come back a little later for another, and maybe even another one after that.

For a buffet event, bite-size desserts are perfect because they are so easy to handle. Whether it's a buffet or serving at the table, there is a lot of flexibility for presenting bite-size desserts because many different platters, trays, and dishes can be used. I like to use decorative pieces of tile or stone as a creative serving surface. And I also

like to use a multitiered plate holder, like those used for serving afternoon tea. For individual servings there are a variety of fun options, from colorful and whimsical paper napkins to petite plates and bowls.

We have all seen those exquisite miniature desserts that look like little jewels. They look like they would be hard to make, but that is a myth. Having made many of these in my career, I can assure you that smaller desserts don't require any more skill or time than regular-size desserts. Also, one thing that I especially like about many small-size desserts is that you can get your hands into shaping and forming them. Several of the desserts in this book, such as scones, shortcakes, galettes, cookies, ice creams, and candies, are made on a small scale, while others are made using small pans, molds, and ramekins, which are very easy to find.

This book starts with a chapter that covers ingredients, equipment, and techniques. Information is provided on many of the ingredients that you will use, including types of sugar, chocolate, and flour, as well as many other basics. Most of the equipment and tools that are needed are discussed, including the staples that all dessert makers should have, as well as some unique, but easy to obtain, pieces that are used to make bite-size desserts. For example, this is where you will find information on small-size pans, molds, and ramekins. Also, in this chapter various techniques for making bite-size desserts are explained.

The recipes are organized by category of desserts. There are seven chapters covering a very large variety of desserts. There is something for everyone, including chapters on cakes, cupcakes, and brownies; scones, shortcakes, muffins, and pastries; tartlets, cobblers, crisps, turnovers, and galettes; mousses, custards, and puddings; cookies; sorbets and ice creams; and candies. You can start anywhere in the book. Just go to the Contents and select the category that you desire. Some recipes may require a few steps and take a little longer to make than others, but everything in this book can be made easily by the novice dessert maker.

Recipes begin with a note that gives information about what makes the dessert special and, where appropriate, makes suggestions for when to serve the dessert, such as a particular season or event. Underneath this you will find the specific yield and the required pan, ramekin, or mold, if necessary. This is followed by a list of the ingredients along with the easy-to-follow instructions for making the recipe. At the end of each recipe is the section called Keeping (storing). Where appropriate, the following are also included: Making a Change (variations), Streamlining (do-ahead), Adding Style (decorating), and Troubleshooting (preventing problems).

At the end of the book is a list of sources for ingredients and equipment, a table of measurement equivalents, a table of metric conversions, and an index.

As with most people, I love desserts and I definitely don't want to give them up. But I don't want to overindulge, which is so easy to do. Whenever I look into those display cases at a bakery, coffee house, or specialty food shop, I say to myself, "Those are such large portions." And the same is true with restaurant desserts. Also, it's too easy to find desserts and confections sold in grocery stores in those extra-large bonus sizes. Bite-Size Desserts is the answer to having fabulous desserts that are easy to make and are just the right size.

It was fun developing and testing all of the recipes for this book. They have become staples in my household, and my hope is that they will become your favorites, too.

chapter one

MAKING BITE-SIZE DESSERTS
ingredients, equipment, and techniques

ingredients

I ALWAYS RECOMMEND USING THE BEST-QUALITY INGREDIENTS. WHEN YOU USE TOP-QUALITY INGREDIENTS, YOUR DESSERTS WILL BE THE BEST THEY CAN BE. SOME OF THE DESSERTS IN THIS BOOK ARE MADE WITH ONLY A FEW INGREDIENTS, MAKING IT HARD TO MASK POOR QUALITY.

BUTTER

All of my recipes use unsalted butter. Different brands of butter have different amounts of salt in them, and it's hard to know what that amount is. By using unsalted butter, you control the amount of salt in the recipes. I used Land O'Lakes unsalted butter to develop all of the recipes in this book. I recommend weighing butter for accuracy. Two tablespoons of butter is equal to one ounce. When a recipe calls for "softened" butter, the butter should be soft enough to hold the indentation of a finger pressed into it, but not so soft that it turns liquid (see Butter Softening page 8). Don't replace butter with margarine or vegetable shortening. They work differently from butter and won't produce the same texture, flavor, or mouthfeel.

CHOCOLATE

Unsweetened, bittersweet, milk, and white chocolate, along with cacao nibs and cocoa powder, are used for the recipes in this book. Unsweetened chocolate is pure chocolate with no added sugar. It provides excellent deep chocolate flavor. Bittersweet chocolate has the highest cacao content after unsweetened chocolate. I use bittersweet chocolate with a cacao content between 62 and 72 percent for these recipes. I don't recommend using chocolate with a cacao content higher than 72 percent because it will react differently with the other ingredients and the outcome won't be the same. Regular milk chocolate has between 10 and 12 percent

cacao content. I prefer to use dark milk chocolate with a cacao content of 38 to 42 percent for the best flavor. Be sure to use real white chocolate made with cocoa butter rather than fake white chocolate made with vegetable fats. It's not a good idea to substitute one type of chocolate for another because each has different amounts of cacao content and body. There are many brands of chocolate on the market. I always suggest tasting chocolate plain to make sure you like it before using it to make desserts. The characteristics to look for when choosing chocolate are appearance, aroma, snap, flavor, mouthfeel, and aftertaste.

There are two types of cocoa powder, natural and Dutch-processed. Natural cocoa powder has acidity and fruity qualities that are softened by adding an alkali to it during processing to create Dutch-processed cocoa. I like both types, but always make sure to use the type called for in the recipes because they react differently to the different types of leavening. In cases where leavening isn't used, it's fine to use either type of cocoa powder.

Cacao nibs are the hulled, roasted, unsweetened kernels of cacao beans that are broken into small pieces. They are great for adding chocolate flavor and texture to recipes.

EGGS

Eggs are one of the basic ingredients and serve many functions in desserts. They provide structure, color, texture, moisture, flavor, and leavening. I use extra-large eggs for all of my desserts. If you have trouble finding extra-large eggs, it is fine to substitute large eggs in the recipes that call for up to four eggs. Always check the date on the carton of eggs and buy them as fresh as possible. Don't use egg substitutes in place of real eggs for making desserts.

FLOUR

Flour provides structure, texture, and color to desserts and is one of the fundamental ingredients in baking. All-purpose flour and cake flour are used for the desserts in this book. All-purpose flour is a blend of hard and soft wheat flours with medium protein (gluten) content. Cake flour has less protein than all-purpose flour and is used to create more delicate textures. Don't use bread flour or pastry flour, which, respectively, have higher and lower gluten content than all-purpose flour and cake flour. Also, don't substitute whole-wheat flour for all-purpose flour in these recipes because it's heavier and denser and will change the texture and consistency of the desserts. If all you have on hand is all-purpose flour, and a recipe calls for cake flour, you can use the all-purpose flour. For each 1 cup of all-purpose flour used in place of cake flour, remove 2 tablespoons. The same is true for cake flour; you can use it in place of all-purpose flour by adding 2 tablespoons for each cup of cake flour.

NUTS

Nuts provide wonderful flavor and texture to desserts, and they make great garnishes. Several different nuts are used in these recipes, including walnuts, almonds, hazelnuts, macadamia nuts, peanuts, and pecans. Most nuts can be substituted for one another in recipes. Try to buy nuts in the form in which you need them—whole (blanched, salted, or unblanched), sliced, slivered, or ground, and toasted, salted, and unsalted.

SALT

One of the main purposes of salt is to help to enhance the flavor of many ingredients used in desserts. I use either coarse kosher salt or fine-grained sea salt in my recipes. Both of these are less salty than table salt, and I prefer their flavor. Because there are many types and colors of sea salt on the market these days, be careful to use a neutral sea salt that won't overpower the flavor of the dessert.

SPICES

Cinnamon, cardamom, cloves, ginger, nutmeg, and vanilla add their vibrant flavors to many recipes in this book. It's possible to substitute one spice for another or to use a single spice instead of a blend. Let your own taste be your guide. Once spices are ground, they begin to lose their flavor, so be sure to buy them in small quantities and use them quickly. Ginger comes in different forms: ground, crystallized, un-crystallized candied (like crystallized but without the outer coating of sugar), and fresh. Some recipes call for ginger in several forms, layering the flavor and making it more pronounced. I always grate nutmeg freshly when using it because it's so easy to do and makes such a distinct difference in flavor. Vanilla is used primarily as extract, but you can always substitute vanilla paste with excellent results.

SUGAR

Sugar is an essential ingredient that adds color, texture, flavor, and moisture to desserts. Granulated, superfine, confectioners', light brown, turbinado, and Demerara sugars are used for the desserts in this book. Superfine sugar is ground finer than granulated sugar so it dissolves very easily, but one can be interchanged for the other. Confectioners' sugar, also known as powdered sugar, is most often used for decorating or garnishing. I like to use light brown sugar to give extra depth of flavor to many desserts. Since light brown sugar has more molasses than granulated sugar, don't substitute one for the other completely; however, you can replace about one-third of the granulated sugar called for in a recipe with light brown sugar. Dark brown sugar has more molasses than light brown sugar, which deepens its flavor. It's fine to substitute dark brown sugar for light brown, but be aware that the flavor will be more pronounced. Turbinado and Demerara sugars are raw brown sugars with coarse crystals. They are primarily used for garnishing but can be used to replace brown sugar in recipes.

equipment

AS WITH INGREDIENTS, BUY THE BEST-QUALITY EQUIPMENT YOU CAN AND IT WILL LAST FOR MANY, MANY YEARS. USING QUALITY EQUIPMENT MAKES YOUR TIME IN THE KITCHEN A PLEASURE AND ALLOWS YOU TO BE THE BEST DESSERT MAKER YOU CAN BE.

BAKING PANS AND RAMEKINS

Several different pans and ramekins are used for making bite-size desserts.

Bundt cupcake pans are used for baking some cakes. They are made of heavy-cast, nonstick aluminum and have 12 cavities, each measuring 2½ × 1¼ inches. Each cavity holds ¼ cup. Because of their size, one of these cakes easily serves two people.

Fluted-edge tartlet pans used for bite-size desserts come in two sizes, 2 × ¾-inch and 1⅝ × ¾ inch. The larger-size tartlet pans hold 4 teaspoons each and the smaller ones hold 2 teaspoons each. The fluted edge of the pans leaves its impression on the tartlets and cookies baked in the pans. Each of these sizes of tartlet pans comes in packages of 24.

Loaf cakes are baked in metal pans that measure 4 × 2¼ × 1¼ inches with a volume of ½ cup. Because these are larger than other bite-size desserts, loaf cakes serve two to three people.

Madeleine cookies are baked in special flat rectangular pans that have shallow shell-shaped, ribbed cavities. These uniquely shaped cavities give madeleines their characteristic shape. For bite-size desserts, use mini madeleine pans that have twenty 1⅝ × 1⅛–inch cavities. Each cavity holds 1 teaspoon.

Mini muffin pans with 12 cavities, measuring 1¾ × 1 inch, are used for muffins, cupcakes, and some cakes. Each cavity holds 2 tablespoons. I prefer the silicone mini muffin pans because they are nonstick and don't have

to be lined with papers. Also, it's very easy to remove the baked goods from them because they are so flexible.

Ramekins made of white porcelain have straight sides and come in several different sizes and shapes. The size most useful for bite-size desserts is round, measuring 2½ inches wide and 1⅝ inches deep. These are used for many custard desserts, such as crème caramel, pots de crème, crème brûlée, puddings, soufflés, and cobblers. For baking crisps, I use oval-shaped ramekins that measure 3¼ × 2¼ inches wide and ¾ inch deep. Both round and oval ramekins have a volume of ¼ cup.

BAKING SHEETS

Baking sheets are used for baking cookies, scones, and galettes, and for holding tartlet, cake, and muffin and cupcake pans as they bake. Heavy-duty metal baking sheets are the best to use because they don't buckle from the heat of the oven. These have 1-inch-high straight sides with rolled rims on all sides. They come in different sizes, so be sure to buy the size that fits your oven and leaves a couple of inches on all sides for the air to circulate in the oven.

CANDY (SUGAR) THERMOMETER

This tool is crucial when cooking sugar mixtures to a particular temperature. A sugar thermometer reads between the ranges of 100° and 400°F in two-degree increments. Be sure that the thermometer takes the temperature of the mixture in the pan, not the bottom of the pan. For this reason, my preference is a Taylor thermometer. It has a metal body with a foot that sits on the bottom of the pan. Clips hold the glass thermometer in place and keep it elevated, so you get an accurate reading.

COOKIE CUTTERS

There are many cookie cutters available, either as sets of graduated sizes or individually. They are usually about 1 inch high, made from either metal or firm plastic, and open at the top and bottom. Some cookie cutters have handles at the top. Make sure your cutters are sharp and sturdy.

FOOD PROCESSOR

A food processor is one of the most useful tools in the dessert kitchen. It makes tart dough and some cookie doughs easily and quickly and is excellent for chopping and grinding nuts of all shapes and sizes. A large-capacity food processor is good to use to accomplish most tasks, but a mini processor is nice to have for chopping or grinding a small quantity of nuts. An extra bowl and metal blade are very handy to have, allowing you to accomplish many tasks without having to stop and clean up in between them.

ICE CREAM SCOOPS

These are great tools for filling mini muffin and cupcake pans, tartlet shells, and for scooping out truffle cream and some cookie doughs. I use a 1-inch round scoop for truffles and doughnut holes and a 1½-inch scoop for most other tasks. My favorite type of ice cream scoop has a round bowl at one end of a shaft with a lever on the handle. When the

lever is squeezed, an arc-shaped strip of metal moves from side to side in the bowl to release what the bowl holds.

MEASURING CUPS AND SPOONS

Use liquid measuring cups with pour spouts for measuring liquids because these have a little extra room at the top for liquids to move around in without spilling out. For dry ingredients, use dry measuring cups that come in nested sets in graduated sizes of ¼ cup, ⅓ cup, ½ cup, and 1 cup. You can fill the measuring cup with the ingredient and level it off at the top using the flat side of a knife or spatula.

Measuring spoons are used for both liquid and dry ingredients. They typically come in sets of ¼ teaspoon, ½ teaspoon, 1 teaspoon, and 1 tablespoon. I like to detach them from the ring and store the same sizes together in small jars on my countertop. This makes it easy to find the size I need quickly without dragging them all around together. I like to have a few sets of measuring spoons because I use them so often.

MICROPLANE GRATERS

These are stainless-steel, razor-sharp graters with non-clogging teeth set into sturdy plastic handles. There are several types of graters designed for specific tasks, such as shaving chocolate, zesting citrus fruit, and grinding spices, like whole nutmeg. Keep them in a place that is easy to reach, like a container on the kitchen counter or in a drawer.

MIXERS

An electric mixer is one of the most important tools for making desserts. A stand mixer allows your hands to be free for adding ingredients or to attend to other tasks while it is mixing. But all desserts can be made using a hand-held mixer. Keep your stand mixer on the countertop where it is easy to reach. If it's buried in a cabinet, you may think twice about making dessert when the mood strikes. Having an extra bowl, flat beater, and wire whip allows you to move from one recipe to another without having to stop and clean up.

PASTRY BAGS AND TIPS

Pastry bags are great for filling baked tartlet shells and cupcake and muffin pans, and for decorating. They are made from a variety of materials, such as nylon, polyester, plastic, and parchment paper. I prefer 10-, 12-, and 14-inch pastry bags because they hold enough without being overfilled. Be careful not to fill a pastry bag more than halfway full or it becomes too difficult to handle.

Pastry tips come in a huge variety of sizes and shapes. A plain round (½-inch) opening and an open star tip will handle most tasks. I prefer to use the 2-inch-tall pastry tips, which can be easily cleaned in the dishwasher.

PASTRY BRUSHES

Pastry brushes have several uses in the dessert kitchen. They butter the inside of pans, brush the tops of scones with liquid, apply glazes, brush excess flour off dough, and wash down the sides of the pan when cooking sugar mixtures. I recommend using natural bristle pastry brushes because they are softer than synthetic materials and won't burn. These usually have a wooden handle and should be washed by hand with hot, soapy water, not in the dishwasher. Pastry brushes come in a variety of sizes. One inch wide is a good size for most tasks. It's a good idea to keep brushes used for butter separate from those used to wash down the sides of pans.

ROLLING PINS

A rolling pin is used to roll out dough for tartlets, galettes, and cookies. There are several types available made from a variety of materials, such as wood, metal, and glass, and one type that is covered with silicone. Which type you choose is a personal preference.

SPATULAS

Rubber and heat-resistant spatulas have several uses in the dessert kitchen, such as stirring mixtures while they cook, blending ingredients together, and scraping down the sides of mixing bowls. It's a good idea to keep a few sizes of spatulas handy. The heat-resistant type comes in a large variety of colors, which is a good way to tell it apart from those that can't take the heat.

An offset spatula is a hand-held tool. It has a flexible, slim, stainless-steel blade with a rounded tip. The blade makes a Z-like shape, stepping down from the wooden handle about 1 inch. This shape allows the blade to fit into many places and is handy for icing and decorative tasks. Offset spatulas come in several sizes, but for bite-size desserts I prefer a 3-inch blade.

TIMERS

A timer is invaluable for knowing when your baked desserts are ready. Use a timer that is easy to read and to use, and become familiar with it before your first use. It's always a good idea to set the timer for the least amount of time called for in the recipe; you can always add more time if necessary.

techniques

USING THE CORRECT TECHNIQUES MAKES DESSERT-MAKING SO MUCH EASIER THAN TRYING TO GUESS THE RIGHT WAY TO ACCOMPLISH A TASK. HERE ARE SEVERAL TECHNIQUES THAT WILL HELP YOU TO EASILY MAKE GREAT BITE-SIZE DESSERTS.

BUTTER

SOFTENING Soften butter by letting it stand at room temperature or microwave it on the lowest power for 5-second bursts, checking its texture after each burst. The butter is at the right texture when you can easily make a thumbprint impression in it.

CHOCOLATE

CHOPPING Use a very sharp chef's knife on a cutting board or a tool called a chocolate chipper to chop chocolate. Chop chocolate from a bar or a chunk that isn't too large. It's best to chop chocolate into matchstick-size pieces so it will melt evenly. I don't recommend chopping chocolate in a food processor because the processor beats up the chocolate too much and may melt it.

DECORATING To drizzle the top of a dessert with melted chocolate, place the chocolate in a parchment paper pastry bag. Roll down the top of the pastry bag tightly and snip off a tiny (1/16 to 1/8 inch) opening at the pointed end. Hold the pastry bag straight up and down and about an inch above the surface to be decorated. Apply slight pressure to the pastry bag with the hand that holds it and use the other hand to help stabilize the bag, while moving your hand from side to side. Or dip the tines of a fork into melted chocolate and swing the fork from side to side while the chocolate drips off. It's a good idea to practice this on waxed paper.

To dip cookies in chocolate, hold a cookie between your thumb and forefinger. Dip it into the bowl of chocolate, then remove it from the bowl and let the excess chocolate drip off. Place the dipped cookie on a lined baking sheet and let the chocolate set up either at room temperature or in the refrigerator for 15 minutes.

MELTING Melt chocolate either in the top pan of a double boiler or in a microwave oven. If using a double boiler, make sure the top pan or bowl fits snugly to the bottom pan so no water or steam can escape. Keep the water level in the lower pan no more than an inch deep and don't let the water touch the bottom of the top pan or bowl. Place the pan over very low heat and stir the chocolate with a rubber spatula frequently as it melts. When removing the top pan of the double boiler, be sure to wipe the bottom and sides dry to remove any possible water drops.

To melt chocolate in a microwave oven, place it in a microwave-safe bowl and melt on the lowest power for 30-second bursts. Stir with a rubber spatula after each burst.

STORAGE Store chocolate at room temperature, not in the refrigerator or freezer. If stored in the refrigerator or freezer, chocolate will develop moisture that will condense on it when it's melted, causing it to seize. If you have a wine cellar, it's the perfect place to store chocolate.

COCONUT

TOASTING Spread the coconut in a single layer in a cake or pie pan and toast it in a 325°F oven for 5 to 7 minutes, stirring every 2 minutes, until it's light golden brown. Remove the pan from the oven and cool completely on a rack.

CREAM

WHIPPING Cold cream whips best because it holds on to the air whipped into it. If possible, chill the bowl and beaters before whipping cream. Use an electric stand mixer or a hand-held mixer and a bowl that is large enough for the cream to increase in volume. Start whipping on medium speed to prevent the cream from sloshing out of the bowl and increase the speed as it thickens. Watch the cream carefully as it whips because it's easy to overwhip it, causing the cream to become too firm. If this happens, repair it by adding another tablespoon or two of cream and whip it on medium speed until the consistency becomes smooth. Whipped cream can be covered and refrigerated for a few hours if you want to make it in advance.

DOUGH

ROLLING Roll out dough on a smooth, flat surface between sheets of lightly floured waxed or parchment paper. Roll from the center out to the edge, give the dough a quarter turn, and repeat. Moving the dough around as you roll makes it easy to roll it out evenly. Occasionally peel off the top piece of paper to make sure the dough isn't sticking. Lightly dust the dough with flour. Turn the package over and do the same thing to make sure the bottom side isn't sticking. Roll the dough until it reaches the thickness or size called for in the recipe.

EGGS AND EGG WHITES

WHIPPING For eggs and egg whites to whip to their full volume, it's best for them to be at room temperature. If they are too cold, let them stand until they warm up or place them in a bowl of warm water for several minutes. Use either an electric stand mixer with the wire whip attachment or a hand-held mixer and a bowl that has enough room for the eggs to triple in volume. Begin whipping on medium speed and increase to medium-high as the eggs increase in size. It's very important that egg whites don't come in contact with any fat or they won't whip properly. Be sure all utensils used to whip egg whites are clean and completely grease free. Egg whites can be frozen and stored up to 6 months. Be sure to defrost them completely and bring them to room temperature before using.

NUTS

CHOPPING AND GRINDING Chop nuts on a cutting board with a chef's knife or in the work bowl of a food processor fitted with the steel blade, pulsing until reaching the chop preferred (coarse, medium, or fine). To grind the nuts, continue pulsing until they are finely ground. All nuts release their natural oils when chopped or ground in a food processor. To keep the nuts from turning into paste, add 1 tablespoon of sugar to each cup of most nuts before grinding. Because hazelnuts and macadamia nuts have more oil than other nuts, add 2 tablespoons of sugar for each cup before grinding.

STORAGE To keep the natural oil in nuts from turning rancid, store the nuts in the freezer in an airtight bag or container for up to a year. They can also be stored in a cool, dry place for short periods of time.

TOASTING Spread the nuts in a single layer in a cake or pie pan or on a baking sheet and toast in a 350°F oven. For all nuts, except hazelnuts, toast for 3 to 5 minutes, shake the pan to stir, and toast another 3 to 5 minutes, until they are light golden brown. Remove the pan from the oven and cool it completely on a rack. Hazelnuts need to toast for 15 to 18 minutes, until the skins split and the nuts turn light golden brown. Remove the pan from the oven and pour the hazelnuts onto a kitchen towel. Rub the towel together to remove most of the skins.

chapter two

CAKES, CUPCAKES, AND BROWNIES

brown sugar and cornmeal bundt cakes with honey whipped cream

EVERYONE WHO EATS THESE LITTLE CAKES LOVES THEM! BROWN SUGAR GIVES THEM A RICH, WARM FLAVOR REMINISCENT OF MAPLE SYRUP, AND CORNMEAL ADDS A PLEASANTLY GRAINY, CHEWY TEXTURE. A SMALL AMOUNT OF LEMON EXTRACT AND LEMON ZEST LIFTS THE OVERALL FLAVOR. BECAUSE THESE ARE LARGER THAN MOST BITE-SIZE DESSERTS, EACH CAKE CAN EASILY SERVE TWO.

MAKES 1 dozen Bundt cakes, 12 to 24 servings | USE one 12-cavity 2½ x 1¼–inch nonstick Bundt cupcake pan

Nonstick baking spray

4 ounces (8 tablespoons, 1 stick) unsalted butter, softened

⅔ cup (4 ounces) firmly packed light brown sugar

2 extra-large eggs, at room temperature

1 extra-large egg yolk, at room temperature

½ cup (2¼ ounces) all-purpose flour

½ cup (3 ounces) fine yellow cornmeal

Pinch of kosher or fine-grained sea salt

¼ teaspoon pure lemon extract

¼ teaspoon pure vanilla extract

Finely grated zest of 2 lemons, divided

⅓ cup heavy whipping cream

2 tablespoons honey

CAKES

Position a rack in the center of the oven and preheat the oven to 325°F. Spray the cavities of the cupcake pan with nonstick baking spray and place the pan on a baking sheet.
• • •
Beat the butter in the bowl of an electric stand mixer with the flat beater attachment or in a large mixing bowl using a hand-held mixer on medium speed until it's fluffy, about 2 minutes. Add the brown sugar and beat together well.
• • •
Use a fork to lightly beat the eggs and egg yolk together in a small bowl. Add to the butter mixture a tablespoon at a time. Stop and scrape down the bottom and sides of the bowl with a rubber spatula a couple of times to help mix evenly. The mixture may look curdled as the eggs are added, but as you scrape down the bowl, the mixture will smooth out.
• • •
In a medium-size bowl, mix together the flour, cornmeal, and salt. Add to the butter mixture in 3 stages, mixing thoroughly after each addition. Add the lemon and vanilla extracts and the zest from 1 lemon and mix thoroughly.
• • •
Use a spoon or a 1½-inch round ice cream scoop to divide the batter evenly among the cavities of the cupcake pan.
• • •
Bake the cakes for 30 minutes, until golden and a cake tester inserted in the center comes out with no crumbs clinging to it. Remove the baking sheet from the oven and transfer the cupcake pan to a rack to cool completely. Invert the pan to remove the cakes.
• • •

HONEY WHIPPED CREAM

Whip the cream in a chilled bowl of an electric stand mixer with the wire whip attachment or in a large mixing bowl using a hand-held mixer on medium speed until frothy. Add the honey and continue to whip until the cream holds soft peaks.
• • •

Fit a 12-inch pastry bag with a large open star tip and fill it partway with the whipped cream. Pipe a rosette of cream in the center indentation of each cake.

• • •

GARNISH
Sprinkle the remaining zest of 1 lemon over the top of the cream on each cake.

• • •

keeping Store the cakes, without the whipped cream, between layers of waxed paper in an airtight container at room temperature up to 3 days. To freeze up to 3 months, wrap the container snugly in several layers of plastic wrap and aluminum foil. Use a large piece of masking tape and an indelible marker to label and date the contents. If frozen, defrost the cakes overnight in the refrigerator and bring to room temperature before serving.

mixed spice and walnut bundt cakes

A WARM BLEND OF SPICES AND TOASTED WALNUTS GIVES THESE LITTLE CAKES LOTS OF FLAVOR. A DUSTING OF CONFECTIONERS' SUGAR IS ALL THE ADORNMENT THEY NEED. THESE ARE PERFECT FOR AFTERNOON COFFEE OR TEA OR WARMED UP FOR BREAKFAST. TRY SERVING THEM FOR DESSERT WITH A SCOOP OF ICE CREAM. BECAUSE THESE ARE LARGER THAN MOST BITE-SIZE DESSERTS, EACH CAKE CAN EASILY SERVE TWO.

MAKES 1 dozen Bundt cakes, 12 to 24 servings | USE one 12-cavity 2½ x 1¼–inch nonstick Bundt cupcake pan

Nonstick baking spray

⅔ cup (3 ounces) finely chopped walnuts

2 ounces (4 tablespoons, ½ stick) unsalted butter, softened

⅓ cup (2 ounces) granulated sugar

¼ cup (1½ ounces) firmly packed light brown sugar

1 extra-large egg, at room temperature

¾ cup (3¼ ounces) cake flour

½ teaspoon baking powder

¼ teaspoon baking soda

¾ teaspoon ground cinnamon

¼ teaspoon ground ginger

⅛ teaspoon ground cloves

½ teaspoon freshly grated nutmeg

⅛ teaspoon kosher or fine-grained sea salt

¾ teaspoon pure vanilla extract

¼ cup buttermilk

1 tablespoon confectioners' sugar

Position a rack in the center of the oven and preheat the oven to 350°F. Spray the cavities of the cupcake pan with nonstick baking spray and place the pan on a baking sheet.
• • •
Place the walnuts in a cake or pie pan and toast in the oven for 6 minutes. Remove the pan from the oven and cool on a rack.
• • •
Beat the butter in the bowl of an electric stand mixer with the flat beater attachment or in a large mixing bowl using a hand-held mixer on medium speed until it's fluffy, about 2 minutes. Gradually add the granulated sugar and brown sugar and beat together well. Add the egg, then stop and scrape down the sides and bottom of the bowl with a rubber spatula. After the egg is added, the mixture may look curdled, but as you scrape down the bowl, the mixture will smooth out.
• • •

Over a medium size bowl, sift together the cake flour, baking powder, baking soda, cinnamon, ginger, and cloves. Add the nutmeg and salt and toss to blend thoroughly.
• • •
Stir the vanilla into the buttermilk. With the mixer on low speed, add the flour mixture to the butter mixture in 3 stages, alternating with the buttermilk mixture. Blend well after each addition and stop often to scrape down the sides and bottom of the bowl with a rubber spatula. Mix in the toasted walnuts on low speed.
• • •
Use a spoon or a 1½-inch round ice cream scoop to divide the batter evenly among the cavities of the cupcake pan. Shake the pan gently to even out the batter and eliminate any air bubbles.
• • •

Bake the cakes for 25 to 30 minutes, until golden and a cake tester inserted in the center comes out with no crumbs clinging to it. Remove the baking sheet from the oven and transfer the cupcake pan to a rack to cool completely. Invert the pan to remove the cakes.

• • •

Dust the tops of the cakes with confectioners' sugar. Cut the cakes in half to serve.

• • •

keeping Store the cakes between layers of waxed paper in an airtight container at room temperature up to 3 days. To freeze up to 3 months, wrap the container snugly in several layers of plastic wrap and aluminum foil. Use a large piece of masking tape and an indelible marker to label and date the contents. If frozen, defrost the cakes overnight in the refrigerator and bring to room temperature before serving.

making a change Use a single spice, such as cinnamon or ginger, instead of the spice blend.

adding style Garnish each serving with a dollop of whipped cream or a scoop of rich vanilla or caramel ice cream.

spiced chocolate-pecan bundt cakes

THESE YUMMY LITTLE CAKES ARE FULL OF SPICES, TOASTED PECANS, AND COCOA POWDER. THEY ARE RICH AND DELICIOUS, PERFECT WHEN YOU WANT A VERY SATISFYING BITE OF CHOCOLATE. BECAUSE THESE ARE LARGER THAN MOST BITE-SIZE DESSERTS, EACH CAKE EASILY SERVES TWO.

MAKES 1 dozen Bundt cakes, 12 to 24 servings | USE one 12-cavity 2½ x 1¼-inch nonstick Bundt cupcake pan

Nonstick baking spray

1⅔ cups (7½ ounces) all-purpose flour

½ cup (1½ ounces) unsweetened Dutch-processed cocoa powder

1 teaspoon baking soda

½ teaspoon ground ginger

¼ teaspoon ground cinnamon

⅛ teaspoon ground cloves

¾ cup (5 ounces) firmly packed light brown sugar

¼ cup freshly grated nutmeg

¼ teaspoon kosher or fine-grained sea salt

⅔ cup (2½ ounces) toasted pecans, finely chopped

1 cup plus 2 tablespoons buttermilk

¾ cup sour cream

1 teaspoon pure vanilla extract

Position a rack in the center of the oven and preheat the oven to 350°F. Spray the cavities of the cupcake pan with nonstick baking spray and place the pan on a baking sheet.

• • •

Over a medium-size bowl, sift together the flour, cocoa powder, baking soda, ginger, cinnamon, and cloves. Add the brown sugar, nutmeg, and salt and toss to blend completely. Add the pecans and stir to blend thoroughly.

• • •

Mix the buttermilk, sour cream, and vanilla in the bowl of an electric stand mixer with the flat beater attachment or in a large mixing bowl using a hand-held mixer on medium speed to blend thoroughly. Add the flour mixture in 4 stages, blending well after each addition. Stop often to scrape down the sides and bottom of the bowl with a rubber spatula.

• • •

Use a spoon or a 1½-inch round ice cream scoop to divide the batter evenly among the cavities of the cupcake pan. Shake the pan gently to even out the batter and eliminate any air bubbles.

• • •

Bake the cakes for 20 to 24 minutes, until a cake tester inserted in the center comes out with no crumbs clinging to it. Remove the baking sheet from the oven and transfer the cupcake pan to a rack to cool completely. Invert the pan to remove the cakes.

• • •

Cut the cakes in half to serve.

• • •

keeping Store the cakes between layers of waxed paper in an airtight container at room temperature up to 3 days. To freeze up to 3 months, wrap the container snugly in several layers of plastic wrap and aluminum foil. Use a large piece of masking tape and an indelible marker to label and date the contents. If frozen, defrost the cakes overnight in the refrigerator and bring to room temperature before serving.

making a change Use a single spice, such as cinnamon or ginger, instead of the spice blend.

dried cherry, toasted pecan, and sour cream pound cakes

I CHOSE TO BAKE THESE CAKES IN SMALL BUNDT PANS INSTEAD OF LOAF PANS BECAUSE OF THE SMALLER SIZE OF THE PANS. BUT ONE OF THESE CAN EASILY SERVE TWO PEOPLE. THESE TRAVEL VERY WELL AND ARE GREAT TO TAKE AS A HOSTESS GIFT. I LIKE THEM WARMED UP FOR AFTERNOON TEA OR AS A SNACK.

MAKES 1 dozen Bundt cakes, 12 to 24 servings | USE one 12-cavity 2½ x 1¼-inch nonstick Bundt cupcake pan

Nonstick baking spray

½ cup (2½ ounces) dried tart cherries

1 teaspoon dark rum

2 ounces (4 tablespoons, ½ stick) unsalted butter, softened

½ cup (3½ ounces) firmly packed light brown sugar

2 extra-large egg yolks, at room temperature

1 teaspoon pure vanilla extract

¾ cup (3¼ ounces) all-purpose flour

¼ cup (1 ounce) cake flour

1 teaspoon baking powder

¼ teaspoon baking soda

¼ teaspoon freshly grated nutmeg

¼ teaspoon kosher or fine-grained sea salt

½ cup sour cream

½ cup (2 ounces) toasted pecans, finely chopped

1 tablespoon confectioners' sugar

Position a rack in the center of the oven and preheat the oven to 350°F. Spray the cavities of the cupcake pan with nonstick baking spray and place the pan on a baking sheet.

• • •

Marinate the cherries in the rum in a small bowl for 15 minutes.

• • •

Beat the butter in the bowl of an electric stand mixer with the flat beater attachment or in a large mixing bowl using a hand-held mixer on medium speed until it's fluffy, about 1 minute. Add the brown sugar and blend thoroughly.

• • •

Use a fork to lightly beat together the egg yolks and vanilla in a small bowl. Add to the butter mixture and blend well. Stop occasionally and scrape down the sides and bottom of the bowl with a rubber spatula.

• • •

Over a medium-size bowl, sift together the all-purpose flour, cake flour, baking powder, and baking soda. Add the nutmeg and salt and toss to blend completely. Add half of this flour mixture to the butter mixture and blend thoroughly. Add the sour cream to the batter and blend well. Then add the remaining flour mixture and blend thoroughly. Stop occasionally and scrape down the sides and bottom of the bowl with a rubber spatula to ensure even mixing.

• • •

Mix the pecans and dried cherries together, then add them to the batter and stir to blend thoroughly.

• • •

Use a spoon or a 1½-inch round ice cream scoop to divide the batter evenly among the cavities of the cupcake pan. Shake the pan gently to even out the batter and eliminate any air bubbles.

Bake the cakes for 25 to 28 minutes, until a cake tester inserted in the center comes out with no crumbs clinging to it. Remove the pan from the oven and transfer the cupcake pan to a rack to cool completely. Invert the pan to remove the cakes.

• • •

Sprinkle the tops of the cakes with confectioners' sugar. Cut the cakes in half to serve. Serve at room temperature.

• • •

keeping Store the cakes between layers of waxed paper in an airtight container at room temperature up to 3 days. To freeze up to 3 months, wrap the container snugly in several layers of plastic wrap and aluminum foil. Use a large piece of masking tape and an indelible marker to label and date the contents. If frozen, defrost the cakes overnight in the refrigerator and bring to room temperature before serving.

making a change Replace the dried cherries with dried cranberries or raisins.

Replace the toasted pecans with toasted walnuts or almonds.

cinnamon-sour cream cupcakes

THE RICH WARMTH OF CINNAMON AND THE SLIGHT TARTNESS OF SOUR CREAM GIVE THESE LITTLE CAKES DISTINCTIVE FLAVOR. THEY ARE FROSTED WITH WHIPPED, INTENSELY FLAVORED BITTERSWEET CHOCOLATE, GANACHE AND DUSTED ON TOP WITH A MIXTURE OF COCOA POWDER AND CINNAMON. THESE ARE JUST RIGHT FOR DESSERT, AFTERNOON TEA OR COFFEE, OR ANYTIME YOU WOULD LIKE A LITTLE TREAT.

MAKES 2 dozen cupcakes | USE two 12-cavity 2-inch round silicone mini muffin pans

---

4 ounces (8 tablespoons, 1 stick) unsalted butter, softened

¾ cup (5 ounces) granulated sugar

1 extra-large egg, at room temperature

1 extra-large egg yolk, at room temperature

½ teaspoon pure vanilla extract

1 cup plus 2 tablespoons (5 ounces) cake flour

2 teaspoons ground cinnamon, divided

1 teaspoon baking powder

¼ teaspoon kosher or fine-grained sea salt

½ cup plus ⅔ cup sour cream

5 ounces bittersweet chocolate (62 to 72% cacao content), finely chopped

2½ ounces (5 tablespoons) unsalted butter, cut into small pieces

¼ teaspoon unsweetened cocoa powder

CUPCAKES

Position a rack in the center of the oven and preheat the oven to 350°F. Place the mini muffin pans on a baking sheet.

• • •

Beat the softened butter in the bowl of an electric stand mixer with the flat beater attachment or in a large mixing bowl using a hand-held mixer on medium speed until it's fluffy, about 2 minutes. Gradually add the sugar and beat until creamy, about 1 minute.

• • •

In a small bowl, use a fork to lightly beat the egg, egg yolk, and vanilla together. Add to the butter mixture in 2 stages, beating well after each addition. Stop and scrape down the sides and bottom of the bowl with a rubber spatula. The mixture may look curdled as the eggs are added, but as you stop and scrape down the bowl, the mixture will smooth out.

• • •

Over a medium-size bowl, sift together the cake flour, 1¼ teaspoons of cinnamon, and baking powder. Add the salt and toss to blend. Add half of this flour mixture to the butter mixture and blend thoroughly. Add ½ cup of sour cream and blend until smooth. Add the remaining flour mixture and blend thoroughly.

• • •

Use a 1½-inch round ice cream scoop to fill the cavities of the mini muffin pans three-fourths full with the batter.

• • •

Bake the cupcakes for 15 to 18 minutes, until light golden and a cake tester inserted in the center comes out clean. Remove the baking sheet from the oven and cool the mini muffin pans on racks. Invert the pans to remove the cupcakes, then turn them right-side up.

• • •

BITTERSWEET CHOCOLATE GANACHE FROSTING

Place the chocolate and the butter pieces in a medium-size microwave-safe bowl. Melt on low power for 30-second bursts, stirring after each burst. Stir for 30 seconds to cool. Add the remaining ⅔ cup of sour cream and ½ teaspoon of cinnamon and blend thoroughly. Cover the bowl with plastic wrap and chill for 20 minutes.

• • •

Whip the ganache in the bowl of an electric stand mixer with the flat beater attachment or a large mixing bowl using a hand-held mixer on medium speed until it holds soft peaks, about 1 minute.

• • •

Fit a 12- or 14-inch pastry bag with a large open star tip and fill it partway with the ganache. Pipe rosettes on top of each cupcake, filling the tops.

• • •

GARNISH

Sift the remaining ¼ teaspoon of cinnamon and the cocoa powder together in a small bowl. Sift the cocoa-cinnamon mixture over the tops of the cupcakes. Serve the cupcakes at room temperature.

• • •

keeping Store the unfrosted cupcakes between layers of waxed paper in a single layer in an airtight plastic container at room temperature up to 4 days. To freeze up to 4 months, wrap the container tightly in several layers of plastic wrap and aluminum foil. Use a large piece of masking tape and an indelible marker to label and date the contents. If frozen, defrost the cupcakes overnight in the refrigerator and bring to room temperature before serving.

The frosted cupcakes can be kept tightly covered in the refrigerator up to 3 days. Serve at room temperature.

streamlining The ganache can be made up to 3 weeks in advance and kept in an airtight container in the refrigerator. Bring it to room temperature or soften it in a microwave oven on low power before whipping.

peanut butter cupcakes with bittersweet chocolate ganache frosting

PEANUT BUTTER AND BITTERSWEET CHOCOLATE ARE A SPECTACULAR FLAVOR COMBINATION THAT IS ONE OF MY FAVORITES. THESE LITTLE CAKES ARE MADE WITH PEANUT BUTTER AND ICED WITH WHIPPED BITTERSWEET CHOCOLATE GANACHE, THEN DECORATED WITH SALTED PEANUTS. ONE OR TWO WILL SURELY SATISFY YOUR PEANUT BUTTER AND CHOCOLATE CRAVING.

MAKES 2 dozen cupcakes | USE two 12-cavity 2-inch round silicone mini muffin pans

¾ cup (3¼ ounces) all-purpose flour

1 teaspoon baking powder

Pinch of kosher or fine-grained sea salt

1½ ounces (3 tablespoons) unsalted butter, softened

⅓ cup (3¼ ounces) smooth peanut butter

⅓ cup (2 ounces) firmly packed light brown sugar

1 extra-large egg, at room temperature

½ teaspoon pure vanilla extract

½ cup half-and-half

4 ounces bittersweet chocolate (66 to 72% cacao content), finely chopped

½ cup heavy whipping cream

¼ cup (1¼ ounces) salted peanuts

CUPCAKES

Position a rack in the center of the oven and preheat the oven to 350°F. Place the mini muffin pans on a baking sheet.

• • •

Over a medium-size bowl, sift together the flour and baking powder. Add the salt and toss together to blend.

• • •

Beat the butter in the bowl of an electric stand mixer with the flat beater attachment or in a large mixing bowl using a hand-held mixer on medium speed until it's fluffy, about 1 minute. Add the peanut butter and blend together until smooth. Add the brown sugar and beat until creamy, about 1 minute.

• • •

In a small bowl, use a fork to lightly beat the egg and vanilla together. Beat this mixture into the peanut butter mixture. Stop frequently and scrape down the sides and bottom of the bowl with a rubber spatula. The mixture may look curdled as the egg is added, but as you stop and scrape down the bowl,

the mixture will smooth out. Add the flour mixture to the peanut butter mixture in 3 stages, alternating with the half-and-half, and blending well after each addition.

• • •

Use a 1½-inch round ice cream scoop to divide the batter evenly among the cavities of the mini muffin pans.

• • •

Bake the cupcakes for 15 minutes, until light golden and a cake tester inserted in the center comes out clean. Remove the baking sheet from the oven and cool the mini muffin pans on racks.

• • •

BITTERSWEET CHOCOLATE GANACHE FROSTING

Place the chopped chocolate in a medium-size bowl.

• • •

Bring the cream to a boil in a small saucepan over medium-high heat. Pour the cream over the chopped chocolate and let it stand for 30 seconds. Use a heat-resistant spatula to stir the mixture together until smooth. Cover the bowl with

plastic wrap and chill until thick but not stiff, 30 minutes to 1 hour.

• • •

Whip the ganache in the bowl of an electric stand mixer with the flat beater attachment or in a large mixing bowl using a hand-held mixer on medium speed until it holds soft peaks, about 1 minute.

• • •

Use a small offset spatula, a rubber spatula, or a spoon to spread the top of each cupcake with the ganache frosting. Or fit a 12- or 14-inch pastry bag with a large open star tip and fill it partway with the ganache. Pipe the ganache onto the cupcakes in rosettes, covering the tops. Serve the cupcakes at room temperature.

• • •

GARNISH
Sprinkle the top of each cupcake with peanuts.

• • •

keeping Store the unfrosted cupcakes between layers of waxed paper in a single layer in an airtight plastic container at room temperature up to 4 days. To freeze up to 4 months, wrap the container tightly in several layers of plastic wrap and aluminum foil. Use a large piece of masking tape and an indelible marker to label and date the contents. If frozen, defrost the cupcakes overnight in the refrigerator and bring to room temperature before frosting.

The frosted cupcakes can be kept tightly covered in the refrigerator up to 3 days. Serve at room temperature.

streamlining The ganache can be made up to 3 weeks in advance and kept in an airtight container in the refrigerator. Bring it to room temperature or soften it in a microwave oven on low power before whipping.

adding style Chop the peanuts finely and sprinkle over the tops of the cupcakes.

bittersweet chocolate five-spice cupcakes

BITTERSWEET CHOCOLATE WITH 70 PERCENT CACAO CONTENT AND FIVE-SPICE POWDER GIVE THESE LITTLE CAKES UNIQUE FLAVOR. THEY ARE TOPPED OFF WITH A RICH WHIPPED BITTERSWEET CHOCOLATE GANACHE. THESE ARE ELEGANT YET FUN, MAKING THEM PERFECT FOR ANY GATHERING. I LOVE CUPCAKES BECAUSE EVERYONE GETS HIS OR HER OWN LITTLE CAKE.

MAKES 2 dozen cupcakes | USE two 12-cavity 2-inch round mini muffin pans and 24 mini cupcake paper baking cups

2 tablespoons (½ ounce) unsweetened Dutch-processed cocoa powder

3 tablespoons boiling water

1½ teaspoons pure vanilla extract, divided

4 ounces (8 tablespoons, 1 stick) unsalted butter, softened

½ cup (3½ ounces) granulated sugar

2 extra-large eggs, at room temperature

10 ounces bittersweet chocolate (70 to 72% cacao content), finely chopped, divided

½ cup (2¼ ounces) cake flour

1¼ teaspoons five-spice powder, divided

½ teaspoon baking powder

⅛ teaspoon kosher or fine-grained sea salt

½ cup heavy whipping cream

CUPCAKES

Position a rack in the center of the oven and preheat the oven to 325°F. Line the cavities of the mini muffin pans with mini cupcake paper baking cups and place the pans on a baking sheet.

• • •

Place the cocoa powder in a small mixing bowl. Add the boiling water and use a heat-resistant spatula to stir together until it forms a smooth paste. Add 1 teaspoon of vanilla and stir together to blend thoroughly.

• • •

Beat the butter in the bowl of an electric stand mixer with the flat beater attachment or in a large mixing bowl using a hand-held mixer on medium speed until it's fluffy, about 2 minutes. Gradually add the sugar and beat until creamy, about 1 minute. One at a time, add the eggs, beating well after each addition and stopping frequently to scrape down the sides and bottom of the bowl with a rubber spatula. The

mixture may look curdled as the eggs are added, but as you stop and scrape down the bowl, the mixture will smooth out. Add the cocoa paste and mix until smooth.

• • •

Melt 4 ounces of chocolate in the top of a double boiler over low heat or in a microwave-safe bowl on low power for 30-second bursts. Stir with a heat-resistant spatula after each burst to ensure even melting. Remove the top of the double boiler, if using, and wipe the bottom and sides very dry. Add the melted chocolate to the batter and blend completely on low speed.

• • •

Over a medium-size bowl, sift together the cake flour, ¾ teaspoon of five-spice powder, and the baking powder. Add the salt and toss together to blend. Add to the batter in 2 stages, blending well after each addition. Stop and scrape down the sides and bottom of the bowl with the spatula.

• • •

Pour the batter into a 2-cup liquid measuring cup. Fill each cupcake paper three-fourths full.

• • •

Bake the cupcakes for 16 minutes, until a cake tester or toothpick inserted in the center comes out slightly moist. Remove the baking sheet from the oven and transfer the mini muffin pans to racks to cool. Gently lift the cupcakes from the pans.

• • •

BITTERSWEET CHOCOLATE GANACHE FROSTING
Place the remaining 6 ounces of chopped chocolate in a medium-size bowl.

• • •

In a small saucepan, warm the cream over medium heat until it boils. Pour the cream over the chopped chocolate. Let it stand for 30 seconds to 1 minute, then stir together using a rubber spatula, whisk, or immersion blender until very smooth. Add the remaining ½ teaspoon of five-spice powder and ½ teaspoon of vanilla and mix completely. Cover the bowl with plastic wrap and chill until thick but not stiff, 30 minutes to 1 hour.

• • •

Whip the ganache in the bowl of an electric stand mixer with the flat beater attachment or in a large mixing bowl using a hand-held mixer on medium speed until it holds soft peaks, about 1 minute.

• • •

Use a small offset spatula, a rubber spatula, or a spoon to spread the top of each cupcake with the ganache frosting. Or fit a 12- or 14-inch pastry bag with a large open star tip and fill it partway with the ganache. Pipe a large rosette on top of each cupcake. Serve the cupcakes at room temperature.

• • •

keeping Store the unfrosted cupcakes between layers of waxed paper in a single layer in an airtight plastic container at room temperature up to 4 days. To freeze up to 4 months, wrap the container tightly in several layers of plastic wrap and aluminum foil. Use a large piece of masking tape and an indelible marker to label and date the contents. If frozen, defrost the cupcakes overnight in the refrigerator and bring to room temperature before frosting.

The frosted cupcakes can be kept tightly covered in the refrigerator up to 3 days. Serve at room temperature.

streamlining The ganache can be made up to 3 weeks in advance and kept in an airtight container in the refrigerator. Bring it to room temperature or soften it in a microwave oven on low power before whipping.

making a change Add ½ cup of finely diced dried apricots or dried cherries to the batter before baking.

Add ½ cup of toasted and finely chopped walnuts or almonds, or toasted and finely ground hazelnuts, to the batter before baking.

adding style Decorate the top of the frosted cupcakes with slivers of dried apricots or dried cherries to match what is used inside.

Sprinkle the top of the frosted cupcakes with finely chopped toasted walnuts, almonds, or ground toasted hazelnuts to match the nuts inside.

Drizzle the top of the frosted cupcakes with melted white or semisweet chocolate in close lines or in concentric circles.

wicked brownie bites

I CALL THESE WICKED BECAUSE THEY ARE INTENSELY FLAVORED, BURSTING WITH DEEP DARK CHOCOLATE AND TOASTED WALNUTS, AND THEY ARE THE MOST DELICIOUS BROWNIES I'VE EVER EATEN. THEY ARE HARD TO RESIST. THESE WILL SURELY SATISFY YOUR MOST INTENSE CHOCOLATE CRAVINGS. I USED A COMBINATION OF MY FAVORITE CHOCOLATES AND COCOA POWDER—SCHARFFEN BERGER UNSWEETENED CHOCOLATE, SCHARFFEN BERGER 70 PERCENT CACAO CONTENT CHOCOLATE, AND PERNIGOTTI COCOA POWDER—TO CREATE THESE.

MAKES 2 dozen brownies | USE two 12-cavity 2-inch round silicone mini muffin pans

1 cup (4½ ounces) coarsely chopped walnuts

3 ounces bittersweet chocolate (70 to 72% cacao content), finely chopped

3 ounces unsweetened chocolate, finely chopped

4 ounces (8 tablespoons, 1 stick) unsalted butter, cut into small pieces

2 extra-large eggs, at room temperature

⅔ cup (4 ounces) granulated sugar

⅔ cup (4 ounces) firmly packed light brown sugar

1 teaspoon pure vanilla extract

½ cup (2¼ ounces) all-purpose flour

2 tablespoons (½ ounce) unsweetened cocoa powder (natural or Dutch-processed)

¼ teaspoon kosher or fine-grained sea salt

Position a rack in the center of the oven and preheat the oven to 350°F. Place the mini muffin pans on a baking sheet.

• • •

Place the walnuts in a cake or pie pan and toast in the oven for 8 minutes. Remove the pan from the oven and cool on a rack.

• • •

Place the bittersweet chocolate, unsweetened chocolate, and butter in the top of a double boiler over low heat. Stir often with a rubber spatula to help the chocolate and butter melt evenly. Remove the top pan of the double boiler and wipe the bottom and sides very dry. Let the mixture cool while mixing the rest of the brownie batter, stirring with a rubber spatula occasionally to prevent a skin from forming on top.

• • •

Or place the chocolates and butter in a microwave-safe bowl and melt on low power for 30-second bursts. Stir with a rubber spatula after each burst to ensure even melting.

• • •

Whip the eggs in the bowl of an electric stand mixer with the wire whip attachment or in a large mixing bowl using a hand-held mixer on medium speed until they are frothy. Add the granulated sugar and brown sugar and whip until the mixture is very thick and pale colored, and holds a slowly dissolving ribbon as the beater is lifted, about 5 minutes. Mix in the vanilla. Add the melted chocolate and butter mixture and blend completely on low speed. Stop and scrape down the sides and bottom of the bowl with the rubber spatula. The mixture will look smooth and dark chocolate colored.

• • •

In a medium-size bowl, sift together the flour and cocoa powder. Add the salt and stir to combine. In 3 stages, add this flour mixture to the chocolate mixture, blending well after each addition. Stop and scrape down the sides and bottom of the bowl with the rubber spatula. Add the walnuts and stir to distribute evenly.

• • •

Use a 1½-inch round ice cream scoop to divide the batter evenly among the cavities of the mini muffin pans, filling each cavity.

• • •

Bake the brownies for 25 minutes, until a cake tester or toothpick inserted in the center comes out slightly moist. Remove the baking sheet from the oven and transfer the mini muffin pans to racks to cool.

• • •

When the brownies are cool, turn the pans over and gently push the brownies out of the cavities, then turn them top-side up. Serve the brownies at room temperature.

• • •

keeping Store the brownies between layers of waxed paper in an airtight plastic container at room temperature up to 4 days. To freeze up to 4 months, wrap the container tightly in several layers of plastic wrap and aluminum foil. Use a large piece of masking tape and an indelible marker to label and date the contents. If frozen, defrost the brownies overnight in the refrigerator and bring to room temperature before serving.

making a change Mix 1 cup of lightly toasted, sweetened shredded coconut into the batter before turning it into the pan to bake.

Replace the walnuts with 1 cup of coarsely chopped toasted hazelnuts or pecans.

adding style Serve the cooled brownies with a dollop of lightly sweetened whipped cream.

Drizzle the top of the cooled brownies with melted white or semisweet chocolate in close lines.

gingerbread bites

THESE SPICY, FRAGRANT GINGERBREAD BITES HAVE A CAKE-LIKE TEXTURE. A BLEND OF GROUND GINGER, UN-CRYSTALLIZED CANDIED GINGER, CINNAMON, CLOVES, AND NUTMEG GIVES THEM FULL-BODIED FLAVOR. I LIKE TO SERVE THESE WITH A DOLLOP OF WHIPPED CREAM PIPED ON TOP AND GARNISHED WITH SLIVERS OF UN-CRYSTALLIZED CANDIED GINGER, BUT THEY ARE EQUALLY GOOD WITH A SCOOP OF VANILLA ICE CREAM.

MAKES 2 dozen bites | USE two 12-cavity 2-inch round silicone mini muffin pans

1¼ cups (5½ ounces) all-purpose flour

1 teaspoon baking soda

1¾ teaspoons ground ginger, divided

½ teaspoon ground cinnamon

¼ teaspoon ground cloves

⅛ teaspoon freshly grated nutmeg

⅛ teaspoon kosher or fine-grained sea salt

½ cup (3 ounces) un-crystallized candied ginger, finely chopped

2 ounces (4 tablespoons, ½ stick) unsalted butter, softened

⅓ cup (2 ounces) firmly packed light brown sugar

½ cup unsulfured molasses

1 extra-large egg, at room temperature

½ cup boiling water

½ cup heavy whipping cream

2 tablespoons confectioners' sugar

24 slivers un-crystallized candied ginger

GINGERBREAD BITES

Adjust the oven racks to the upper and lower thirds and preheat the oven to 350°F. Place the mini muffin pans on a baking sheet.

• • •

In a medium-size bowl, sift together the flour, baking soda, 1½ teaspoons of ground ginger, cinnamon, and cloves. Add the nutmeg and salt and toss to blend. Add the chopped ginger and toss to coat completely.

• • •

Beat the butter in the bowl of an electric stand mixer with the flat beater attachment or in a large mixing bowl using a hand-held mixer on medium speed until light and fluffy, about 2 minutes. Add the brown sugar and beat until smooth. Stop and scrape down the sides and bottom of the bowl with a rubber spatula.

• • •

Use a fork to lightly beat together the molasses and egg in a liquid measuring cup and add to the butter mixture. The egg will sit on top of the mixture so stop after adding it and scrape down the sides and bottom of the bowl with a rubber spatula to help mix evenly. The mixture may look curdled but will smooth out when the flour mixture is added. Add the boiling water and beat to blend thoroughly. Adjust the mixer speed to low and add the flour mixture in 4 stages, blending thoroughly after each addition. Stop and scrape down the sides and bottom of the bowl with a rubber spatula.

• • •

Pour the gingerbread batter into a 2-cup liquid measuring cup and fill the cavities of the mini muffin pan three-fourths full.

• • •

Bake for 25 minutes, until a cake tester inserted in the center comes out clean. Remove the baking sheet from the oven and transfer the mini muffin pans to racks to cool completely. Turn the mini muffin pans upside down and press the gingerbread bites out, then turn them right-side up.

• • •

GARNISH

Whip the cream in the bowl of an electric stand mixer with the wire whip attachment or in a large mixing bowl using a hand-held mixer on medium speed until frothy. Add the confectioners' sugar and remaining ¼ teaspoon of ground ginger and continue to whip until the cream holds soft peaks.

• • •

Top each gingerbread bite with a dollop of whipped cream and garnish with a sliver of un-crystallized candied ginger.

Or fit a 12- to -14-inch pastry bag with a large open star tip and fill it partway with the whipped cream. Pipe rosettes on top of each bite and garnish with a sliver of un-crystallized candied ginger. Serve at room temperature.

• • •

keeping Store the gingerbread bites, without the garnish, tightly wrapped in aluminum foil at room temperature up to 4 days. To freeze up to 4 months, wrap them tightly in several layers of plastic wrap and aluminum foil. Use a large piece of masking tape and an indelible marker to label and date the contents. If frozen, defrost the bites overnight in the refrigerator and bring to room temperature before serving.

adding style Serve the gingerbread bites with a scoop of vanilla ice cream.

apricot-orange loaf cakes

DRIED APRICOTS SOAKED IN ORANGE LIQUEUR, ORANGE ZEST, AND A HINT OF ORANGE EXTRACT GIVE THESE CAKES DEPTH OF FLAVOR AND TEXTURE. THEY ARE LARGER THAN MOST BITE-SIZE DESSERTS, SO ONE OF THEM WILL EASILY SERVE TWO OR THREE PEOPLE. I LIKE TO SERVE THESE WITH RASPBERRY SAUCE (SEE PAGE 36) AND A FEW FRESH RASPBERRIES, RASPBERRY (SEE PAGE 158) OR CANTALOUPE SORBET (SEE PAGE 160), OR HONEY WHIPPED CREAM (SEE PAGE 12).

MAKES 1 dozen loaf cakes | USE twelve 4 x 2¼–inch loaf pans

Nonstick baking spray

⅔ cup (4 ounces) dried apricots, finely chopped

2 tablespoons Grand Marnier or other orange liqueur

6 ounces (12 tablespoons, 1½ sticks) unsalted butter, softened

¾ cup (5 ounces) granulated sugar

¾ cup (4½ ounces) firmly packed light brown sugar

2 extra-large eggs, at room temperature

1 extra-large egg yolk, at room temperature

1 teaspoon pure vanilla extract

¼ teaspoon pure orange extract

Finely grated zest of 1 large orange

2 cups (9 ounces) all-purpose flour

½ teaspoon baking powder

¼ teaspoon baking soda

¼ teaspoon kosher or fine-grained sea salt

½ cup buttermilk

½ cup (2¼ ounces) walnuts, coarsely chopped

Position a rack in the center of the oven and preheat the oven to 325°F. Spray the inside of the loaf pans generously with nonstick baking spray and place the pans on a baking sheet.

• • •

Place the chopped apricots in a small bowl and pour the Grand Marnier or other orange liqueur over them. Cover the bowl tightly with plastic wrap and let the apricots marinate for at least 15 minutes.

• • •

Beat the butter in the bowl of an electric stand mixer with the flat beater attachment or in a large mixing bowl using a hand-held mixer on medium speed until it's fluffy, about 2 minutes. Add the sugars and beat together well. Stop occasionally and scrape down the sides and bottom of the bowl with a rubber spatula.

• • •

In a small bowl, use a fork to lightly beat the eggs and egg yolk together. Add the vanilla, orange extract, and orange zest and blend well. Add this to the butter mixture. Stop occasionally to scrape down the sides and bottom of the bowl with a rubber spatula. The mixture may look curdled as the eggs are added, but as you stop and scrape down the bowl, the mixture will smooth out.

• • •

In a medium-size bowl, sift together the flour, baking powder, and baking soda. Add the salt and toss together. Add the flour mixture in 3 stages, alternating with the buttermilk. Stop after each addition and scrape down the sides and bottom of the bowl. Blend the mixture until smooth. Mix in the chopped walnuts on low speed.

• • •

Use a 1½-inch round ice cream scoop to transfer the mixture to the loaf pans, filling each three-fourths full. Use a rubber spatula to spread the thick batter evenly into the corners of the pans.

• • •

Bake the cakes for 30 minutes, until a cake tester inserted in the center comes out clean. Remove the baking sheet from the oven and transfer the loaf pans to racks to cool. Invert the pans to remove the cakes. If necessary, run a very thin blade between the loaves and the sides of the pans.

• • •

Slice the loaves into ½-inch-thick slices and serve with your choice of accompaniment at room temperature.

• • •

keeping Store the loaf cakes tightly wrapped in aluminum foil up to 4 days at room temperature. To freeze up to 4 months, wrap them tightly in several layers of plastic wrap and aluminum foil. Use a large piece of masking tape and an indelible marker to label and date the contents. If frozen, defrost the cakes overnight in the refrigerator and bring to room temperature before serving.

making a change Replace the walnuts with pecans, almonds, or macadamia nuts.

petite cheesecakes with raspberry sauce

EVERYONE LOVES CHEESECAKE BECAUSE IT IS SO SCRUMPTIOUS, BUT A REGULAR-SIZE SERVING IS USUALLY TOO MUCH TO EAT. THESE LITTLE CAKES ARE JUST RIGHT FOR INDULGING IN A SMALL SERVING OF DELECTABLE CHEESECAKE. MAKE THESE AT LEAST A DAY BEFORE SERVING SO THEY HAVE TIME TO COOL AND SET.

MAKES 2 dozen cheesecakes | USE two 12-cavity 2-inch round silicone mini muffin pans

2 teaspoons plus 2 tablespoons (1 ounce) unsalted butter, melted

2 ounces (about 7) butter cookie wafers or biscuits

2 teaspoons plus ¼ cup (1½ ounces) firmly packed light brown sugar

⅛ teaspoon freshly grated nutmeg

8 ounces cream cheese, softened

¼ cup (1½ ounces) granulated sugar

Pinch of kosher or fine-grained sea salt

1 extra-large egg, at room temperature

⅓ cup sour cream

2 tablespoons heavy whipping cream

1½ teaspoons pure vanilla extract or vanilla paste

1 quart boiling water

1 cup (4½ ounces) fresh or fresh-frozen raspberries, defrosted

1 tablespoon (¼ ounce) superfine sugar

1 teaspoon freshly squeezed lemon juice

1 tablespoon framboise, Chambord, kirsch, or Grand Marnier

Fresh raspberries, for garnish

Position a rack in the center of the oven and preheat the oven to 350°F. Use a pastry brush to coat the cavities of the mini muffin pan with 2 teaspoons of melted butter.

• • •

BUTTER COOKIE CRUST

Place the cookies, 2 teaspoons of brown sugar, and nutmeg in the work bowl of a food processor fitted with the steel blade. Pulse until the cookies are finely ground, about 1 minute. With the food processor running, pour the remaining 2 tablespoons of melted butter through the feed tube. Process the mixture until it begins to hold together.

• • •

Press 1 teaspoon of the cookie mixture into each cavity of the mini muffin pans so it clings to the bottom and goes a little

way up the sides. Place the mini muffin pans on a baking sheet and chill the crust while preparing the cheesecake batter.

• • •

CHEESECAKE FILLING

Beat the cream cheese in the bowl of an electric stand mixer with the flat beater attachment or in a large mixing bowl using a hand-held mixer on medium speed until fluffy, about 2 minutes. Add the granulated sugar, salt, and remaining ¼ cup of brown sugar. Beat until well blended, stopping occasionally to scrape down the sides and bottom of the bowl with a rubber spatula. Add the egg and blend well. Stop to scrape down the sides and bottom of the bowl with a rubber spatula. Add the sour cream, whipping cream, and vanilla, and blend thoroughly.

• • •

Pour the batter into a 2-cup liquid measuring cup. Fill each cavity of the mini muffin pans three-fourths full. Place the baking sheet in the oven and carefully pour the boiling water into the baking sheet until it comes halfway up the sides of the mini muffin pans.

• • •

Bake the cheesecakes for 25 minutes. Turn off the oven and let them stand for 25 minutes. The tops should be light golden and set, but jiggle slightly when the pan is moved. Remove the baking sheet from the oven and transfer the mini muffin pans to racks to cool.

• • •

Gently turn the pans over and push the cheesecakes out, then turn the cheesecakes right-side up. Transfer the cheesecakes to a plate, cover the tops with waxed paper, and wrap tightly with aluminum foil. Refrigerate for at least 3 hours before serving.

• • •

RASPBERRY SAUCE
Place the 1 cup of raspberries in the work bowl of a food processor fitted with the steel blade or in a blender. Pulse until the berries are pureed into liquid, about 1 minute.

• • •

Using a rubber spatula or wooden spoon and a fine-mesh strainer, strain the raspberry puree into a medium-size bowl. Push through the strainer as much of the liquid as possible, without the seeds. Add the superfine sugar, lemon juice, and liqueur to the raspberry puree and blend thoroughly.

• • •

Serve each cheesecake with a spoonful of raspberry sauce and garnish with a few fresh raspberries. Serve at room temperature.

• • •

keeping Store the cheesecakes in a single layer tightly covered with aluminum foil in the refrigerator up to 4 days. To freeze up to 2 months, wrap them tightly in several layers of plastic wrap and aluminum foil. Use a large piece of masking tape and an indelible marker to label and date the contents. If frozen, defrost the cheesecakes overnight in the refrigerator.

making a change Add 1 cup of fresh raspberries or blueberries to the batter before baking.

Add 1 cup of toasted and finely chopped walnuts or almonds, or toasted and finely ground hazelnuts, to the batter before baking.

walnut and lemon tea cakes

THESE LITTLE CAKES ARE PACKED WITH FLAVOR. THEY ARE PERFECT FOR AFTERNOON TEA, AS A SNACK, OR TO PACK INTO A LOVED ONE'S LUNCH BOX.

MAKES 2 dozen tea cakes | USE two 12-cavity 2-inch round silicone mini muffin pans

4 ounces (8 tablespoons, 1 stick) unsalted butter, softened

⅓ cup (2 ounces) firmly packed light brown sugar

⅓ cup (2 ounces) granulated sugar

1 extra-large egg, at room temperature

1 extra-large egg yolk, at room temperature

½ teaspoon pure lemon extract

Finely grated zest of 1 large lemon

1¼ cups (5½ ounces) all-purpose flour

1 teaspoon baking powder

½ teaspoon baking soda

Pinch of kosher or fine-grained sea salt

2 tablespoons heavy whipping cream

¾ cup (3¼ ounces) walnuts, coarsely chopped

2 tablespoons confectioners' sugar, sifted

Position a rack in the center of the oven and preheat the oven to 350°F. Place the mini muffin pans on a baking sheet.

• • •

Beat the butter in the bowl of an electric stand mixer with the flat beater attachment or in a large mixing bowl using a hand-held mixer on medium speed until it's fluffy, about 2 minutes. Add the brown sugar and granulated sugar and beat together well. Stop occasionally and scrape down the sides and bottom of the bowl with a rubber spatula.

• • •

Use a fork to lightly beat the egg and yolk together in a small bowl. Add to the butter mixture. Stop to scrape down the sides and bottom of the bowl. The mixture may look curdled as the eggs are added, but as you stop and scrape down the bowl, the mixture will smooth out. Add the lemon extract and lemon zest and blend thoroughly.

• • •

Over a medium-size bowl, sift together the flour, baking powder, and baking soda. Add the salt and toss together to blend. Add the flour mixture to the butter mixture in 3 stages, alternating with the cream. Stop after each addition and scrape down the sides and bottom of the bowl. Add the chopped walnuts and blend thoroughly on low speed.

• • •

Use a 1½-inch round ice cream scoop to divide the batter evenly among the cavities of the mini muffins pans.

• • •

Bake the cakes for 20 minutes, until a cake tester inserted in the center of the cakes comes out clean. Remove the baking sheet from the oven and transfer the mini muffin pans to racks to cool. Invert the muffin pans to remove the cakes.

• • •

Dust the tops of the cakes with confectioners' sugar before serving. Serve at room temperature.

• • •

keeping Store the tea cakes tightly wrapped in plastic wrap at room temperature up to 4 days. To freeze up to 4 months, tightly wrap them in several layers of plastic wrap and aluminum foil. Use a large piece of masking tape and an indelible marker to label and date the contents. If frozen, defrost the cakes overnight in the refrigerator and bring to room temperature before serving.

making a change Replace the walnuts with pecans or almonds.

maple walnut tea cakes

I LOVE THE WARM, RICH FLAVOR OF MAPLE AND FIND IT VERY COMFORTING IN COLD WEATHER. MAPLE AND WALNUTS IS A DIVINE FLAVOR BLEND THAT BRINGS OUT THE BEST IN EACH INGREDIENT. THESE LITTLE CAKES ARE PERFECT WITH A STEAMING CUP OF TEA OR COFFEE.

MAKES 1½ dozen tea cakes | USE two 12-cavity 2-inch round silicone mini muffin pans

½ ounce (1 tablespoon) unsalted butter, softened

¼ cup (1½ ounces) firmly packed light brown sugar

1 extra-large egg yolk, at room temperature

3 tablespoons pure maple syrup

1 tablespoon unsulfured molasses

½ teaspoon pure vanilla extract

¾ cup (3¼ ounces) all-purpose flour

½ teaspoon baking soda

Pinch of kosher or fine-grained sea salt

¼ cup sour cream

⅓ cup (1½ ounces) walnuts, coarsely chopped

2 tablespoons confectioners' sugar

Position a rack in the center of the oven and preheat the oven to 350°F. Place the mini muffin pans on a baking sheet.
• • •
Beat the butter in the bowl of an electric stand mixer with the flat beater attachment or in a large mixing bowl using a hand-held mixer on medium speed until it's light and fluffy, about 1 minute. Add the brown sugar and beat until smooth. Stop and scrape down the sides and bottom of the bowl with a rubber spatula. Add the egg yolk. It will sit on top of the mixture, so be sure to scrape down the sides and bottom of the bowl with a rubber spatula. Add the maple syrup, molasses, and vanilla, and blend thoroughly.
• • •
In a medium-size bowl, sift together the flour and baking soda. Add the salt and toss to blend. Add the flour mixture to the butter mixture in 3 stages, alternating with the sour cream. Blend thoroughly, stopping to scrape down the sides and bottom of the bowl after each addition. Add the walnuts and blend well.
• • •
Use a 1½-inch round ice cream scoop to divide the batter evenly among the 18 cavities of the mini-muffin pans, filling each halfway. (Fill the remaining 6 cavities with water.)
• • •

Bake the cakes for 15 minutes, until light golden and a cake tester inserted in the center comes out clean. Remove the baking sheet from the oven and transfer the mini muffin pans to racks to cool completely. Turn the mini muffin pans upside down and press the cakes out, then turn the cakes right-side up.
• • •
Lightly dust the tops of the cakes with the confectioners' sugar. Serve the cakes at room temperature.
• • •
keeping Store the tea cakes tightly wrapped in aluminum foil at room temperature up to 4 days. To freeze up to 4 months, wrap them tightly in several layers of plastic wrap and aluminum foil. Use a large piece of masking tape and an indelible marker to label and date the contents. If frozen, defrost the cakes overnight in the refrigerator and bring to room temperature before serving.

adding style Make a stencil of a maple leaf and hold it over the top of each cake, then dust with confectioners' sugar. Carefully lift off the stencil to leave a maple leaf on top of each cake.

mini pistachio tea cakes

THESE SUBLIME LITTLE CAKES ARE THE PERFECT ACCOMPANIMENT FOR AFTERNOON TEA OR COFFEE. PISTACHIO PASTE GIVES THEM SUBTLE YET LUSCIOUS FLAVOR. PISTACHIO PASTE IS SIMILAR TO ALMOND PASTE IN TEXTURE AND CONSISTENCY. IT CAN BE FOUND IN VACUUM-SEALED CANS IN SOME COOKWARE AND SPECIALTY FOOD SHOPS AND THROUGH CATALOG AND ONLINE SOURCES.

MAKES 2 dozen tea cakes | USE two 12-cavity 2-inch round silicone mini muffin pans

3 ounces (6 tablespoons, ¾ stick) unsalted butter, softened

½ cup (3½ ounces) granulated sugar

⅓ cup (3 ounces) packed pistachio paste

½ teaspoon pure vanilla extract

2 extra-large eggs, at room temperature

½ cup (2¼ ounces) all-purpose flour

¼ teaspoon kosher or fine-grained sea salt

2 tablespoons confectioners' sugar

Position a rack in the upper third of the oven and preheat the oven to 400°F. Place the mini muffin pans on a baking sheet.

• • •

Beat the butter in the bowl of an electric stand mixer with the flat beater attachment or in a large mixing bowl using a hand-held mixer until it's light and fluffy, about 2 minutes. Add the granulated sugar and beat until smooth. Stop and scrape down the sides and bottom of the bowl with a rubber spatula. Add the pistachio paste and vanilla and mix until smooth and thoroughly combined. One at a time, add the eggs. They will sit on top of the mixture, so be sure to scrape down the sides and bottom of the bowl with a rubber spatula. Blend thoroughly.

• • •

Sift the flour into a medium-size bowl. Add the salt and toss to blend. Add this mixture to the butter mixture in 2 stages, blending well after each addition. Stop after each addition and scrape down the sides and bottom of the bowl.

• • •

Pour the batter into a 2-cup liquid measuring cup and divide it evenly among the cavities of the mini muffin pans.

• • •

Bake the cakes for 13 to 15 minutes, until light golden and a cake tester inserted in the center comes out clean. Remove the baking sheet from the oven and transfer the mini muffin pans to racks to cool completely. Turn the mini muffin pans upside down and press the cakes out, then turn them right-side up.

• • •

Dust the tops of the cakes with the confectioners' sugar. Serve the cakes at room temperature.

• • •

keeping Store the tea cakes tightly wrapped in aluminum foil at room temperature up to 4 days. To freeze up to 4 months, wrap them tightly in several layers of plastic wrap and aluminum foil. Use a large piece of masking tape and an indelible marker to label and date the contents. If frozen, defrost the cakes overnight in the refrigerator and bring to room temperature before serving.

adding style Top each cake with 2 or 3 toasted pistachio nuts before baking.

almond-cornmeal cakes

CORNMEAL GIVES A CRUNCHY TEXTURE TO THESE MOIST ALMOND CAKES. THESE ARE GREAT SERVED WITH STRAWBERRY SAUCE (BELOW) OR RASPBERRY SAUCE (SEE PAGE 36) AND FRESH BERRIES. THEY ARE ALSO EXCELLENT SERVED WARM WITH BUTTER AND JAM FOR BREAKFAST, BRUNCH, OR AFTERNOON TEA. THEY CAN BE REWARMED IN A 350°F OVEN FOR 8 TO 10 MINUTES.

MAKES 2 dozen cakes | USE two 12-cavity 2-inch round silicone mini muffin pans

1 roll (7 ounces) almond paste

½ cup (3½ ounces) granulated sugar

6 ounces (12 tablespoons, 1½ sticks) unsalted butter, softened

2 extra-large eggs, at room temperature

2 extra-large egg yolks, at room temperature

½ cup (2¼ ounces) cake flour

¾ teaspoon baking powder

½ cup (3 ounces) fine yellow cornmeal

Pinch of kosher or fine-grained sea salt

1 pint (16 ounces) fresh strawberries, washed, dried, and hulled

2 tablespoons (¾ ounce) superfine sugar

½ teaspoon freshly squeezed lemon juice

CAKES

Position a rack in the center of the oven and preheat the oven to 350°F. Place the mini muffin pans on a baking sheet.

• • •

Beat the almond paste and granulated sugar together in the bowl of an electric stand mixer with the flat beater attachment or in a large mixing bowl using a hand-held mixer on medium speed until it's crumbly, about 2 minutes. Add the butter and beat together until very smooth. Stop occasionally and scrape down the sides and bottom of the bowl to mix evenly. One at a time, add the eggs and egg yolks, beating until smooth after each addition.

• • •

In a medium-size bowl, sift together the cake flour and baking powder. Add the cornmeal and salt and toss together to blend. Add the flour mixture to the batter in 3 stages. Stop after each addition and scrape down the sides and bottom of the bowl. Beat to blend the mixture thoroughly.

• • •

Use a 1½-inch round ice cream scoop to divide the batter evenly among the cavities of the mini muffin pans.

• • •

Bake the cakes for 25 minutes, until light golden and they spring back when lightly touched on top. Remove the baking sheet from the oven and transfer the mini muffin pans to racks to cool. Invert the pans to remove the cakes, then turn them right-side up.

• • •

STRAWBERRY SAUCE

Reserve half of the berries for garnish and cut them in half.

• • •

Puree the rest of the strawberries with the superfine sugar and lemon juice in the work bowl of a food processor fitted with a steel blade or in a blender.

• • •

Serve each cake at room temperature with a spoonful of strawberry sauce or place the sauce in a squeeze bottle and place dots of sauce around the cake. Scatter each plate with the cut strawberries.

• • •

keeping Store the cakes, without the sauce, tightly wrapped in aluminum foil at room temperature up to 4 days. To freeze up to 4 months, tightly wrap them in several layers of plastic wrap and aluminum foil. Use a large piece of masking tape and an indelible marker to label and date the contents. If frozen, defrost the cakes overnight in the refrigerator and bring to room temperature before serving.

streamlining The sauce can be made up to 4 days in advance and kept in a tightly covered container in the refrigerator.

triple lemon pound cakes

NEXT TO CHOCOLATE, LEMON IS MY FAVORITE FLAVOR. WHEN I CREATED THESE POUND CAKES, I WANTED THEM TO TASTE DISTINCTLY OF LEMON. IF YOU ARE ALSO A LEMON LOVER, THESE CAKES ARE FOR YOU! THEY ARE DELICIOUS ON THEIR OWN, BUT ALSO SCRUMPTIOUS SERVED WITH WHIPPED CREAM AND FRESH BERRIES, SLICED PEACHES, OR SLICED POACHED PEARS. BECAUSE THESE CAKES ARE LARGER THAN MOST BITE-SIZE DESSERTS, ONE OF THEM EASILY SERVES TWO OR THREE PEOPLE.

MAKES 8 cakes, 16 to 24 servings | USE two 4-cavity 4 x 2½ x 1¼–inch mini loaf pans

Nonstick baking spray

5 ounces (1 stick plus 2 tablespoons) unsalted butter, softened

1 cup (6½ ounces) plus 2 tablespoons superfine sugar, divided

3 extra-large eggs, at room temperature

1 teaspoon pure lemon extract

3 tablespoons freshly squeezed lemon juice, divided

Finely grated zest of 3 large lemons

1¼ cups (5½ ounces) cake flour

1 teaspoon baking powder

¼ teaspoon kosher or fine-grained sea salt

POUND CAKES

Position a rack in the center of the oven and preheat the oven to 325°F. Spray the inside of the mini loaf pans with nonstick baking spray, and place the pans on a baking sheet.

• • •

Beat the butter in the bowl of an electric stand mixer with the flat beater attachment or in a large mixing bowl using a hand-held mixer on medium speed until it's fluffy, about 2 minutes. Gradually add 1 cup of sugar and beat until it's very fluffy, about 2 minutes. One at a time, add the eggs, beating well after each addition. Stop frequently and scrape down the sides and bottom of the bowl with a rubber spatula to help mix the batter evenly. The mixture may look curdled as the eggs are added, but as you stop and scrape down the bowl, the mixture will smooth out. Add the lemon extract, 1 tablespoon of lemon juice, and zest and blend thoroughly. The mixture will look curdled.

• • •

In a medium-size bowl, sift together the cake flour and baking powder. Add the salt and toss to blend. Add this flour mixture to the batter in 3 stages. Stop to scrape down the sides and bottom of the bowl with the rubber spatula to blend well after each addition.

• • •

Divide the batter evenly among the cavities of the loaf pans, filling each about two-thirds full. Shake the pans gently to spread out the batter.

• • •

Bake the pound cakes for 30 minutes, until light golden and a cake tester or toothpick inserted in the center comes out clean. Remove the baking sheet from the oven and place the loaf pans on racks to cool.

• • •

Run a small flexible-blade spatula or knife around the rim of each pan. Turn the pans upside down and gently shake out the cakes, then turn them right-side up.

• • •

LEMON SYRUP

Place the remaining 2 tablespoons of sugar and 2 tablespoons of lemon juice in a small saucepan and stir over medium heat until the sugar dissolves, about 3 minutes. Continue to cook the syrup until it thickens slightly, 2 to 3 minutes. Remove the pan from the heat and brush the tops of the pound cakes with some of the syrup.

• • •

Use a toothpick to poke 4 or 5 holes in the top of each cake and brush the cakes again with the lemon syrup. Let the cakes stand 5 minutes. Brush the tops of the cakes again with any remaining lemon syrup and let them cool completely.

• • •

Serve the cakes at room temperature.

• • •

keeping Store the pound cakes in a single layer in an airtight plastic container at room temperature up to 4 days. To freeze up to 4 months, wrap the container tightly in several layers of plastic wrap and aluminum foil. Use a large piece of masking tape and an indelible marker to label and date the contents. If frozen, defrost the cakes overnight in the refrigerator and bring to room temperature before serving.

making a change Add ½ cup of lightly toasted unsweetened shredded coconut to the batter before baking.

Add ½ cup of toasted and finely chopped walnuts or pecans to the batter before baking.

adding style Garnish each serving with a scoop of whipped cream and fresh berries, sliced peaches, or sliced poached pears.

chapter three

SCONES, SHORTCAKES, MUFFINS, AND PASTRIES

cornmeal-dried cherry scones

I LOVE TO USE CORNMEAL IN BAKING BECAUSE IT PROVIDES LOTS OF TEXTURE. IT WORKS DELICIOUSLY WITH THE DRIED TART CHERRIES IN THESE SCONES. THESE ARE LOVELY FOR BREAKFAST, AFTERNOON TEA, AND AS A SNACK. THEY TASTE BEST WHEN WARM AND CAN BE REHEATED IN A 350°F OVEN FOR 7 TO 9 MINUTES.

MAKES 2 dozen 2-inch round scones

¾ cup (3¼ ounces) all-purpose flour

⅔ cup (4 ounces) fine yellow cornmeal

1 tablespoon (¼ ounce) plus 1 teaspoon granulated sugar

1½ teaspoons baking powder

⅛ teaspoon kosher or fine-grained sea salt

2 ounces (4 tablespoons, ½ stick) unsalted butter, chilled

⅔ cup (3½ ounces) dried tart cherries

⅓ cup plus 2 teaspoons heavy whipping cream

1 extra-large egg, at room temperature

½ teaspoon pure vanilla extract

Adjust the oven racks to the upper and lower thirds and preheat the oven to 350°F. Line 2 baking sheets with parchment paper or nonstick liners.

• • •

Pulse together the flour, cornmeal, 1 tablespoon of sugar, baking powder, and salt in the work bowl of a food processor fitted with a steel blade.

• • •

Cut the butter into small pieces and add it to the flour mixture. Pulse until the butter is cut into very tiny pieces, about 30 seconds. The texture should be sandy with very tiny lumps throughout. Add the dried cherries and pulse a few times to mix.

• • •

Use a fork to lightly beat ⅓ cup of cream with the egg and vanilla in a liquid measuring cup. With the food processor running, pour this mixture through the feed tube and process until the dough forms itself into a ball, about 30 seconds.

• • •

Dust a large piece of waxed or parchment paper with flour and turn the dough out onto it. Knead the dough briefly and form it into a round about ¾ inch thick. Dip a 1½-inch round plain-edge biscuit cutter in flour and use it to cut straight down through the dough and lift straight up, without twisting, to form the scones. Twisting seals the edges of the dough and keeps the scones from rising well as they bake. Gather the scraps together, knead briefly, and roll and cut the remaining dough into scones. Transfer the scones to the lined baking sheets, leaving at least 1 inch of space between them so they have room to expand as they bake.

• • •

GARNISH

Brush the tops of the scones with the remaining 2 teaspoons of cream, taking care that it doesn't run down the sides and under the scones. If it does, wipe it up because it can cause the bottoms of the scones to burn. Lightly sprinkle the tops of the scones with the remaining 1 teaspoon of sugar.

• • •

Bake for 9 minutes. Switch the baking sheets and bake another 9 minutes, until the scones are light golden. Remove the baking sheets from the oven and cool the scones completely on the baking sheets on racks.

• • •

keeping Store the scones in an airtight plastic container between layers of waxed paper at room temperature up to 4 days. To freeze up to 4 months, wrap the container tightly in several layers of plastic wrap and aluminum foil. Use a large piece of masking tape and an indelible marker to label and date the contents. If frozen, defrost the scones overnight in the refrigerator and bring to room temperature before serving.

making a change Add ⅓ cup of coarsely chopped toasted walnuts or pecans with the cherries.

Replace the dried tart cherries with dried cranberries or dried blueberries.

raisin and walnut scones

RAISINS, WALNUTS, LIGHT BROWN SUGAR, AND BUTTERMILK COMBINE TO MAKE THESE SCRUMPTIOUS SCONES. I FIND IT HARD TO EAT ONLY ONE OF THEM, SO IT'S A GOOD THING THEY ARE SMALL. THEY ARE DELICIOUS WITH AFTERNOON TEA, SERVED WITH BUTTER AND JAM, AND ARE EQUALLY GOOD FOR BREAKFAST. THESE SCONES ARE BEST SERVED WARM AND ARE EASILY REHEATED IN A 350°F OVEN FOR 7 TO 9 MINUTES.

MAKES 2 dozen 1½-inch triangular scones

1¼ cups (5½ ounces) all-purpose flour

1 tablespoon (¼ ounce) firmly packed light brown sugar

1 teaspoon baking powder

¼ teaspoon baking soda

⅛ teaspoon kosher or fine-grained sea salt

2 ounces (4 tablespoons, ½ stick) unsalted butter, chilled

⅔ cup (3½ ounces) raisins

½ cup (2¼ ounces) coarsely chopped walnuts

¼ cup buttermilk

1 extra-large egg, at room temperature

½ teaspoon pure vanilla extract

2 teaspoons heavy whipping cream

1 teaspoon turbinado or Demerara sugar

Position a rack in the center of the oven and preheat the oven to 350°F. Line a baking sheet with parchment paper or a nonstick liner.

• • •

Pulse together the flour, brown sugar, baking powder, baking soda, and salt in the work bowl of a food processor fitted with a steel blade.

• • •

Cut the butter into small pieces and add it to the flour mixture. Pulse until the butter is cut into very tiny pieces, about 30 seconds. The texture should be sandy with very tiny lumps throughout. Add the raisins and walnuts and pulse a few times to mix.

• • •

Use a fork to lightly beat together the buttermilk, egg, and vanilla in a liquid measuring cup. With the food processor running, pour this mixture through the feed tube and process until the dough forms itself into a ball, about 30 seconds.

• • •

Dust a large piece of waxed or parchment paper with flour and turn the dough out onto it. Knead the dough briefly and divide it into 6 equal pieces. Form each piece of dough into a disk about 3 inches in diameter. Using a sharp knife dipped in flour, quarter each disk into 4 equal wedges. Transfer the scones to the lined baking sheet, leaving at least 1 inch of space between them so they have room to expand as they bake.

• • •

GARNISH

Brush the tops of the scones with cream, taking care that it doesn't run down the sides and under the scones. If it does, wipe it up because it can cause the bottoms of the scones to burn. Lightly sprinkle the tops of the scones with turbinado or Demerara sugar.

• • •

Bake the scones for 15 minutes, until light golden. Remove the baking sheet from the oven and cool the scones completely on the baking sheet on a rack.

• • •

keeping Store the scones in an airtight plastic container between layers of waxed paper at room temperature up to 4 days. To freeze up to 4 months, wrap the container tightly in several layers of plastic wrap and aluminum foil. Use a large piece of masking tape and an indelible marker to label and date the contents. If frozen, defrost the scones overnight in the refrigerator and bring to room temperature before serving.

making a change Replace the raisins with finely chopped dried apricots, dried tart cherries, or dried cranberries.

Replace the walnuts with almonds or pecans.

macadamia nut and toasted coconut scones

TOASTED MACADAMIA NUTS AND TOASTED COCONUT GIVE THESE CLASSIC SCONES A TROPICAL FLAVOR. THEY ARE NOT TOO SWEET AND HAVE THE PERFECT TEXTURE THAT IS LIGHT YET DENSE, CRUMBLY ON THE INSIDE AND CRISP ON THE OUTSIDE. THESE BITE-SIZE MORSELS WILL QUICKLY BECOME YOUR FAVORITES FOR BREAKFAST, AFTERNOON TEA, AND SNACKS. THESE ARE BEST SERVED WARM AND CAN BE REHEATED IN A 350°F OVEN FOR 7 TO 9 MINUTES.

MAKES 2 dozen 1½-inch triangular scones

⅓ cup (¾ ounce) sweetened shredded coconut

1¼ cups (5½ ounces) all-purpose flour

1 tablespoon (¼ ounce) plus 1 teaspoon granulated sugar

1½ teaspoons baking powder

⅛ teaspoon kosher or fine-grained sea salt

2 ounces (4 tablespoons, ½ stick) unsalted butter, chilled

½ cup (2¾ ounces) coarsely chopped, toasted unsalted macadamia nuts

⅓ cup plus 2 teaspoons heavy whipping cream

1 extra-large egg, at room temperature

½ teaspoon pure vanilla extract

Position a rack in the center of the oven and preheat the oven to 350°F. Line a baking sheet with parchment paper or a nonstick liner.

• • •

Place the coconut in a cake or pie pan and toast in the oven for 4 minutes. Shake the pan and toast another 3 to 4 minutes, until light golden brown. Remove the pan from the oven and cool on a rack. Raise the oven temperature to 425°F.

• • •

Pulse together the flour, 1 tablespoon of sugar, baking powder, and salt in the work bowl of a food processor fitted with a steel blade.

• • •

Cut the butter into small pieces and add it to the flour mixture. Pulse until the butter is cut into very tiny pieces, about 30 seconds. The texture should be sandy with very tiny lumps throughout. Add the macadamia nuts and toasted coconut and pulse a few times to mix them in.

• • •

Use a fork to lightly beat ⅓ cup of cream with the egg and vanilla in a liquid measuring cup. With the food processor running, pour this mixture through the feed tube and process until the dough forms itself into a ball, about 30 seconds.

• • •

Dust a large piece of waxed or parchment paper with flour and turn the dough out onto it. Knead the dough briefly and divide it into 6 equal pieces. Form each piece of dough into a disk about 3 inches in diameter. Using a sharp knife dipped in flour, quarter each disk into 4 equal wedges. Transfer the scones to the lined baking sheet, leaving at least 1 inch of space between them so they have room to expand as they bake.

• • •

GARNISH

Brush the tops of the scones with the remaining 2 teaspoons of cream, taking care that it doesn't run down the sides and under the scones. If it does, wipe it up because it can cause the bottoms of the scones to burn. Lightly sprinkle the tops of the scones with the remaining 1 teaspoon of sugar.

• • •

Bake the scones for 15 to 17 minutes, until light golden. Remove the baking sheet from the oven and cool the scones completely on a rack.

• • •

keeping Store the scones in an airtight plastic container between layers of waxed paper at room temperature up to 4 days. To freeze up to 4 months, wrap the container tightly in several layers of plastic wrap and aluminum foil. Use a large piece of masking tape and an indelible marker to label and date the contents. If frozen, defrost the scones overnight in the refrigerator and bring to room temperature before serving.

making a change Add ¼ cup of finely chopped dried apricots or dried tart cherries with the nuts and coconut.

Replace the toasted macadamia nuts with toasted walnuts, almonds, or pecans.

lemon-cornmeal shortcakes

CORNMEAL ADDS BOTH DISTINCTIVE FLAVOR AND TEXTURE TO THESE SHORTCAKES, WHICH ARE FILLED WITH LEMON CREAM AND FRESH BLUEBERRIES. THESE ARE A WONDERFUL SPRINGTIME DESSERT.

MAKES *fourteen 1½-inch round shortcakes*

¾ cup (3¼ ounces) all-purpose flour

3 tablespoons (1 ounce) fine yellow cornmeal

1 tablespoon (¼ ounce) granulated sugar

1¼ teaspoons baking powder

Finely grated zest of 1 large lemon

⅛ teaspoon kosher or fine-grained sea salt

2 ounces (4 tablespoons, ½ stick) unsalted butter, chilled in the freezer for 20 minutes

3 tablespoons plus ⅓ cup heavy whipping cream

1 extra-large egg yolk, at room temperature

¼ teaspoon pure lemon extract

¼ teaspoon pure vanilla extract

1 teaspoon turbinado or Demerara sugar

1 cup Lemon Curd (see page 78)

2 cups (10 ounces) fresh blueberries

SHORTCAKES

Position a rack in the center of the oven and preheat the oven to 400°F. Line a baking sheet with parchment paper or a nonstick liner.

• • •

Pulse together the flour, cornmeal, granulated sugar, baking powder, lemon zest, and salt in the work bowl of a food processor fitted with a steel blade.

• • •

Cut the butter into small pieces and add it to the flour mixture. Pulse until the butter is cut into pea-size pieces, about 30 seconds. The mixture should be crumbly. Don't cut the butter too small or the shortcakes will lose their flaky quality.

• • •

Use a fork to lightly beat 2 tablespoons of cream with the egg yolk, lemon extract, and vanilla in a liquid measuring cup. With the food processor running, pour this mixture through the feed tube and process until all the ingredients are combined and the dough is moist, about 30 seconds.

• • •

Turn the dough out onto a lightly floured flat surface. Dust your hands with flour and shape the dough into a disk or rectangle about ¾ inch thick. Dip a 1½-inch round plain-edge biscuit cutter in flour and use it to cut out the shortcakes. Cut straight down through the dough without twisting the cutter, which seals the edges of the dough and keeps the shortcakes from rising well in the oven. Transfer them to the lined baking sheet, leaving at least 1 inch of space between them so they have room to expand as they bake. Gather the scraps together and knead slightly. Pat them into a ¾-inch-thick disk or rectangle and proceed as above to get 14 shortcakes. Brush any excess flour off the shortcakes.

• • •

GARNISH

Brush the tops of the shortcakes with 1 tablespoon of cream, being careful that it doesn't run down the sides and under the shortcakes. If it does, wipe it up because it can cause the bottoms of the shortcakes to burn. Lightly sprinkle the tops of the shortcakes with the turbinado or Demerara sugar. Using this type of sugar on top adds extra texture to the shortcakes.

• • •

Bake the shortcakes for 10 to 11 minutes, until light golden. Remove the baking sheet from the oven and cool the shortcakes completely on the baking sheet on a rack.

• • •

ASSEMBLY

Stir the lemon curd in a medium-size bowl with a whisk or rubber spatula to remove any lumps.

• • •

Whip the remaining ⅓ cup of cream in a chilled bowl of an electric stand mixer with the wire whip attachment or in a medium-size mixing bowl using a hand-held mixer on medium speed until frothy. Fold the lemon curd and whipped cream together until thoroughly blended.

• • •

Using a serrated knife, slice each shortcake in half horizontally. Place the bottom of a shortcake on a serving plate and cover with a small scoop of the lemon cream. Place 1 tablespoon of blueberries on top of the lemon cream and cover the blueberries with another small scoop of lemon cream.

Lightly place the top of the shortcake on top of the berries or arrange it at an angle to the bottom of the shortcake. Scatter a few blueberries around the plate. Repeat with the remaining shortcakes, lemon cream, and blueberries.

• • •

Serve immediately or cover with aluminum foil and refrigerate up to 3 hours before serving.

• • •

keeping The shortcakes can be baked up to 4 days in advance of assembly. Store them in an airtight plastic container between layers of waxed paper at room temperature. To freeze for up to 4 months, wrap the container tightly in several layers of plastic wrap and aluminum foil. Use a large piece of masking tape and an indelible marker to label and date the contents. If frozen, defrost the shortcakes overnight in the refrigerator and bring to room temperature before serving.

making a change Replace the blueberries with blackberries or raspberries, or use a combination of berries.

raspberry, ginger, and honey shortcakes

FLAKY SHORTCAKES ACCENTED WITH GINGER ARE FILLED WITH A DELECTABLE COMBINATION OF FRESH RASPBERRIES AND HONEY WHIPPED CREAM. I LIKE TO USE CLOVER HONEY WHEN I MAKE THESE, BUT TRY USING DIFFERENT TYPES OF HONEY TO CREATE DISTINCTIVE FLAVORS.

MAKES *fourteen 1½-inch round shortcakes*

¾ cup (3¼ ounces) all-purpose flour

1 tablespoon (¼ ounce) firmly packed light brown sugar

1¼ teaspoons baking powder

2 tablespoons (1 ounce) finely chopped crystallized ginger

¼ teaspoon freshly grated nutmeg

⅛ teaspoon kosher or fine-grained sea salt

2 ounces (4 tablespoons, ½ stick) unsalted butter, chilled in the freezer for 20 minutes

3 tablespoons plus ½ cup heavy whipping cream

1 extra-large egg yolk, at room temperature

½ teaspoon pure vanilla extract

1 teaspoon Demerara or crystal sugar

2 cups (9 ounces) fresh raspberries

2 tablespoons (¾ ounce) superfine sugar

1 tablespoon Grand Marnier or other orange liqueur, or Chambord (optional)

2 tablespoons clover honey

1 tablespoon (¼ ounce) thinly sliced crystallized ginger

SHORTCAKES

Position a rack in the center of the oven and preheat the oven to 400°F. Line a baking sheet with parchment paper or a nonstick liner.

• • •

Pulse together the flour, brown sugar, baking powder, chopped crystallized ginger, nutmeg, and salt in the work bowl of a food processor fitted with a steel blade.

• • •

Cut the butter into small pieces and add it to the flour mixture. Pulse until the butter is cut into pea-size pieces, about 30 seconds. The mixture should be crumbly. Don't cut the butter too small or the shortcakes will lose their flaky quality.

• • •

Use a fork to lightly beat 2 tablespoons of cream with the egg yolk and vanilla in a liquid measuring cup. With the food processor running, pour this mixture through the feed tube and process until all the ingredients are combined and the dough is moist, about 30 seconds.

• • •

Turn the dough out onto a lightly floured flat surface. Dust your hands with flour and shape the dough into a disk or rectangle about ¾ inch thick. Dip a 1½-inch round plain-edge biscuit cutter in flour and use it to cut out the short-cakes. Cut straight down through the dough without twisting the cutter, which seals the edges of the dough and keeps the shortcakes from rising well in the oven. Place them on the lined baking sheet, leaving at least 1 inch of space between them so they have room to expand as they bake. Gather the scraps together and knead slightly. Pat them into a ¾-inch-thick disk or rectangle and proceed as above to get 14 short-cakes. Brush any excess flour off of the shortcakes.

• • •

GARNISH

Brush the tops of the shortcakes with 1 tablespoon of cream, being careful that it doesn't run down the sides and under the shortcakes. If it does, wipe it up because it can cause the bottoms of the shortcakes to burn. Lightly sprinkle the tops of the shortcakes with the Demerara or crystal sugar. Using these types of sugar on top adds extra texture to the shortcakes.

• • •

Bake the shortcakes for 10 to 11 minutes, until light golden. Remove the baking sheet from the oven and cool the shortcakes completely on the baking sheet on a rack.

• • •

ASSEMBLY

Place the raspberries in a medium-size bowl. Add the superfine sugar and Grand Marnier, if using. Toss lightly to coat the berries completely. Cover the bowl tightly with plastic wrap and let the raspberries marinate for 15 to 30 minutes.

• • •

Whip the remaining ½ cup of cream in a chilled bowl of an electric stand mixer with the wire whip attachment or in a medium-size bowl using a hand-held mixer on medium speed until frothy. Add the honey and continue to whip the cream until it holds soft peaks.

• • •

Using a serrated knife, slice each shortcake in half horizontally. Place the bottom of a shortcake on a serving plate and cover with a small scoop of whipped cream. Place 1 tablespoon of raspberries on top of the cream and cover the raspberries with another small scoop of whipped cream. Lightly place the top of the shortcake on top of the raspberries or arrange it at an angle to the bottom of the shortcake. Top with a sliver of crystallized ginger at an angle in the cream. Scatter a few raspberries around the plate. Repeat with the remaining shortcakes, whipped cream, raspberries, and slivers of crystallized ginger.

• • •

Serve immediately or cover with aluminum foil and refrigerate up to 3 hours before serving.

• • •

keeping The shortcakes can be baked up to 4 days in advance of assembly. Store them in an airtight plastic container between layers of waxed paper at room temperature. To freeze for up to 4 months, wrap the container tightly in several layers of plastic wrap and aluminum foil. Use a large piece of masking tape and an indelible marker to label and date the contents. If frozen, defrost the shortcakes overnight in the refrigerator and bring to room temperature before serving.

making a change Replace the raspberries with blackberries, blueberries, or thinly sliced strawberries, or use a combination of berries.

apricot, almond, and toasted coconut muffins

DRIED APRICOTS, TOASTED ALMONDS, AND TOASTED COCONUT COMBINE TO MAKE THESE TASTY MUFFINS. THEY ARE GREAT TO EAT ANY TIME OF DAY. I LIKE THEM EITHER AT ROOM TEMPERATURE OR REWARMED IN A 350°F OVEN FOR 8 TO 10 MINUTES.

MAKES 22 muffins | USE two 12-cavity 2-inch round silicone mini muffin pans

⅓ cup (½ ounce) sweetened shredded coconut

1 cup (4½ ounces) all-purpose flour

⅓ cup (2 ounces) firmly packed light brown sugar

1½ teaspoons baking powder

¼ teaspoon freshly grated nutmeg

¼ teaspoon kosher or fine-grained sea salt

1 extra-large egg, at room temperature

½ cup heavy whipping cream

2 ounces (4 tablespoons, ½ stick) unsalted butter, melted

1 teaspoon pure vanilla extract or vanilla paste

⅓ cup (2 ounces) finely chopped dried apricots

⅓ cup (1¾ ounces) toasted whole almonds, coarsely chopped

Position a rack in the center of the oven and preheat the oven to 350°F. Place the mini muffin pans on a baking sheet.

• • •

Place the coconut in a cake or pie pan. Toast in the oven for 5 to 7 minutes, until light golden brown, shaking the pan every 2 minutes. Remove the pan from the oven and cool on a rack. Raise the oven temperature to 400°F.

• • •

In a large mixing bowl, stir together the flour, brown sugar, baking powder, nutmeg, and salt.

• • •

In a medium-size bowl, use a fork to beat together the egg, cream, melted butter, and vanilla. Add this mixture to the flour mixture and blend together to moisten. The batter doesn't have to be totally smooth. Add the dried apricots, chopped almonds, and toasted coconut to the batter and stir briefly to mix evenly.

• • •

Use a 1½-inch round ice cream scoop to divide the batter evenly among 22 cavities of the muffin pans, filling them three-fourths full.

• • •

Bake the muffins for 15 minutes, until golden and a cake tester inserted in the center comes out clean. Remove the baking sheet from the oven and transfer the mini muffin pans to cooling racks. When the muffins are cool, invert the pans to remove them, then turn them right-side up.

• • •

keeping Store the muffins in an airtight plastic container between layers of waxed paper at room temperature up to 4 days. To freeze up to 4 months, wrap the container tightly in several layers of plastic wrap and aluminum foil. Use a large piece of masking tape and an indelible marker to label and date the contents. If frozen, defrost the muffins overnight in the refrigerator and bring to room temperature before serving.

making a change Replace the dried apricots with dried tart cherries, dried cranberries, diced dried figs, or raisins.

coconut–macadamia nut muffins

COCONUT AND MACADAMIA NUTS BLEND TOGETHER TO GIVE THESE MUFFINS GREAT TEXTURE AND FLAVOR. THEY ARE DELICIOUS AT ROOM TEMPERATURE AND EQUALLY GOOD WARMED UP IN A 350°F OVEN FOR 7 TO 9 MINUTES FOR BREAKFAST, AFTERNOON TEA, OR AS A SNACK.

MAKES 1 dozen muffins | USE a 12-cavity 2-inch round silicone mini muffin pan

½ cup plus 1 tablespoon (2¾ ounces) all-purpose flour

⅛ teaspoon baking soda

Pinch of kosher or fine-grained sea salt

1 ounce (2 tablespoons, ¼ stick) unsalted butter, softened

3 tablespoons (1¼ ounces) granulated sugar

1 extra-large egg yolk, at room temperature

1 teaspoon pure vanilla extract

2 tablespoons buttermilk

⅓ cup (½ ounce) sweetened shredded coconut

¼ cup (1¼ ounces) coarsely chopped, toasted unsalted macadamia nuts

Position a rack in the center of the oven and preheat the oven to 375°F. Place the mini muffin pan on a baking sheet.

• • •

Over a medium-size bowl, sift together the flour and baking soda. Add the salt and toss together to blend.

• • •

Beat the butter in the bowl of an electric stand mixer with the flat beater attachment or in a large bowl using a hand-held mixer on medium speed until fluffy, about 1 minute. Add the sugar and beat together well.

• • •

Use a fork to lightly beat the egg yolk and vanilla together in a small bowl and add to the butter mixture. Stop occasionally and scrape down the sides and bottom of the bowl with a rubber spatula to mix evenly. Add the flour mixture to the butter mixture in 3 stages, alternating with the buttermilk and blending well after each addition. Add the coconut and macadamia nuts and blend thoroughly.

• • •

Use a 1½-inch round ice cream scoop to divide the batter evenly among the cavities of the muffin pan.

• • •

Bake the muffins for 14 minutes, until they spring back when lightly touched on top. Remove the baking sheet from the oven and transfer the mini muffin pan to a cooling rack. When the muffins are cool, invert the pan to remove them, then turn them right-side up.

• • •

keeping Store the muffins in an airtight plastic container between layers of waxed paper at room temperature up to 4 days. To freeze up to 4 months, wrap the container tightly in several layers of plastic wrap and aluminum foil. Use a large piece of masking tape and an indelible marker to label and date the contents. If frozen, defrost the muffins overnight in the refrigerator and bring to room temperature before serving.

making a change Add ¼ cup of finely chopped dried apricots, dried pineapple, or dried tart cherries with the coconut and macadamia nuts.

Replace the macadamia nuts with walnuts, almonds, or pecans.

spiced buttermilk doughnut holes

LIKE MOST PEOPLE, I'VE EATEN MY SHARE OF DOUGHNUTS, AND THESE REMIND ME OF THE DOUGHNUT HOLES I ATE AS A CHILD. I'VE SPICED THESE UP WITH CINNAMON, GINGER, AND NUTMEG TO MAKE THEM IRRESISTIBLE. ENJOY!

MAKES 5 dozen doughnut holes

4 cups canola or safflower oil

1½ cups (10 ounces) granulated sugar, divided

2¼ teaspoons ground cinnamon, divided

1 teaspoon freshly grated nutmeg, divided

¾ teaspoon ground ginger, divided

1 cup (4½ ounces) all-purpose flour

¾ cup (2¼ ounces) cake flour

1 teaspoon baking powder

½ teaspoon baking soda

¼ teaspoon kosher or fine-grained sea salt

1 extra-large egg, at room temperature

½ cup buttermilk

1 tablespoon unsalted butter, melted

1 teaspoon finely grated lemon zest

½ teaspoon pure vanilla extract

Pour the oil into a 3- or 4-quart heavy-duty saucepan. Insert a candy or instant-read deep-fry thermometer into the oil and heat the oil over medium heat until it registers 375°F. Line a baking sheet with a double layer of paper towels.

• • •

Place 1 cup of sugar in a small bowl or plastic bag and add 2 teaspoons of cinnamon, ½ teaspoon of nutmeg, and ½ teaspoon of ginger. Stir or shake together until well blended. Set this spiced sugar aside while making the doughnut holes.

• • •

Over a medium-size bowl, sift together the flours, baking powder, baking soda, the remaining ¼ teaspoon of cinnamon, and ¼ teaspoon of ginger. Add the remaining ½ cup of sugar, ½ teaspoon of nutmeg, and the salt and toss to blend.

• • •

Whisk the egg in a large bowl. Add the buttermilk, melted butter, lemon zest, and vanilla and whisk until smooth. Add the flour mixture in 2 stages, folding together gently with a rubber spatula until thoroughly mixed.

• • •

Using a 1-inch round ice cream scoop, place 5 or 6 scoops of the batter into the hot oil. Cook for 2 to 3 minutes, until golden brown, turning once.

• • •

Use a skimmer or slotted spoon to remove the doughnut holes from the oil and place them on the lined baking sheet. Let them cool slightly, then roll them in the spiced sugar. If the spiced sugar is in a plastic bag, shake 2 or 3 doughnut holes at a time in the spiced sugar to coat. Place the doughnut holes back on the baking sheet and cool them slightly. Repeat with the remaining batter. Serve the doughnut holes warm or at room temperature.

• • •

keeping Although the doughnut holes are best eaten the day they are made, they will keep for 3 days. Store them on a plate, tightly covered with aluminum foil. They can be rewarmed in a 350°F oven for 10 minutes.

caramelized pear and dried cherry strudel

WHEN MY GOOD FRIEND KITTY MORSE CAME FOR THANKSGIVING DINNER, SHE BROUGHT A DELICIOUS SAVORY STRUDEL AS AN APPETIZER. IT INSPIRED ME TO CREATE THIS SWEET STRUDEL MADE WITH SHEETS OF FILO DOUGH FILLED WITH CARAMELIZED PEARS AND DRIED TART CHERRIES. SERVE THIS AT ROOM TEMPERATURE OR WARM. IT CAN BE REHEATED IN A 350°F OVEN FOR ABOUT 8 MINUTES. FOR AN EXTRA TREAT, SERVE THIS STRUDEL WITH SMALL SCOOPS OF VANILLA OR CARDAMOM ICE CREAM. BE SURE TO DEFROST THE FILO DOUGH A DAY IN ADVANCE BEFORE USING IT.

MAKES *two 9 × 3–inch strudels, 16 to 18 servings*

½ cup (2 ounces) pecans

3 ripe Bosc or Anjou pears (1 to 1¼ pounds)

⅓ cup (1¾ ounces) dried tart cherries

2 tablespoons dark rum

1 teaspoon pure vanilla bean paste

¼ teaspoon freshly grated nutmeg

¼ cup (1½ ounces) firmly packed light brown sugar

2 tablespoons water

½ ounce (1 tablespoon) unsalted butter

8 half-size (9 × 12–inch) sheets frozen filo pastry dough, thawed

2 ounces (4 tablespoons, ½ stick) unsalted butter, melted

1 to 2 tablespoons confectioners' sugar

Position a rack in the center of the oven and preheat the oven to 350°F. Line a baking sheet with parchment paper or a nonstick liner.

• • •

Place the pecans in a cake or pie pan and toast in the oven for 8 minutes. Remove the pan from the oven and cool on a rack. Chop the pecans finely.

• • •

Peel, quarter, and core the pears, then cut them into 1-inch-thick slices. Put them in a large bowl and add the cherries, rum, vanilla paste, and nutmeg. Toss to coat the pears completely and let stand for 10 minutes.

• • •

Combine the brown sugar and water in a 3-quart saucepan or large frying pan and bring to a boil over medium-high heat. Cook for about 5 minutes, until the bubbles are large and the mixture caramelizes. Add the ½ ounce of butter and stir until it is completely melted.

• • •

Stir the pear mixture into the caramel and cook for 8 to 10 minutes, until most of the liquid has evaporated. Stir in the chopped toasted pecans. Remove the pan from the heat and cool.

• • •

Place the filo dough on a smooth, flat surface and cover with a damp paper towel to keep it from drying out. Take 1 sheet of filo dough and lay it across the width of the baking sheet. Use a pastry brush to lightly spread some of the melted butter over the filo. Repeat with 3 more sheets of filo dough and melted butter.

• • •

Spread half of the caramelized pear mixture lengthwise along the center of the filo, leaving a 2-inch border along the short ends and a 3-inch border along the long ends. Fold the short ends of the filo dough toward the center and over the filling and brush lightly with butter. Fold the long ends over the filling and brush lightly with butter. Use a long-blade offset spatula to turn the strudel over on the baking sheet so the seam is on the bottom. Repeat with the remaining sheets of filo dough, melted butter, and filling.

• • •

Bake the strudels for 20 minutes, until light golden brown. Remove the baking sheet from the oven and cool the strudels on the baking sheet on a rack.

• • •

Dust the tops of the strudels with confectioners' sugar. Cut the strudels crosswise into 1-inch-thick slices and serve.

• • •

keeping Store the cooled strudel tightly covered with aluminum foil at room temperature for 3 days.

making a change Replace the pecans with walnuts.

Replace the dried tart cherries with dried cranberries or dried blueberries.

chapter four

TARTLETS, COBBLERS, CRISPS, TURNOVERS, AND GALETTES

double lemon meringue tartlets

IF YOU LIKE LEMON MERINGUE PIE, YOU WILL LOVE THESE. LEMON CURD FILLING IS NESTLED INSIDE OF LEMON-ACCENTED PASTRY SHELLS, THEN TOPPED WITH A LIGHTLY TOASTED MERINGUE. BOTH THE PASTRY DOUGH AND THE LEMON CURD NEED TO BE MADE IN ADVANCE SO THEY HAVE TIME TO CHILL. SINCE THE PASTRY SHELLS ALSO NEED TO BE BAKED WITHOUT THE FILLING, THEY CAN BE MADE UP TO TWO DAYS AHEAD, MAKING IT EASY TO ASSEMBLE THESE NOT LONG BEFORE SERVING.

MAKES 2 dozen tartlets | USE forty-eight 2 × 1–inch round fluted-edge tartlet pans

1 cup (4½ ounces) all-purpose flour

1 tablespoon (¼ ounce) plus ¼ cup (1½ ounces) granulated sugar

⅛ teaspoon kosher or fine-grained sea salt

Finely grated zest of ½ large lemon

3 ounces (6 tablespoons, ¾ stick) unsalted butter, chilled

1 extra-large egg yolk, at room temperature, divided

1 tablespoon heavy whipping cream

1 recipe Lemon Curd (page 78)

2 extra-large egg whites, at room temperature

LEMON PASTRY DOUGH

Pulse together the flour, 1 tablespoon of sugar, salt, and lemon zest in the work bowl of a food processor fitted with a steel blade.

• • •

Cut the chilled butter into small pieces and add to the flour mixture. Pulse until the butter is cut into very tiny pieces, about 30 seconds. The texture will be sandy with very tiny lumps throughout.

• • •

In a small bowl, use a fork to mix the egg yolk with the cream. With the food processor running, pour this mixture through the feed tube. Process the dough until the mixture wraps itself around the blade, about 1 minute.

• • •

Shape the dough into a flat disk and wrap tightly in a double layer of plastic wrap. Chill in the refrigerator until firm before using, about 2 hours. If the dough is too cold and

firm, let it stand at room temperature for 10 to 15 minutes to become more pliable before rolling out.

• • •

On a smooth, flat surface, roll out the pastry dough between sheets of lightly floured waxed or parchment paper to a large disk about 12 inches in diameter. Carefully peel the paper off the top of the dough and brush off any excess flour. Dip a 2½-inch plain round biscuit cutter into flour and cut out 24 circles of dough. Gently place each dough circle into a tartlet pan, fit it against the bottom and sides of the pan, and pinch off any excess dough at the top edge.

• • •

Top the dough in each tartlet pan with another tartlet pan to act as a weight as it bakes. Place the pans on a baking sheet. Chill in the freezer for 15 to 20 minutes.

• • •

Position a rack in the center of the oven and preheat the oven to 375°F.

• • •

Bake the tartlet shells for 8 minutes. Remove the top tartlet pans. If the bottoms of the pastry shells puff up, gently pierce them with a fork or the point of a knife to release the air. Bake another 8 to 10 minutes, until light golden brown. Remove the baking sheet from the oven and transfer it to a rack to cool completely. To remove the tartlet shells from their pans, gently tap each pan on the countertop.

• • •

LEMON CURD

Make one recipe of Lemon Curd according to the procedure given on page 78 of the Almond, Lemon, and Berry Tartlets. Note that the lemon curd must chill for 3 to 4 hours before assembly.

• • •

MERINGUE

Place the egg whites and remaining ¼ cup of sugar in a grease-free large mixing bowl and place the bowl over a large saucepan of simmering water. Whisk constantly until the egg whites are warm. Remove the bowl from the pan of water and wipe the bottom and sides dry. Whip the egg whites in an electric stand mixer with a grease-free wire whip attachment or in a medium bowl using a hand-held mixer on medium-high speed until they hold shiny and firm but not stiff peaks.

• • •

ASSEMBLY

Stir the lemon curd vigorously with a whisk or rubber spatula to eliminate any lumps. Fit a 12- or 14-inch pastry bag with a ½-inch-diameter plain tip and fill the bag partway with the lemon curd. Pipe about ½ teaspoon of lemon curd into each tartlet shell.

• • •

Fit another 12- or 14-inch pastry bag with a large open star tip and fill the bag partway with the meringue. Pipe the meringue on top of each tartlet in a rosette. Use a butane kitchen torch to lightly brown the meringue.

• • •

Serve immediately or chill in the refrigerator, lightly covered with waxed paper, then loosely wrapped with plastic wrap, up to 3 hours before serving.

• • •

keeping Store the tartlets in a single layer on a baking sheet. Cover the tops of the tartlets with a large piece of waxed paper to keep the surface from becoming marred. Tightly wrap the pan with plastic wrap and keep in the refrigerator up to 1 day.

streamlining The pastry dough can be made in advance and kept in the refrigerator, tightly wrapped in a double layer of plastic wrap up, up to 4 days before using. To freeze up to 4 months, wrap it in a double layer of plastic wrap and enclose it in a freezer bag. Use a large piece of masking tape and an indelible marker to label and date the contents. If frozen, defrost the dough in the refrigerator overnight before using. If it is too cold to roll out, let it stand at room temperature to become pliable.

The tartlet shells can be baked and held at room temperature up to 2 days before filling. After they are completely cool, place them on a jelly-roll pan, cover with waxed paper, and tightly wrap the pan in aluminum foil.

The lemon curd can be made up to 1 month in advance. Store it in a tightly covered plastic container in the refrigerator.

bittersweet chocolate and hazelnut tartlets

BITTERSWEET CHOCOLATE AND HAZELNUT IS ONE OF MY FAVORITE FLAVOR COMBINATIONS. A TOUCH OF ORANGE ZEST IN THE BACKGROUND HELPS TO HIGHLIGHT THE FLAVORS. THESE ARE GREAT TO SERVE WHENEVER YOU WOULD LIKE AN ELEGANT DESSERT.

MAKES 2 dozen tartlets | USE twenty-four 1⅝ × ¾–inch round fluted-edge tartlet pans

1 cup (4½ ounces) plus 1 teaspoon all-purpose flour

5 tablespoons (2¼ ounces) granulated sugar, divided

⅛ teaspoon baking powder

Pinch of kosher or fine-grained sea salt

Finely grated zest of 1 medium orange, divided

1½ ounces (3 tablespoons) unsalted butter, chilled

2 extra-large egg yolks, at room temperature, divided

1 to 2 tablespoons heavy whipping cream

1½ teaspoons pure vanilla extract, divided

½ cup (2½ ounces) raw hazelnuts

1 ounce (2 tablespoons, ¼ stick) unsalted butter, softened

1¾ ounces bittersweet chocolate (62 to 72% cacao content), finely chopped

PASTRY DOUGH

Pulse together briefly 1 cup of flour, 2 tablespoons of sugar, baking powder, salt, and zest from ½ orange in the work bowl of a food processor fitted with the steel blade.

• • •

Cut the chilled butter into small pieces and add it to the flour mixture. Pulse until the butter is cut into very tiny pieces, about 30 seconds. The texture will be sandy with very tiny lumps throughout.

• • •

In a small bowl, use a fork to beat 1 egg yolk, 1 tablespoon of cream, and ½ teaspoon of vanilla together. With the food processor running, pour this mixture through the feed tube. Process the dough until the mixture wraps itself around the blade, about 1 minute. If the dough is dry, add the remaining tablespoon of cream and process.

• • •

Shape the dough into a flat disk and wrap tightly in a double layer of plastic wrap. Chill in the refrigerator until firm before using, about 2 hours. If the dough is too cold and firm, let it stand at room temperature for 10 to 15 minutes to become more pliable before rolling out.

• • •

On a smooth, flat surface, roll out the pastry dough between sheets of lightly floured waxed or parchment paper to a large disk about 12 inches in diameter. Carefully peel the paper off the top of the dough and brush off any excess flour. Dip a 2-inch round plain biscuit cutter into flour and cut out circles of dough.

• • •

Gently place each dough circle into a tartlet pan and fit it against the bottom and sides of the pan. Pinch off any excess dough at the top edge of the pans. Place the tartlet pans on a baking sheet. Gather together any scraps, knead briefly, roll out, cut, and fit into the remaining tartlet pans. Chill while preparing the filling.

• • •

Position a rack in the center of the oven and preheat the oven to 350°F.

• • •

CHOCOLATE AND HAZELNUT FILLING

Place the hazelnuts in a single layer in a cake or pie pan and toast for 15 to 18 minutes, until the skins split and the nuts turn light golden brown.

• • •

Remove the pan from the oven and transfer the hazelnuts to a kitchen towel. Fold the towel around the hazelnuts and rub them together to remove most of the skins.

• • •

Pulse together the hazelnuts and 1 tablespoon of sugar in the work bowl of a food processor fitted with the steel blade until the nuts are finely ground, about 1 minute.

• • •

Beat the softened butter in the bowl of an electric stand mixer with the flat beater attachment or in a large bowl using a hand-held mixer on medium speed until it's fluffy, about 1 minute. Add the remaining 2 tablespoons of sugar and beat together thoroughly. Stop occasionally and scrape down the sides and bottom of the bowl with a rubber spatula.

• • •

In a small bowl, whisk together the remaining 1 egg yolk and zest from ½ orange to blend. Adjust the mixer speed to low and add the egg mixture to the butter mixture. The eggs will sit on top of the butter mixture, so stop and scrape down the sides and bottom of the bowl with a rubber spatula to help mix evenly. Add the remaining 1 teaspoon of flour and chopped chocolate and blend thoroughly. Add the remaining 1 teaspoon of vanilla extract and the finely ground hazelnuts and blend thoroughly.

• • •

Use a spoon or 1-inch round ice cream scoop to place about 1 teaspoon of filling in each unbaked tartlet shell.

• • •

Bake the tartlets for 20 to 25 minutes, until the filling is puffed and light golden brown. Remove the baking sheet from the oven and transfer it to a rack to cool completely. To remove the tartlets from their pans, gently tap each pan on the countertop.

• • •

keeping Store the tartlets in a single layer on a baking sheet. Cover the tops of the tartlets with a large piece of waxed paper. Tightly wrap the baking sheet with aluminum foil and keep at room temperature for up to 4 days.

Streamlining The pastry dough can be made in advance and kept in the refrigerator, tightly wrapped in a double layer of plastic wrap, up to 4 days before using. To freeze up to 4 months, wrap it in a double layer of plastic wrap and enclose it in a freezer bag. Use a large piece of masking tape and an indelible marker to label and date the contents. If frozen, defrost the dough in the refrigerator overnight before using. If it is too cold to roll out, let it stand at room temperature to become pliable.

The filling can be made and kept in a tightly covered container in the refrigerator up to 3 days before using.

adding style Serve each tartlet with a star, rosette, or dollop of whipped cream on top.

cacao nib—walnut ganache tartlets

THESE ARE A CHOCOLATE LOVER'S IDEA OF HEAVEN. CACAO NIBS ARE THE HULLED UNSWEETENED CENTERS OF THE CACAO BEAN THAT ARE ROASTED AND BROKEN INTO SMALL PIECES. THEY ARE CRUNCHY AND FULL OF CHOCOLATE FLAVOR. THEY CAN BE FOUND WHEREVER FINE-QUALITY CHOCOLATE IS SOLD AND THROUGH ONLINE SOURCES. IN THE PASTRY DOUGH FOR THESE TARTLETS, CACAO NIBS AND WALNUTS PROVIDE A LOT OF TEXTURE AND FLAVOR. AFTER THE PASTRY SHELLS ARE BAKED AND COOLED THEY ARE FILLED WITH A VELVETY GANACHE MIXTURE.

MAKES 22 tartlets | USE forty-four 1⅝ × ¾–inch round fluted-edge tartlet pans

Nonstick baking spray

⅓ cup (1½ ounces) walnuts

⅔ cup (3 ounces) all-purpose flour

2 tablespoons (¾ ounce) firmly packed light brown sugar

⅛ teaspoon kosher or fine-grained sea salt

2 ounces (4 tablespoons, ½ stick) unsalted butter, chilled

¼ cup (1 ounce) cacao nibs

1 extra-large egg yolk, at room temperature

½ teaspoon pure vanilla extract

6½ ounces bittersweet chocolate (62 to 72% cacao content), finely chopped

½ cup heavy whipping cream

CACAO NIB PASTRY DOUGH

Position a rack in the center of the oven and preheat the oven to 350°F. Spray the inside of each tartlet pan with non-stick baking spray and place the pans on a baking sheet.

• • •

Place the walnuts in a cake or pie pan and toast in the oven for 7 to 8 minutes, until light golden. Remove the pan from the oven and cool on a rack. Chop the walnuts finely.

• • •

Pulse together the flour, brown sugar, and salt in the work bowl of a food processor fitted with a steel blade.

• • •

Cut the butter into small pieces and add it to the flour mixture. Pulse until the butter is cut into very tiny pieces, about 30 seconds. The texture will be sandy with very tiny lumps throughout. Add the cacao nibs and chopped walnuts and pulse briefly to blend.

• • •

In a small bowl, use a fork to beat the egg yolk and vanilla together. With the food processor running, pour this mixture through the feed tube. Process the dough until the mixture wraps itself around the blade, about 1 minute.

• • •

Break off walnut-size pieces of the dough and press them into the tartlet pans. Pinch off any excess dough at the top edge of the pans. Place another tartlet pan on top of each tartlet to act as a weight while it bakes.

• • •

Bake the tartlet shells for 7 minutes. Remove the top tartlet pans. If the bottoms of the pastry shells puff up, gently pierce them with a fork or the point of a knife to release the air. Bake another 7 to 8 minutes, until light golden and set. Remove the baking sheet from the oven and transfer it to a rack to cool completely. To remove the tartlet shells from their pans, gently tap each pan on the countertop.

• • •

GANACHE FILLING

Place the chopped chocolate in a 2-quart bowl.

• • •

Place the cream in a medium saucepan and bring to a boil over medium heat. Pour the cream over the chocolate. Let it stand for 15 seconds, then stir together with a rubber spatula, whisk, or immersion blender until very smooth.

• • •

ASSEMBLY

Use a 1-inch round ice cream scoop to fill each tartlet shell to the top with ganache. Chill for 15 minutes to set the filling, or let it set at room temperature for 30 minutes to 1 hour.

• • •

Serve at room temperature.

• • •

keeping Store the tartlets in a single layer on a baking sheet. Cover the tops of the tartlets with a large piece of waxed paper to keep the surface from becoming marred. Tightly wrap the pan with aluminum foil and keep in the refrigerator up to 3 days.

streamlining The pastry dough can be made in advance and kept in the refrigerator, tightly wrapped in a double layer of plastic wrap, up to 4 days before using. To freeze up to 4 months, wrap it in a double layer of plastic wrap and enclose it in a freezer bag. Use a large piece of masking tape and an indelible marker to label and date the contents. If frozen, defrost the dough in the refrigerator overnight before using. If it is too cold to roll out, let it stand at room temperature to become pliable.

The tartlet shells can be baked and held at room temperature up to 2 days before filling. After they are completely cool, place them on a jelly-roll pan, cover with waxed paper, and tightly wrap the pan in aluminum foil.

caramelized walnut tartlets

A CREAMY CARAMELIZED FILLING CHOCK-FULL OF WALNUTS IS NESTLED IN WALNUT-ACCENTED SWEET
PASTRY DOUGH TO MAKE THESE TINY TARTLETS. A DOT OF DARK CHOCOLATE ON TOP IS ALL THESE
NEED FOR A GARNISH. THESE ARE PERFECT TWO-BITE DESSERTS THAT WILL RECEIVE RAVE REVIEWS.

MAKES 2½ dozen tartlets | USE thirty 1⅝ × ¾–inch round fluted-edge tartlet pans

---

¾ cup (3¼ ounces) all-purpose flour

1¼ cups (5½ ounces) finely chopped walnuts, divided

1 tablespoon (½ ounce) plus ⅔ cup (4 ounces) granulated sugar

⅛ teaspoon kosher or fine-grained sea salt

2 ounces (4 tablespoons, ½ stick) unsalted butter, chilled

1 extra-large egg yolk, at room temperature

1½ teaspoons pure vanilla extract, divided

Nonstick baking spray

¼ cup water

2 teaspoons honey

⅓ cup heavy whipping cream

1 teaspoon unsalted butter, softened

1 ounce bittersweet chocolate (62 to 72% cacao content), finely chopped

---

WALNUT PASTRY DOUGH

Pulse the flour, ¼ cup of walnuts, 1 tablespoon of sugar, and salt in the work bowl of a food processor fitted with a steel blade until the walnuts are finely ground, about 2 minutes.

• • •

Cut the chilled butter into small pieces and add to the flour mixture. Pulse until the butter is cut into very tiny pieces, about 30 seconds. The texture will be sandy with very tiny lumps throughout.

• • •

In a small bowl, use a fork to beat the egg yolk and ½ teaspoon of vanilla together. With the food processor running, pour this mixture through the feed tube. Process the dough until the mixture wraps itself around the blade, about 1 minute.

• • •

Coat the inside of each tartlet pan with nonstick baking spray. Break off walnut-size pieces of the dough and press them into the tartlet pans. Pinch off any excess dough at the top edge of the pans. Place the tartlet pans on a baking sheet and chill for 15 minutes.

• • •

Position a rack in the center of the oven and preheat the oven to 350°F.

• • •

CARAMELIZED WALNUT FILLING

Cook the remaining ⅔ cup of sugar, water, and honey in a 2-quart heavy-duty saucepan over high heat, without stirring, until the mixture begins to boil. Place a wet pastry brush at the point where the sugar syrup meets the sides of the pan and sweep it around completely. Do this two times to prevent the sugar from crystallizing. Cook the mixture over high heat, without stirring, until it turns amber colored, about 10 minutes.

• • •

At the same time, heat the cream in a small saucepan until it begins to boil. Pour the hot cream into the caramel mixture. Stir together using a long-handled wooden spoon or heat-resistant spatula. Be very careful because the mixture will bubble and splatter. Stir for a minute or two to dissolve any lumps.

• • •

Add the remaining 1 cup of chopped walnuts and stir them into the caramel mixture to coat completely.

• • •

Stir in the softened butter until completely melted. Then stir in the remaining 1 teaspoon of vanilla. Remove the saucepan from the heat.

• • •

Use a 1-inch round ice cream scoop to fill each tartlet shell with the walnut mixture.

• • •

Bake the tartlets for 20 minutes, until the edges are light golden brown and the filling bubbles thickly. Remove the baking sheet from the oven and transfer it to a rack to cool completely. To remove the tartlets from their pans, gently tap each pan on the countertop.

• • •

GARNISH

Place two-thirds of the chocolate in the top of a double boiler over hot water or in a microwave-safe bowl and melt on low power in the microwave for 30-second bursts. Stir after each burst to be sure the chocolate is melting. Remove the top pan of the double boiler, if using, and wipe the bottom and sides very dry. Stir in the remaining one-third of the chocolate in 2 or 3 batches, making sure each is melted before adding the next.

• • •

Pour the chocolate into a small parchment paper pastry cone. Fold down the top of the pastry cone securely. Snip off a small opening at the pointed end. Holding the pastry

bag slightly above the center of each tartlet, pipe out a small chocolate dot on top of each tartlet. Or use a spoon to drop a dot of chocolate on top of each tartlet. Chill the tartlets for 15 minutes to set the chocolate.

• • •

Serve at room temperature.

• • •

keeping Store the tartlets in a single layer on a baking sheet. Cover the tops of the tartlets with a large piece of waxed paper to keep the surface from becoming marred. Tightly wrap the pan with aluminum foil and keep at room temperature up to 3 days.

streamlining The pastry dough can be made in advance and kept in the refrigerator, tightly wrapped in a double layer of plastic wrap, up to 4 days before using. To freeze up to 4 months, wrap it in a double layer of plastic wrap and enclose it in a freezer bag. Use a large piece of masking tape and an indelible marker to label and date the contents. If frozen, defrost the dough in the refrigerator overnight before using. If it is too cold to roll out, let it stand at room temperature to become pliable.

making a change Replace the walnuts with almonds or pecans.

Serve the tartlets without the chocolate garnish on top.

venetian almond tartlets

WHEN I WORKED IN VENICE, ITALY, MANY YEARS AGO, ALL THE PASTRY SHOP WINDOWS HAD BEAUTIFUL DISPLAYS OF VENETIAN ALMOND TARTLETS IN A HUGE VARIETY OF SIZES AND SHAPES. THESE TARTLETS ARE ONE OF MY VERY FAVORITE DESSERTS, NOT ONLY BECAUSE THEY BRING BACK GREAT MEMORIES, BUT BECAUSE THEY ARE SCRUMPTIOUS.

MAKES 2 dozen tartlets | USE twenty-four 1⅝ × ¾–inch round fluted-edge tartlet pans

1 cup (4½ ounces) all-purpose flour

2 tablespoons (¾ ounce) plus ¼ cup (1½ ounces) granulated sugar

Pinch of kosher or fine-grained sea salt

3 ounces (6 tablespoons, ¾ stick) unsalted butter, chilled

2 extra-large egg yolks, at room temperature

¾ teaspoon pure vanilla extract, divided

½ cup (1¾ ounces) sliced or slivered almonds

1½ ounces (3 tablespoons) unsalted butter, softened

¼ teaspoon almond extract

⅓ cup (1¾ ounces) whole unblanched almonds

1 to 2 tablespoons confectioners' sugar, optional

PASTRY DOUGH

Pulse together the flour, 2 tablespoons of granulated sugar, and salt in the work bowl of a food processor fitted with a steel blade.

• • •

Cut the chilled butter into small pieces and add it to the flour mixture. Pulse until the butter is cut into very tiny pieces, about 30 seconds. The texture will be sandy with very tiny lumps throughout.

• • •

In a small bowl, use a fork to beat one egg yolk and ½ teaspoon of vanilla together. With the food processor running, pour this mixture through the feed tube. Process the dough until the mixture wraps itself around the blade, about 1 minute.

• • •

Shape the dough into a flat disk and wrap tightly in a double layer of plastic wrap. Chill in the refrigerator until firm before using, about 2 hours. If the dough is too cold and firm, let it stand at room temperature for 10 to 15 minutes to become more pliable before rolling out.

• • •

On a smooth, flat surface, roll out the pastry dough between sheets of lightly floured waxed or parchment paper to a large disk about 12 inches in diameter. Carefully peel the paper off the top of the dough and brush off any excess flour. Dip a 2-inch round plain-edge biscuit cutter into flour and cut out circles of dough.

• • •

Gently place each dough round into a tartlet pan and fit it against the bottom and sides of the pan. Pinch off any excess dough at the top edge of the pans. Place the tartlet pans on a baking sheet. Gather together any scraps, knead briefly, roll out, cut, and fit into the remaining tartlet pans. Chill while preparing the filling.

• • •

Position a rack in the center of the oven and preheat it to 375°F.

• • •

ALMOND FILLING

Pulse the sliced or slivered almonds and remaining ¼ cup of granulated sugar in the work bowl of a food processor fitted with a steel blade until finely ground, about 1 minute. Add the softened butter and pulse to blend together well.

• • •

In a small bowl, whisk together the remaining egg yolk, almond extract, and the remaining ¼ teaspoon of vanilla. With the food processor running, pour this mixture through the feed tube and process until the mixture is smooth and creamy.

• • •

Place about 1 teaspoon of the filling in each tartlet shell. Place 4 or 5 whole unblanched almonds on top of the filling in each tartlet shell. Press the almonds down lightly.

• • •

Bake the tartlets for 16 to 18 minutes, until the filling is puffed and light golden brown. Remove the baking sheet from the oven and transfer it to a rack to cool completely. To remove the tartlets from their pans, gently tap each pan on the countertop.

• • •

OPTIONAL GARNISH

Lightly dust the tops of the tartlets with confectioners' sugar.

• • •

keeping Store the tartlets in a single layer on a baking sheet. Cover the tops of the tartlets with a large piece of waxed paper. Tightly wrap the baking sheet with aluminum foil and keep at room temperature up to 4 days.

streamlining The pastry dough can be made in advance and kept in the refrigerator, tightly wrapped in a double layer of plastic wrap, up to 4 days before using. To freeze up to 4 months, wrap it in a double layer of plastic wrap and enclose it in a freezer bag. Use a large piece of masking tape and an indelible marker to label and date the contents. If frozen, defrost the dough in the refrigerator overnight before using. If it is too cold to roll out, let it stand at room temperature to become pliable.

The filling can be made and kept in a tightly covered container in the refrigerator up to 3 days before using.

making a change Replace the almonds with walnuts, pine nuts, or pecans.

almond, lemon, and berry tartlets

A BUTTERY ALMOND PASTRY DOUGH HOLDS A CREAMY LEMON CURD FILLING, TOPPED WITH FRESH RASPBERRIES AND BLUEBERRIES IN THESE TINY TARTLETS. THEY REMIND ME OF LITTLE JEWELS WHEN THEY ARE ARRANGED ON A SERVING PLATTER. BE SURE TO MAKE THE LEMON CURD FILLING IN ADVANCE SO IT HAS TIME TO COOL AND THICKEN.

MAKES 2 dozen 1⅝ × ¾–inch round tartlets or sixteen 2 × 1–inch round tartlets | USE forty-eight 1⅝ × ¾–inch round fluted-edge tartlet pans or thirty-two 2 × 1–inch round fluted-edge tartlet pans

⅓ cup (1 ounce) sliced almonds

⅔ cup (3 ounces) all-purpose flour

4 tablespoons plus 1 teaspoon (2 ounces) granulated sugar

⅛ teaspoon kosher or fine-grained sea salt

2 ounces (4 tablespoons, ½ stick) unsalted butter, chilled

1 tablespoon plus 1 teaspoon heavy whipping cream

¼ teaspoon pure almond extract

¼ teaspoon pure vanilla extract

1 large lemon

2 extra-large egg yolks, at room temperature

1 ounce (2 tablespoons, ¼ stick) unsalted butter, melted

⅓ cup (1½ ounces) fresh raspberries

½ cup (2½ ounces) fresh blueberries

ALMOND PASTRY DOUGH

Position a rack in the center of the oven and preheat the oven to 350°F.

• • •

Place the almonds in a cake or pie pan and toast in the oven for 5 to 8 minutes, until light golden. Remove the pan from the oven and cool on a rack. Raise the oven temperature to 375°F.

• • •

Pulse together the toasted almonds, flour, 1 tablespoon plus 1 teaspoon of sugar, and salt in the work bowl of a food processor fitted with a steel blade until the almonds are finely ground, about 2 minutes.

• • •

Cut the chilled butter into small pieces and add it to the flour mixture. Pulse until the butter is cut into very tiny pieces, about 30 seconds. The texture will be sandy with very tiny lumps throughout.

• • •

In a small bowl, use a fork to mix the cream, almond extract, and vanilla extract together. With the food processor running, pour this mixture through the feed tube. Process the dough until the mixture wraps itself around the blade, about 1 minute.

• • •

Break off walnut-size pieces of the dough and press into the tartlet pans. Pinch off any excess dough at the top edge of the pans. Place another tartlet pan on top of each tartlet to act as weights while they bake. Place the tartlet pans on a baking sheet.

• • •

Bake the tartlet shells for 7 minutes, then remove the top tartlet pans. If the bottoms of the pastry shells puff up, gently pierce them with a fork or the point of a knife to release the air. Bake another 12 to 14 minutes, until light golden and set. Remove the baking sheet from the oven and transfer it to a rack to cool completely. To remove the tartlet shells from their pans, gently tap each pan on the countertop.

• • •

LEMON CURD

Use a fine grater to remove the outer yellow rind of the lemon. Or use a zester to remove the lemon zest and chop it very finely with a chef's knife. Cut the lemon in half, squeeze out the juice, and strain it to remove any seeds. Measure out 2 tablespoons of the juice and reserve the rest for another use.

• • •

Place the egg yolks and remaining 3 tablespoons of sugar in the top pan of a double boiler over simmering water. Stir together constantly to dissolve the sugar, about 3 minutes. Add the lemon zest, lemon juice, and melted butter. Stir the mixture constantly with a heat-resistant spatula or wooden spoon until it thickens, about 12 minutes. To see if the mixture is at the right consistency, dip the spatula into it. Hold the blade of the spatula parallel to the top of the pan and draw your finger in a parallel line across the middle of the spatula. If the mixture does not run over the line, it's thick enough. The mixture will thicken more as it cools and chills.

• • •

Remove the top pan of the double boiler and wipe the bottom and sides dry. Transfer the lemon curd to a bowl or plastic container. Cover tightly with plastic wrap or the container lid. Cool to room temperature, then place in the refrigerator until thoroughly chilled, 3 to 4 hours.

• • •

ASSEMBLY

Stir the lemon curd vigorously with a whisk or rubber spatula to eliminate any lumps. Drop about 1 teaspoon of lemon curd into each tartlet shell, filling it three-fourths full. Place a raspberry in the center of half of the tartlets and mound blueberries on the filling of the other tartlets.

• • •

keeping Store the tartlets in a single layer on a baking sheet. Cover the tops of the tartlets with a large piece of waxed paper to keep the surface from becoming marred. Tightly wrap the baking sheet with plastic wrap and keep in the refrigerator up to 2 days.

streamlining The pastry dough can be made in advance and kept in the refrigerator, tightly wrapped in a double layer of plastic wrap, up to 4 days before using. To freeze up to 4 months, wrap it in a double layer of plastic wrap and enclose it in a freezer bag. Use a large piece of masking tape and an indelible marker to label and date the contents. If frozen, defrost the dough in the refrigerator overnight before using. If it is too cold to roll out, let it stand at room temperature to become pliable.

The tartlet shells can be baked and held at room temperature up to 2 days before filling. After they are completely cool, place them on a baking sheet, cover with waxed paper, and tightly wrap the pan in aluminum foil.

The lemon curd can be made up to 1 month in advance. Store it in a tightly covered plastic container in the refrigerator.

making a change Replace the lemon curd filling with ⅓ cup of mascarpone cheese, whipped to soft peaks.

pavlovas with passion fruit sauce

PAVLOVA IS A LIGHT, CRISP MERINGUE SHELL FILLED WITH WHIPPED CREAM AND TOPPED WITH TROPICAL FRUIT. I CHOOSE TO PAIR IT WITH A PASSION FRUIT SAUCE TO ACCENT ITS TROPICAL NATURE. THIS CLASSIC DESSERT WAS CREATED TO HONOR THE VISIT TO AUSTRALIA OF ANNA PAVLOVA, A FAMOUS RUSSIAN PRIMA BALLERINA, IN 1926. THE MERINGUE SHELLS CAN BE MADE SEVERAL DAYS IN ADVANCE OF ASSEMBLING THE DESSERT, WHICH MAKES IT EASY TO FIT INTO A BUSY LIFE. YOUR GUESTS WILL BE VERY APPRECIATIVE THAT YOU DID. PASSION FRUIT CONCENTRATE FOR THE SAUCE IS AVAILABLE THROUGH PERFECT PURÉE OF NAPA VALLEY. THEIR WEB SITE IS WWW.PERFECTPUREE.COM.

MAKES 2½ dozen pavlovas

2 extra-large egg whites, at room temperature

⅛ teaspoon cream of tartar

¾ cup (5 ounces) plus 1 tablespoon superfine sugar

2 teaspoons cornstarch, sifted

¼ teaspoon distilled white vinegar

1¾ teaspoons pure vanilla extract, divided

¾ cup heavy whipping cream

½ cup (2½ ounces) fresh raspberries, blueberries, or blackberries

1 to 2 kiwifruit, peeled and thinly sliced

1 cup passion fruit concentrate

MERINGUE SHELLS

Adjust the oven racks to the upper and lower thirds and preheat the oven to 400°F. Line two baking sheets with aluminum foil. Using a 1½-inch round plain cutter or a glass as a guide, trace 30 circles onto the dull side of the foil with a pencil, then turn the foil over on the baking sheets.

• • •

Whip together the egg whites and cream of tartar in a grease-free bowl of an electric stand mixer with the wire whip attachment or in a large grease-free mixing bowl using a hand-held mixer on medium speed until frothy. Slowly sprinkle on ½ cup of sugar and continue beating the egg whites until they hold firm peaks, about 3 minutes. Turn the mixer speed to low and sprinkle on the cornstarch. Blend

together well, then thoroughly fold in the white vinegar and ¼ teaspoon of vanilla.

• • •

Fit a 12- or 14-inch pastry bag with a ½-inch-diameter plain tip and fill the bag partway with the meringue mixture. Using the traced circles as a guide, pipe out 2-inch round mounds. Dampen the back of a spoon and push the center of the meringue toward the outer edges so they are a little thicker than the center, creating a shallow bowl.

• • •

Place the baking sheets in the oven, lower the oven temperature to 250°F, and dry the meringues for 1½ hours. Turn off the oven, prop open the oven door with a wooden spoon, and leave the meringues in the oven until they are cool.

• • •

Remove the baking sheets from the oven and carefully peel the foil off the back of the meringues. Place the meringues on a baking sheet lined with waxed or parchment paper.

• • •

CREAM FILLING

Whip the cream in a chilled bowl of an electric stand mixer with a chilled wire whip attachment or in a chilled large mixing bowl using a hand-held mixer on medium speed until it thickens. Gradually sprinkle on 1 tablespoon of sugar, then beat in ½ teaspoon of vanilla and whip the cream until it holds soft peaks.

• • •

ASSEMBLY

Fit another 12- or 14-inch pastry bag with a large open star tip and fill the bag partway with the whipped cream. Pipe the cream in a circle into the center cavity and to the outer edges of each meringue mound. Arrange the fruit attractively over the cream.

• • •

PASSION FRUIT SAUCE

Bring the passion fruit concentrate and the remaining ¼ cup of sugar to a boil in a 1-quart saucepan over medium heat and reduce to half the original amount. Remove the saucepan from the heat and cool. Add the remaining 1 teaspoon of vanilla and blend thoroughly.

• • •

To serve, place a pavlova on a plate and drizzle the sauce around it.

• • •

keeping Although the pavlovas are best eaten the day they are made, they can last up to 2 days. Store them, loosely covered with waxed paper and then tightly wrapped with aluminum foil, in the refrigerator.

streamlining The meringues can be made up to 1 week in advance. Store them at room temperature, tightly wrapped in aluminum foil to protect them from moisture, which will make them soft.

mixed berry cobblers

I LOVE TO MAKE THESE COBBLERS DURING THE HEIGHT OF BERRY SEASON. THE COBBLERS CAN BE MADE WITH ANY BERRIES YOU CHOOSE, EXCEPT STRAWBERRIES, WHICH ARE TOO WATERY. I USE A MIXTURE OF RASPBERRIES, BLUEBERRIES, AND BLACKBERRIES.

MAKES 8 cobblers | USE eight 2½ × 1⅝–inch round ramekins

2 cups (10½ ounces) mixed fresh berries (raspberries, blueberries, and blackberries)

3 tablespoons (1¼ ounces) firmly packed light brown sugar, divided

½ teaspoon freshly grated nutmeg, divided

Finely grated or minced zest of ½ large lemon

1 teaspoon freshly squeezed lemon juice

1 ounce (2 tablespoons, ¼ stick) unsalted butter, softened

½ cup (2¼ ounces) all-purpose flour

¼ cup (¾ ounce) sliced almonds

¼ teaspoon baking soda

Pinch of kosher or fine-grained sea salt

1½ ounces (3 tablespoons) unsalted butter, chilled

3 tablespoons buttermilk

½ teaspoon pure vanilla extract

1 teaspoon granulated sugar

⅓ cup heavy whipping cream

2 teaspoons confectioners' sugar

Position a rack in the center of the oven and preheat the oven to 375°F. Place the ramekins in a 2-quart baking dish.

• • •

BERRY FILLING
Place the berries in a medium-size mixing bowl. Add 2 tablespoons of brown sugar, ¼ teaspoon of nutmeg, lemon zest, and lemon juice to the berries and toss together to coat them completely.

• • •

Divide the filling evenly among the ramekins, filling each three-fourths full. Cut the softened butter into small pieces and distribute it evenly over the berries.

• • •

DOUGH TOPPING
Pulse together the flour, almonds, baking soda, salt, remaining 1 tablespoon of brown sugar, and remaining ¼ teaspoon of nutmeg in the work bowl of a food processor fitted with the steel blade until the almonds are finely chopped.

• • •

Cut the chilled butter into small pieces and add it to the flour mixture. Pulse until the butter is cut into very tiny pieces, about 1 minute.

• • •

In a small bowl or a liquid measuring cup, combine the buttermilk and vanilla. With the food processor running, pour this mixture through the feed tube. Process until the dough wraps itself around the blade, about 30 seconds.

• • •

Drop spoonfuls of the dough over the berry filling in the ramekins, dividing the dough evenly. Sprinkle the topping with the granulated sugar.

• • •

Bake the cobblers for 30 minutes, until the topping is light golden and set. Remove the baking dish from the oven and transfer the ramekins to a rack to cool.

• • •

GARNISH

Whip the cream in the bowl of an electric stand mixer with the wire whip attachment or in a large mixing bowl using a hand-held mixer on medium speed until frothy. Add the confectioners' sugar and continue whipping the cream until it holds soft peaks.

• • •

Serve each cobbler with a dollop of whipped cream.

• • •

keeping Although the cobblers are best eaten the day they are made, they can last up to 2 days. Store them, without the whipped cream, tightly covered with aluminum foil in the refrigerator. Garnish right before serving.

streamlining The dough topping can be made in advance. Shape it into a disk and keep in the refrigerator, tightly wrapped in a double layer of plastic wrap, up to 4 days. To freeze up to 3 months, wrap the dough snugly in several layers of plastic wrap and enclose it in a freezer bag. Use a large piece of masking tape and an indelible marker to label and date the contents. If frozen, defrost the topping overnight in the refrigerator and bring to room temperature before using.

adding style Serve each cobbler with a scoop of vanilla, coconut, or cardamom ice cream.

peachy cobblers

FRESH, SWEET PEACHES, TOPPED WITH A BISCUIT CRUST, STAR IN THESE MINI COBBLERS. THE NAME COBBLER COMES FROM THE LOOK OF THE BISCUIT TOPPING OF THIS DESSERT, WHICH HAS A COBBLED OR "BROKEN" APPEARANCE. THIS IS A PERFECT SUMMERTIME DESSERT.

MAKES 8 cobblers | USE eight 2½ × 1⅝–inch round ramekins

1 pound fresh peaches (3 large or 4 medium)

2 tablespoons (¾ ounce) firmly packed light brown sugar

½ teaspoon freshly grated nutmeg, divided

Finely grated or minced zest of ½ large lemon

1 teaspoon freshly squeezed lemon juice

1 ounce (2 tablespoons, ¼ stick) unsalted butter, softened

½ cup (2¼ ounces) all-purpose flour

1 tablespoon (½ ounce) plus 1 teaspoon granulated sugar

1 teaspoon baking powder

Pinch of kosher or fine-grained sea salt

1½ ounces (3 tablespoons) unsalted butter, chilled

3 tablespoons plus ⅓ cup heavy whipping cream

½ teaspoon pure vanilla extract

2 teaspoons confectioners' sugar

Position a rack in the center of the oven and preheat the oven to 375°F. Place the ramekins in a 2-quart baking dish.

• • •

PEACH FILLING

Bring a large saucepan or stockpot of water to a boil over high heat. Using a sharp knife, score a small X in the bottom of each peach. Add the peaches to the water and let them boil for 1 to 2 minutes. Use a slotted spoon or skimmer to remove the peaches from the boiling water. Place them into a bowl of cold water to stop them from cooking.

• • •

Starting at the X, use a small sharp knife to gently peel the skin off the peaches. It should slip off easily. If the peaches are too hot, peel them under cold running water. Cut the peaches in half and remove the stone. Cut each half into ½-inch-thick slices, then cut the slices in thirds across the width and place them in a mixing bowl.

• • •

Add the brown sugar, ¼ teaspoon of nutmeg, lemon zest, and lemon juice to the peaches and toss together to coat them completely.

• • •

Divide the filling evenly among the ramekins, filling each three-fourths full. Cut the softened butter into small pieces and distribute it evenly over the peaches.

• • •

BISCUIT DOUGH TOPPING

Pulse together the flour, 1 tablespoon of granulated sugar, baking powder, salt, and remaining ¼ teaspoon of nutmeg in the work bowl of a food processor fitted with the steel blade.

• • •

Cut the chilled butter into small pieces and add to the flour mixture. Pulse until the butter is cut into very tiny pieces, about 1 minute.

• • •

In a small bowl or a liquid measuring cup, combine 3 tablespoons of cream and vanilla. With the food processor running, pour the cream mixture through the feed tube. Process until the dough wraps itself around the blade, about 30 seconds.

• • •

Drop spoonfuls of the dough over the peach filling in the ramekins, dividing it evenly. Sprinkle the topping with the remaining 1 teaspoon of granulated sugar.

• • •

Bake the cobblers for 30 to 35 minutes, until the biscuit topping is light golden and set. Remove the baking dish from the oven and transfer the ramekins to racks to cool.

• • •

GARNISH

Whip the remaining ⅓ cup of cream in the bowl of an electric stand mixer with the wire whip attachment or in a large mixing bowl using a hand-held mixer on medium speed until frothy. Add the confectioners' sugar and continue whipping the cream until it holds soft peaks.

• • •

Serve each cobbler with a dollop of whipped cream.

• • •

keeping Although the cobblers are best eaten the day they are made, they can last up to 2 days. Store them, without the whipped cream, tightly covered with aluminum foil in the refrigerator. Garnish right before serving.

streamlining The biscuit dough can be made in advance. Shape it into a disk and keep in the refrigerator, tightly wrapped in a double layer of plastic wrap, up to 4 days. To freeze up to 3 months, wrap the dough snugly in several layers of plastic wrap and enclose it in a freezer bag. Use a large piece of masking tape and an indelible marker to label and date the contents. If frozen, defrost the dough overnight in the refrigerator and bring to room temperature before using.

making a change Replace the peaches with apricots, nectarines, plums, or pluots. It's not necessary to remove the skins from these fruits.

adding style Serve each cobbler with a scoop of vanilla or cardamom ice cream.

pear and triple ginger cobblers

FRESH GINGER, CRYSTALLIZED GINGER, AND GROUND GINGER GIVE THE PEARS THEIR SWEET-HOT FLAVOR IN THESE YUMMY COBBLERS. DRIED CHERRIES ALSO ADD EXTRA TEXTURE AND FLAVOR. ALTHOUGH THESE ARE DELICIOUS ON THEIR OWN, TRY SERVING THEM WITH SMALL SCOOPS OF VANILLA OR HONEY ICE CREAM.

MAKES 8 cobblers | USE eight 3¼ × 2¼ × ¾–inch oval ramekins

1 pound ripe pears (3 medium), such as Bosc or Anjou

¼ cup (1½ ounces) dried tart cherries

4 tablespoons (1 ounce) finely chopped crystallized ginger, divided

3 tablespoons (1¼ ounces) firmly packed light brown sugar, divided

2 tablespoons finely grated peeled fresh gingerroot

½ teaspoon freshly grated nutmeg, divided

½ teaspoon ground ginger, divided

Finely grated or minced zest of ½ large lemon

1 teaspoon freshly squeezed lemon juice

1 ounce (2 tablespoons, ¼ stick) unsalted butter, softened

½ cup (2¼ ounces) all-purpose flour

1 teaspoon baking powder

Pinch of kosher or fine-grained sea salt

1½ ounces (3 tablespoons) unsalted butter, chilled

¼ cup heavy whipping cream

½ teaspoon pure vanilla extract

1 teaspoon granulated sugar

Position a rack in the center of the oven and preheat the oven to 375°F. Place the ramekins in a 2-quart baking dish.

• • •

PEAR FILLING

Use a vegetable peeler to peel the pears, then cut them lengthwise into quarters. Scoop out the core and cut each quarter across the width into ½-inch-thick chunks. Place them in a large mixing bowl. Add the dried cherries, 2 tablespoons of crystallized ginger, 2 tablespoons of brown sugar, fresh gingerroot, ¼ teaspoon of nutmeg, ¼ teaspoon of ground ginger, lemon zest, and lemon juice to the pears and toss together to coat them completely.

• • •

Divide the filling evenly among the ramekins. Cut the softened butter into small pieces and distribute it evenly over the pears.

• • •

GINGER DOUGH TOPPING

Pulse together the flour, baking powder, salt, and remaining 2 tablespoons of crystallized ginger, 1 tablespoon of brown sugar, ¼ teaspoon of nutmeg, and ¼ teaspoon of ground ginger in the work bowl of a food processor fitted with the steel blade.

• • •

Cut the chilled butter into small pieces and add to the flour mixture. Pulse until the butter is cut into very tiny pieces, about 1 minute.

• • •

In a small bowl or a liquid measuring cup, combine the cream and vanilla. With the food processor running, pour the cream mixture through the feed tube. Process until the dough wraps itself around the blade, about 30 seconds.

• • •

Drop spoonfuls of the dough over the pear filling in the ramekins, dividing it evenly. Sprinkle the topping with granulated sugar.

• • •

Bake the cobblers for 30 to 35 minutes, until the biscuit topping is light golden and set. Remove the baking dish from the oven and transfer the ramekins to racks to cool.

• • •

keeping Although the cobblers are best eaten the day they are made, they can last up to 2 days. Store them tightly covered with aluminum foil in the refrigerator.

streamlining The dough topping can be made in advance. Shape it into a disk and keep in the refrigerator, tightly wrapped in a double layer of plastic wrap, up to 4 days. To freeze up to 3 months, wrap the dough snugly in several layers of plastic wrap and enclose it in a freezer bag. Use a large piece of masking tape and an indelible marker to label and date the contents. If frozen, defrost the topping overnight in the refrigerator and bring to room temperature before using.

adding style Serve each cobbler with a scoop of vanilla or honey ice cream.

raspberry–blueberry crisps

CRISPS ARE RUSTIC, EASY-TO-PREPARE, CLASSIC DESSERTS. A CRUMBLY TOPPING IS SCATTERED OVER FRESH RASPBERRIES AND BLUEBERRIES IN SMALL RAMEKINS AND THE DESSERTS ARE BAKED. CRISPS ARE SCRUMPTIOUS EATEN WARM OR AT ROOM TEMPERATURE. USE RIPE BERRIES WITH LOTS OF FLAVOR TO MAKE THE BEST-TASTING CRISPS.

MAKES 8 crisps | USE eight 3¼ × 2¼ × ¾–inch oval ramekins

---

1 cup (4½ ounces) fresh raspberries

1 cup (5 ounces) fresh blueberries

2 tablespoons (¾ ounce) granulated sugar

1 teaspoon freshly squeezed lemon juice

¼ teaspoon pure vanilla extract

⅛ teaspoon plus ¼ teaspoon freshly grated nutmeg

3 tablespoons (½ ounce) sliced or slivered almonds

⅓ cup (1 ounce) old-fashioned rolled oats

2 tablespoons (½ ounce) all-purpose flour

3 tablespoons (1¼ ounces) firmly packed light brown sugar

Pinch of kosher or fine-grained sea salt

1½ ounces (3 tablespoons) unsalted butter, chilled

⅓ cup heavy whipping cream

2 teaspoons confectioners' sugar

Position a rack in the center of the oven and preheat the oven to 350°F.

• • •

BERRY FILLING

Place the berries in a large mixing bowl. Sprinkle the granulated sugar, lemon juice, vanilla, and ⅛ teaspoon of nutmeg over the berries and toss them lightly to coat them evenly.

• • •

Divide the berry mixture evenly among the ramekins. Place the ramekins on a baking sheet.

• • •

TOPPING

Place the almonds in a single layer in a cake or pie pan. Toast in the oven for 4 minutes. Shake the pan to stir the almonds and toast for another 4 to 6 minutes, until light golden. Remove from the oven and cool the pan on a rack.

• • •

Spread the oats in a single layer in another cake or pie pan. Toast in the oven for 5 minutes. Shake the pan to stir the oats and toast another 5 to 7 minutes, until light golden. Remove from the oven and cool the pan on a rack. Raise the oven temperature to 375°F.

• • •

Pulse together the flour, brown sugar, salt, and remaining ¼ teaspoon of nutmeg in the work bowl of a food processor fitted with the steel blade. Add the toasted almonds and toasted oats and pulse until they are finely chopped.

• • •

Cut the chilled butter into small pieces and add to the flour mixture. Pulse until the butter is cut into very small pieces, 30 seconds to 1 minute.

• • •

Evenly sprinkle the topping over the berries.

• • •

Bake the crisps for 25 to 27 minutes, until the topping is light golden. Remove the baking sheet from the oven and transfer the ramekins to racks to cool.

• • •

GARNISH

Whip the cream in the bowl of an electric stand mixer with the wire whip attachment or in a large mixing bowl using a hand-held mixer on medium speed until frothy. Add the confectioners' sugar and continue whipping the cream until it holds soft peaks.

• • •

Serve each crisp with a dollop of whipped cream.

• • •

keeping Although the crisps are best eaten the day they are made, they can last up to 2 days. Store them tightly covered with aluminum foil in the refrigerator.

streamlining The topping can be made in advance. Store it in a tightly covered plastic container in the refrigerator up to 4 days.

making a change Use one type of berry instead of a mixture.

Use fresh-frozen berries if fresh berries are not available. It's not necessary to defrost the fresh-frozen berries before using, but bake the crisps about 3 minutes longer.

adding style Serve the crisps with vanilla or cardamom ice cream.

apple—walnut crisps

A TASTY COMBINATION OF APPLES AND WALNUTS WITH A LITTLE GROUND CORIANDER THAT ADDS ITS SLIGHTLY TANGY, CITRUSY FLAVOR GIVES THESE CRISPS AN INTRIGUING AROMA AND FLAVOR. I LIKE TO MAKE THESE IN THE FALL, WHEN APPLES ARE AT THEIR PEAK. THEY ARE EVEN MORE DELICIOUS SERVED WITH A SMALL SCOOP OF VANILLA OR HONEY ICE CREAM.

MAKES 8 crisps | USE eight 3¼ × 2¼ × ¾–inch oval ramekins

2 small Granny Smith or Gala apples (8 to 9 ounces total)

5 tablespoons (2 ounces) firmly packed light brown sugar, divided

1 teaspoon freshly squeezed lemon juice

Finely grated zest of 1 small lemon

½ teaspoon ground coriander, divided

2 pinches of kosher or fine-grained sea salt, divided

⅔ cup (3 ounces) walnuts

2 tablespoons (½ ounce) all-purpose flour

1½ ounces (3 tablespoons) unsalted butter, chilled

⅓ cup heavy whipping cream

1 tablespoon (½ ounce) superfine sugar

Position a rack in the center of the oven and preheat the oven to 350°F.

• • •

APPLE FILLING

Peel, quarter, and core the apples. Cut each quarter into 3 or 4 lengthwise pieces, then cut them crosswise into ½-inch-thick chunks. Place the chunks in a large mixing bowl. Sprinkle 2 tablespoons of brown sugar, lemon juice, lemon zest, ¼ teaspoon of coriander, and a pinch of salt over the apples and toss them lightly to coat evenly.

• • •

Divide the apple mixture evenly among the ramekins. Place the ramekins on a baking sheet.

• • •

TOPPING

Toast the walnuts in a cake or pie pan for 4 minutes. Shake the pan to stir the walnuts and toast for another 3 to 4 minutes. Remove from the oven and cool the pan on a rack. Raise the oven temperature to 375°F.

• • •

Pulse together the flour, remaining 3 tablespoons of brown sugar, remaining ¼ teaspoon of coriander, 1 pinch of salt, and toasted walnuts in the work bowl of a food processor fitted with the steel blade until the nuts are coarsely chopped.

• • •

Cut the butter into small pieces and add to the flour mixture. Pulse until the butter is cut into very small pieces, 30 seconds to 1 minute.

• • •

Sprinkle the topping evenly over the apple filling in the ramekins.

• • •

Bake the crisps for 25 to 28 minutes, until the topping is light golden. Remove the baking sheet from the oven and transfer the ramekins to racks to cool.

• • •

GARNISH

Whip the cream in the bowl of an electric stand mixer with the wire whip attachment or in a large mixing bowl using a hand-held mixer on medium speed until frothy. Add the superfine sugar and continue whipping the cream until it holds soft peaks.

• • •

Serve each crisp with a dollop of whipped cream.

• • •

keeping Although the crisps are best eaten the day they are made, they can last up to 2 days. Store them tightly covered with aluminum foil in the refrigerator.

streamlining The topping can be made in advance. Store it in a tightly covered plastic container in the refrigerator up to 4 days.

adding style Serve the crisps with vanilla or honey ice cream.

blueberry turnovers

THIS DOUGH IS ONE OF MY FAVORITES BECAUSE IT'S VERY EASY TO WORK WITH AND TASTES GREAT. IF YOU'RE NOT IN THE MOOD TO MAKE YOUR OWN DOUGH, YOU CAN USE STORE-BOUGHT PUFF PASTRY TO MAKE THESE TURNOVERS. TURNOVERS ARE DELICIOUS FOR DESSERT BUT ARE JUST AS GOOD WARMED UP FOR BREAKFAST.

MAKES sixteen 3-inch turnovers

3 ounces (6 tablespoons, ¾ stick) unsalted butter, chilled

⅔ cup (3 ounces) all-purpose flour

2 teaspoons plus 1 tablespoon (¼ ounce) granulated sugar

Pinch of kosher or fine-grained sea salt

2½ ounces cream cheese, chilled

2 tablespoons heavy whipping cream, divided

1 cup (5 ounces] fresh blueberries

1 tablespoon (¼ ounce) cornstarch, sifted

Finely grated zest of 1 small lemon

1 teaspoon freshly squeezed lemon juice

1 to 2 teaspoons water

1 extra-large egg yolk, at room temperature

1 tablespoon (½ ounce) turbinado or Demerara sugar

PASTRY DOUGH

Cut the butter into small pieces and freeze for 20 minutes.

• • •

Pulse the flour, 2 teaspoons of sugar, and salt in the work bowl of a food processor fitted with a steel blade.

• • •

Cut the cream cheese into small pieces and add to the flour mixture. Pulse to cut the cream cheese into very tiny pieces. The texture should be sandy with very tiny lumps throughout. Add the chilled butter and pulse until it is cut into pea-size pieces, 30 to 45 seconds. Remove the top of the food processor and sprinkle on 1 tablespoon of cream. Replace the top and pulse until the dough begins to hold together, about 30 seconds.

• • •

Shape the dough into a flat disk and wrap it tightly in a double layer of plastic wrap. Chill in the refrigerator until firm before using, at least 1 hour.

• • •

On a smooth, flat surface, roll out the dough between sheets of lightly floured waxed or parchment paper to a 12-inch square. Carefully peel the waxed or parchment paper off the top of the dough and brush off any excess flour.

• • •

Use a sharp knife or pastry wheel to trim off any rough edges. Cut the dough horizontally into four equal-size strips. Use a ruler to mark four 3-inch horizontal lines on each strip. Then cut each strip into four 3-inch squares, forming 16 squares total.

• • •

Adjust an oven rack to the lower third and preheat the oven to 400°F. Line a baking sheet with parchment paper or a nonstick liner.

• • •

BLUEBERRY FILLING

Place the blueberries in a large bowl. Add the remaining 1 tablespoon of granulated sugar, cornstarch, lemon zest, and lemon juice and gently toss the fruit to coat completely.

• • •

Place about 1 teaspoon of this mixture in the center of each dough square. Use a pastry brush to brush the outer edges of each square with water. Be sure to brush only the inner part of the dough, not the outside. This will help the pastry dough stick together when the turnovers are formed.

• • •

Bring opposite corners together and fold each pastry square diagonally in half, lining up all the edges and points and forming a triangle. Pinch the edges together firmly. Use a fork to press the edges together and imprint a design.

• • •

Place the turnovers on the lined baking sheet, leaving at least 1 inch of space between them.

EGG WASH AND GARNISH

Use a fork to lightly beat the egg yolk and remaining 1 tablespoon of cream together in a small bowl. Use a pastry brush to brush the top of each turnover with the egg wash. Be careful that the egg wash doesn't run down the sides and underneath the turnovers. If it does, wipe it up because it can cause the bottoms of the turnovers to burn. Sprinkle the turbinado or Demerara sugar evenly over the tops of the turnovers. Using this type of sugar gives the turnovers extra texture.

• • •

Bake the turnovers for 20 to 25 minutes, until light golden and the fruit is thickly bubbling inside. Remove the pan from the oven and cool on a rack for 10 minutes.

• • •

Serve the turnovers warm or at room temperature.

• • •

keeping Store the turnovers, loosely covered with waxed paper, then tightly wrapped with aluminum foil, at room temperature up to 2 days. To rewarm, place them in a single layer on a baking sheet lined with parchment paper or a nonstick liner and bake at 350°F for 10 to 15 minutes.

streamlining The dough can be made in advance and kept in the refrigerator, tightly wrapped in a double layer of plastic wrap, up to 4 days. To freeze up to 3 months, wrap it snugly in several layers of plastic wrap and enclose it in a freezer bag. Use a large piece of masking tape and an indelible marker to label and date the contents. If frozen, defrost the dough overnight in the refrigerator before using.

troubleshooting Don't overprocess the dough or it will be tough and not flaky.

making a change Use a mixture of berries instead of the blueberries.

Replace 2 tablespoons of flour in the dough with sliced or slivered almonds. Pulse with the remaining flour in the recipe until the almonds are very finely ground.

Replace the pastry dough with store-bought puff pastry.

adding style Add 2 tablespoons finely grated or minced lemon zest to the dough before adding the butter.

nectarine and walnut galettes

THESE FREE-FORM TARTLETS ARE MADE WITH DELECTABLE WALNUT PASTRY DOUGH THAT ENCLOSES A CREAMY WALNUT FILLING AND FRESH NECTARINES. THESE ARE PERFECT SUMMERTIME DESSERTS WHEN LUSCIOUS NECTARINES ARE RIPE. I LIKE TO SERVE THEM WITH A SCOOP OF CARDAMOM OR VANILLA ICE CREAM.

MAKES *eight 3-inch galettes*

¾ cup (3¼ ounces) plus 2 teaspoons all-purpose flour

⅔ cup (3 ounces) walnuts, divided

2 teaspoons plus 1 tablespoon (¼ ounce) granulated sugar

⅛ teaspoon kosher or fine-grained sea salt

3 ounces (6 tablespoons, ¾ stick) plus 2 teaspoons unsalted butter, chilled, divided

1 to 2 tablespoons ice water

1 teaspoon freshly squeezed lemon juice

Finely grated zest of ½ large lemon

¾ pound fresh nectarines (2 to 3 medium), halved and pitted

2 tablespoons (¾ ounce) firmly packed light brown sugar

1 extra-large egg yolk, at room temperature

½ teaspoon pure vanilla extract

1 ounce (2 tablespoons) unsalted butter, softened

1 tablespoon heavy whipping cream

¼ cup apricot preserves

1 tablespoon amaretto, Cognac, or water

WALNUT PASTRY DOUGH

Pulse together ¾ cup of flour, ⅓ cup of walnuts, 1 teaspoon of granulated sugar, and salt in the work bowl of a food processor fitted with the steel blade until the walnuts are very finely ground, about 1 minute.

• • •

Cut 3 ounces of chilled butter into small pieces and add to the flour mixture. Pulse until the butter is cut into very tiny pieces, about 30 seconds. The texture should be sandy with very tiny lumps throughout.

• • •

In a small bowl, combine 1 tablespoon of water, lemon juice, and lemon zest. With the food processor running, pour this mixture through the feed tube. Process until the dough wraps itself around the blade, 30 seconds to 1 minute. If the dough seems dry, add the remaining 1 tablespoon of water and process until the dough comes together.

• • •

Shape the dough into a flat disk and wrap tightly in a double layer of plastic wrap. Chill in the refrigerator until firm before using, about 2 hours. If the dough is too cold and firm, it will splinter and break when rolled out. Let it stand at room temperature for 10 to 15 minutes to become more pliable.

• • •

NECTARINE FILLING

Cut the nectarines into ½-inch-thick slices and cut each slice in half across the width. You should have approximately 3 cups of sliced fruit.

• • •

Place the sliced nectarines in a large mixing bowl. Add the brown sugar and toss together to distribute evenly. Taste the fruit to see if it needs any more brown sugar.

• • •

WALNUT FILLING

Pulse the remaining ⅓ cup of walnuts and 1 tablespoon of granulated sugar together in the work bowl of a food processor fitted with a steel blade until the walnuts are very finely ground, about 1 minute. Add the egg yolk and vanilla and pulse to blend together.

• • •

Cut the softened butter into small pieces and add it to the walnut mixture. Pulse several times until the butter is cut into tiny pieces. Add the remaining 2 teaspoons of flour and pulse until the mixture is smooth, about 15 seconds.

• • •

ASSEMBLY

Position a rack in the center of the oven and preheat the oven to 375°F. Line a baking sheet with parchment paper or a nonstick liner.

• • •

On a smooth, flat surface, roll out the pastry dough between sheets of lightly floured waxed or parchment paper to a large disk about 14 inches in diameter. Carefully peel the paper off the top of the dough and brush off any excess flour.

• • •

Dip a 4-inch round plain biscuit cutter into flour or use a small knife to cut out 4-inch rounds of dough. Use an offset spatula to lift up the dough rounds and transfer them to the lined baking sheet, leaving at least 1 inch of space between them.

• • •

Divide the walnut filling evenly among the dough rounds. Use a spoon or small offset spatula to spread the filling over the center of the pastry dough, leaving a 1-inch border all around. Mound the sliced nectarines over the walnut filling in the center of each dough circle.

• • •

Cut the remaining 2 teaspoons of chilled butter into small pieces and distribute them evenly over the sliced nectarines.

• • •

Fold the border of each dough round up so that it partially encloses the nectarines and walnut filling. It will naturally form pleats as it is folded. Brush the borders of each dough

round with some of the cream, being careful that it doesn't run down the sides and under the galettes. If it does, wipe it up because it can cause the bottoms of the galettes to burn. Gently lift back the folds of the dough and brush those areas with more cream, then replace the folds. Evenly sprinkle the remaining 1 teaspoon of granulated sugar over the dough borders.

• • •

Bake the galettes for 35 to 40 minutes, until the crusts are light golden. Remove the baking sheet from the oven and transfer it to a rack to cool.

• • •

APRICOT GLAZE

Combine the apricot preserves and amaretto, Cognac, or water in a small saucepan. Bring to a boil over medium heat. Remove the saucepan from the heat and strain the glaze into a small bowl, pushing through as much of the pulp as possible.

• • •

Use a goose-feather pastry brush to lightly brush the top of each galette with the glaze.

• • •

keeping Although the galettes are best eaten the day they are made, they can last up to 2 days. Store them tightly covered with aluminum foil at room temperature.

streamlining The pastry dough can be made in advance and kept in the refrigerator, tightly wrapped in a double layer of plastic wrap, up to 4 days before using. To freeze up to 4 months, wrap it in a double layer of plastic wrap and enclose it in a freezer bag. Use a large piece of masking tape and an indelible marker to label and date the contents. If frozen, defrost the dough in the refrigerator overnight before using. If the dough is too cold to roll out, let it stand at room temperature to become pliable.

making a change Replace the nectarines with other stone fruit, such as apricots, plums, pluots, and peeled peaches.

Use a combination of fruit instead of a single type.

pear and pecan galettes

RICH PECAN PASTRY DOUGH SPREAD WITH PECAN FILLING AND TOPPED WITH CHUNKS OF RIPE PEARS
MAKE UP THESE YUMMY FREE-FORM TARTLETS. MY FAVORITE PEARS ARE BOSCS, BUT IT'S FINE TO USE
ANY TYPE OF PEARS YOU PREFER. JUST MAKE SURE THEY ARE RIPE BUT NOT TOO SOFT. A DOLLOP OF
WHIPPED CREAM OR A SCOOP OF VANILLA ICE CREAM IS THE PERFECT ACCOMPANIMENT.

MAKES *eight 3-inch galettes*

¾ cup (3¾ ounces) plus 2 teaspoons all-purpose flour

⅔ cup (2½ ounces) toasted pecans, divided

2 teaspoons (¼ ounce) plus 1 tablespoon (½ ounce) granulated sugar

⅛ teaspoon kosher or fine-grained sea salt

3 ounces (6 tablespoons, ¾ stick) plus 2 teaspoons unsalted butter, chilled

3 tablespoons heavy whipping cream, divided

¾ pound ripe Bosc pears (2 medium)

2 tablespoons (¾ ounce) firmly packed light brown sugar

1 teaspoon pure vanilla extract, divided

1 extra-large egg yolk, at room temperature

1 ounce (2 tablespoons, ¼ stick) unsalted butter, softened

PECAN PASTRY DOUGH

Pulse ¾ cup of flour, ⅓ cup of pecans, 1 teaspoon of granulated sugar, and salt in the work bowl of a food processor until the pecans are very finely ground, about 1 minute.

• • •

Cut 3 ounces of chilled butter into small pieces and add to the flour mixture. Pulse until the butter is cut into very tiny pieces, about 30 seconds. The texture should be sandy with very tiny lumps throughout. With the food processor running, pour 2 tablespoons of cream through the feed tube. Process until the dough wraps itself around the blade, 30 seconds to 1 minute.

• • •

Shape the dough into a flat disk and wrap tightly in a double layer of plastic wrap. Chill in the refrigerator until firm before using, about 2 hours. If the dough is too cold and

firm, it will splinter and break when rolled out. Let it stand at room temperature for 10 to 15 minutes to become more pliable.

• • •

PEAR FILLING

Use a vegetable peeler to peel the pears, then cut them lengthwise into quarters. Scoop out the core and cut each quarter across the width into ½-inch-thick chunks. Place them in a large bowl.

• • •

Add the brown sugar and ½ teaspoon of vanilla to the pears and toss together to coat them evenly.

• • •

PECAN FILLING

Pulse the remaining ⅓ cup of pecans and 1 tablespoon of sugar in the work bowl of a food processor fitted with a steel blade until the pecans are very finely ground, about 1 minute.

Add the egg yolk and remaining ½ teaspoon of vanilla and pulse to blend together.

• • •

Cut the softened butter into small pieces and add to the pecan mixture. Pulse several times to combine. Add the remaining 2 teaspoons of flour and pulse until the mixture is smooth, about 15 seconds.

• • •

ASSEMBLY

Position a rack in the center of the oven and preheat the oven to 375°F. Line a baking sheet with parchment paper or a nonstick liner.

• • •

On a smooth, flat surface, roll out the pastry dough between sheets of lightly floured waxed or parchment paper to a large disk about 14 inches in diameter. Carefully peel the paper off the top of the dough and brush off any excess flour.

• • •

Dip a 4-inch round plain-edge biscuit cutter into flour or use a small knife to cut out 4-inch rounds of dough. Use an offset spatula to lift up the dough rounds and transfer them to the lined baking sheet, leaving at least 1 inch of space between them.

• • •

Divide the pecan filling evenly among the dough rounds. Use a spoon or small offset spatula to spread the filling over the center of the pastry dough, leaving a 1-inch border all around. Mound the pear filling over the pecan filling in the center of each dough round.

• • •

Cut the remaining 2 teaspoons of chilled butter into small pieces and distribute them evenly over the pears.

• • •

Fold up the border of each dough round so that it partially encloses the pears and pecan filling. The dough naturally forms pleats as it is folded. Brush the borders of each dough round with some of the remaining 1 tablespoon of cream, being careful that it doesn't run down the sides and under the galettes. If it does, wipe it up because it can cause the bottoms of the galettes to burn. Gently lift back the folds of the dough and brush those areas with more cream, then replace the folds. Evenly sprinkle the remaining 1 teaspoon of granulated sugar over the dough borders.

• • •

Bake the galettes for 35 to 40 minutes, until the crusts are light golden. Remove the baking sheet from the oven and transfer it to a rack to cool.

• • •

keeping Although the galettes are best eaten the day they are made, they can last up to 2 days. Store them tightly covered with aluminum foil at room temperature.

streamlining The pastry dough can be made in advance and kept in the refrigerator, tightly wrapped in a double layer of plastic wrap, up to 4 days before using. To freeze up to 4 months, wrap it in a double layer of plastic wrap and enclose it in a freezer bag. Use a large piece of masking tape and an indelible marker to label and date the contents. If frozen, defrost the dough in the refrigerator overnight before using. If it is too cold to roll out, let it stand at room temperature to become pliable.

The pecan filling can be made up to 4 days in advance and kept in a tightly sealed container in the refrigerator. To freeze up to 4 months, enclose the container in a freezer bag. Use a large piece of masking tape and an indelible marker to label and date the contents. If frozen, defrost the filling in the refrigerator overnight before using.

making a change Replace the Bosc pears with other types of pears or with apples.

chapter five

MOUSSES, CUSTARDS, AND PUDDINGS

creamy caramel mousse

I LOVE THE FLAVOR OF CARAMEL, AND WHEN I MADE THIS MOUSSE, I FOUND MYSELF CLEANING THE BOWL AND LICKING THE SPATULA. IT HAS JUST WHAT I WANT IN CARAMEL MOUSSE—A RICH, DEEP CARAMEL FLAVOR AND A VELVETY, CREAMY TEXTURE.

MAKES 6 servings | USE six 2-ounce mini martini glasses or bowls

1 cup heavy whipping cream, divided

¼ cup (1½ ounces) granulated sugar

¼ cup (1½ ounces) firmly packed light brown sugar

2 tablespoons water

1 teaspoon honey

½ teaspoon pure vanilla paste

1 ounce (2 tablespoons, ¼ stick) unsalted butter, softened

MOUSSE

Bring ⅓ cup of cream to a boil in a ½-quart saucepan over medium heat.

• • •

Cook the granulated sugar, brown sugar, water, honey, and vanilla paste in a 2-quart heavy-duty saucepan over high heat, without stirring, until the mixture comes to a boil. Brush around the inside of the pan with a damp pastry brush at the point where the sugar syrup meets the sides of the pan to prevent the sugars from crystallizing. Do this two times. Cook the mixture over high heat, without stirring, until it turns amber colored, 6 to 8 minutes.

• • •

Lower the heat to medium and slowly add the hot cream while stirring constantly with a long-handled heat-resistant spatula. The cream will bubble and foam. Continue to stir to make sure there are no lumps. Remove the saucepan from the heat and stir in the butter until it is completely melted.

• • •

Transfer the caramel sauce to a 2-quart mixing bowl, cover tightly with plastic wrap, cool to room temperature, then chill until thick, about 2 hours.

• • •

Whip the remaining ⅔ cup of cream in the bowl of an electric stand mixer with the wire whip attachment or in a large mixing bowl using a hand-held mixer on medium speed until it holds soft peaks. Set aside ⅓ cup of the whipped cream and fold the remaining whipped cream into the chilled caramel sauce in 3 stages.

• • •

Use a large ice cream scoop or spoon to fill each mini martini glass or bowl with the mousse. Cover the glasses or bowls loosely with waxed paper, then tightly wrap with plastic wrap and chill for at least 2 hours.

• • •

GARNISH

Fit a 12- or 14-inch pastry bag with a large open star tip and fill the bag with the remaining ⅓ cup of whipped cream. Pipe a rosette or star of whipped cream on top of each mousse.

• • •

adding style Pipe the mousse into Tuile Cookie Cups (page 155) right before serving.

keeping The mousse, without the garnish, will keep up to 2 days, tightly wrapped with plastic wrap, in the refrigerator.

mocha mousse

A TOUCH OF ESPRESSO POWDER ENHANCES THE FLAVOR OF DEEP, DARK CHOCOLATE IN THIS MOUSSE. I LIKE TO SERVE IT IN ESPRESSO CUPS OR MINI MARTINI GLASSES FOR A STYLISH LOOK, BUT YOU CAN USE SMALL BOWLS OR OTHER GLASSES, AS WELL.

MAKES 6 servings | USE six 2-ounce espresso cups, mini martini glasses, or bowls

3 ounces bittersweet chocolate (66 to 72% cacao content), finely chopped

⅓ cup plus ½ cup heavy whipping cream

1 teaspoon instant espresso powder

½ teaspoon pure vanilla extract

1 extra-large egg white, at room temperature

2 tablespoons (¾ ounce) plus 1 teaspoon superfine sugar

6 chocolate-coated espresso beans

Place the finely chopped chocolate in a 2-quart mixing bowl.

• • •

Bring ⅓ cup of cream to a boil in a ½-quart saucepan over medium heat. Turn off the heat, add the espresso powder, and stir until dissolved. Cover the pan and steep for 10 minutes.

• • •

Uncover the saucepan and bring the cream back to a boil. Strain the cream over the bowl of chopped chocolate. Let the mixture stand for 30 seconds, then whisk together until smooth and all the chocolate is melted. Add the vanilla and stir to blend well.

• • •

Whip the remaining ½ cup of cream in the bowl of an electric stand mixer with the wire whip attachment or in a large mixing bowl using a hand-held mixer on medium speed until it holds soft peaks. Set aside ⅓ cup of the whipped cream and fold the remaining whipped cream into the chocolate mixture in 3 stages.

• • •

Place 2 inches of water in a large saucepan and warm over medium heat. Place a grease-free bowl of an electric stand mixer or a large grease-free mixing bowl over the saucepan

of water. Whisk the egg white until it registers 160°F on an instant-read thermometer. Immediately remove the bowl from the water, wipe the bottom and sides dry, and whip the egg white on medium-high speed until frothy. Gradually sprinkle on the sugar and whip the egg white until it holds firm but not stiff peaks. Fold the whipped egg white into the chocolate mixture in 3 stages, blending well.

• • •

Fit a 12- or 14-inch pastry bag with a large open star tip and fill the bag partway with the mousse mixture. Pipe the mousse into the espresso cups, mini martini glasses, or bowls, filling them completely. Cover the cups, glasses, or bowls loosely with waxed paper, then tightly with plastic wrap and chill for at least 2 hours.

• • •

GARNISH

Fit a clean 10- or 12-inch pastry bag with a large open star tip and fill the bag with the reserved ⅓ cup of whipped cream. Pipe a rosette or star of whipped cream on top of each mousse. Decorate the top of each mousse with a chocolate-coated espresso bean.

• • •

keeping The mousse, without the garnish, will keep up to 2 days, tightly wrapped with plastic wrap, in the refrigerator. With the garnish, the mousse will keep up to 3 hours, loosely covered with waxed paper and then tightly wrapped with plastic wrap, in the refrigerator. Pipe the whipped cream rosettes or stars on top of each mousse before serving.

making a change Leave out the espresso powder and increase the vanilla extract to 1 teaspoon.

cardamom pots de crème

THE SWEET, WARM, SLIGHTLY LEMONY FLAVOR OF CARDAMOM IS ONE OF MY FAVORITES. IT'S THE PERFECT FLAVOR FOR THESE LUSCIOUS, CREAMY POTS DE CRÈME. CARDAMOM COMES IN PODS THAT MEASURE ABOUT ½ INCH LONG. THE PAPERY OUTER PODS ARE DISCARDED, AND THE SEEDS WITHIN ARE USED TO IMPART THEIR FLAVOR. CARDAMOM CAN BE BOUGHT GROUND, BUT IT LOSES ITS FLAVOR RAPIDLY. I HIGHLY RECOMMEND THAT YOU USE THE PODS TO OBTAIN THE MOST FLAVOR.

MAKES eight ¼-cup servings | USE eight 2½ × 1⅝–inch round ramekins

1⅔ cups plus ¼ cup heavy whipping cream

1 tablespoon cardamom seeds

4 extra-large egg yolks, at room temperature

½ cup (3½ ounces) firmly packed light brown sugar

Pinch of kosher or fine-grained sea salt

½ teaspoon pure vanilla extract

2 to 3 cups boiling water

2 teaspoons confectioners' sugar

POTS DE CRÈME

Bring 1⅔ cups of cream to a boil in a 1-quart saucepan over medium heat. Turn off the heat, add the cardamom seeds, cover the saucepan, and let the mixture steep for 30 minutes.
• • •
Position a rack in the center of the oven and preheat the oven to 325°F. Place the ramekins in a 2-quart baking dish.
• • •
Whisk the egg yolks in a large mixing bowl to break them up. Add the brown sugar and salt and whisk to blend smoothly.
• • •
Uncover the saucepan and bring the cream to a boil over medium heat. Strain the cream into the egg yolk mixture, whisking constantly. Add the vanilla and blend thoroughly. Pour the mixture into a 2-cup liquid measuring cup and divide it evenly among the ramekins, filling each almost to the top.
• • •

Carefully pour the boiling water into the baking dish until it reaches partway up the sides of the ramekins. Cover the baking dish tightly with aluminum foil. Bake for 28 to 30 minutes, until the custards are set around the edges but slightly soft in the center.
• • •
Remove the baking dish from the oven. Remove the ramekins from the water bath and cool on a rack. Cover loosely with waxed paper and then tightly wrap with plastic wrap and chill at least 2 hours.
• • •

GARNISH

Whip the remaining ¼ cup of cream in the bowl of an electric stand mixer with the wire whip attachment or in a medium mixing bowl using a hand-held mixer on medium speed until frothy. Add the confectioners' sugar and continue whipping the cream until it holds soft peaks.
• • •

Fit a 10- or 12-inch pastry bag with a large open star tip and fill the bag partway with the whipped cream. Pipe a rosette or a star in the center of each custard, or add a dollop of whipped cream on top.

• • •

keeping The baked pots de crème, without the whipped cream, will keep up to 2 days, tightly covered with aluminum foil, in the refrigerator. Pipe the whipped cream rosettes or stars, or add a dollop of whipped cream, on the pots de crème before serving.

chocolate—espresso pots de crème

IF YOU LIKE THE FLAVOR OF CHOCOLATE AND ESPRESSO, YOU WILL LOVE THESE LUSCIOUS, VELVETY CUSTARDS. WHEN THEY ARE EATEN WARM, THE TEXTURE IS SOFT. ONCE THESE ARE CHILLED, THE TEXTURE BECOMES FIRMER. EITHER WAY, THEY ARE SURE TO BECOME YOUR NEW FAVORITES.

MAKES *eight ¼-cup servings* | USE *eight 2½ × 1⅝–inch round ramekins*

1½ cups heavy whipping cream, divided

2 teaspoons instant espresso powder

3 ounces bittersweet chocolate (62 to 72% cacao content), finely chopped

3 extra-large egg yolks, at room temperature

1 tablespoon (½ ounce) granulated sugar

½ teaspoon pure vanilla extract

Pinch of kosher or fine-grained sea salt

2 to 3 cups boiling water

2 teaspoons confectioners' sugar

8 chocolate-coated espresso beans

POTS DE CRÈME

Boil 1¼ cups of cream and the espresso powder together in a 1-quart saucepan over medium heat, stirring to dissolve the powder. Remove the saucepan from the heat and stir in the chocolate until completely smooth.

• • •

Position a rack in the center of the oven and preheat the oven to 325°F. Place the ramekins in a 2-quart baking dish.

• • •

Whisk the egg yolks in the mixing bowl of a stand mixer using the wire whip attachment or a hand-held mixer on low speed to break them up. Add the granulated sugar, vanilla, and salt and whisk to blend smoothly. Add the chocolate mixture and blend thoroughly. Strain the mixture into a 2-cup liquid measuring cup and divide it evenly among the ramekins, filling each almost to the top.

• • •

Carefully pour the boiling water into the baking dish until it reaches partway up the sides of the ramekins. Cover the baking dish tightly with aluminum foil. Bake for 25 to 28 minutes, until the custards are set around the edges but slightly soft in the center.

• • •

Remove the baking dish from the oven. Remove the ramekins from the water bath and cool on a rack. Cover loosely with waxed paper and then tightly wrap with plastic wrap and chill at least 2 hours.

• • •

GARNISH

Whip the remaining ¼ cup of cream in the bowl of an electric stand mixer with the wire whip attachment or in a large mixing bowl using a hand-held mixer on medium speed until frothy. Add the confectioners' sugar and continue whipping the cream until it holds soft peaks.

• • •

Fit a 10- or 12-inch pastry bag with a large open star tip and fill the bag partway with the whipped cream. Pipe the whipped cream into rosettes or stars on the pots de crème before serving. Place a chocolate-coated espresso bean on top of the whipped cream on each custard.

• • •

keeping The baked pots de crème, without the whipped cream, will keep up to 2 days, tightly covered with aluminum foil, in the refrigerator.

maple pots de crème

MAPLE GIVES THESE SILKY-SMOOTH CUSTARDS A RICH, DEEP FLAVOR. MAPLE IS PERFECT FOR FALL AND WINTER WHEN WE'RE IN THE MOOD FOR WARM, FULL-BODIED FLAVOR. BE SURE TO USE GOOD-QUALITY PURE MAPLE SYRUP, SUCH AS GRADE A OR B.

MAKES *eight ¼-cup servings* | USE *eight 2½ × 1⅝-inch round ramekins*

1⅓ cups plus ¼ cup heavy whipping cream

4 extra-large egg yolks, at room temperature

¼ cup (3½ ounces) firmly packed light brown sugar

Pinch of kosher or fine-grained sea salt

¼ cup plus 1 teaspoon pure maple syrup

½ teaspoon pure vanilla extract

2 to 3 cups boiling water

POTS DE CRÈME

Position a rack in the center of the oven and preheat the oven to 325°F. Place the ramekins in a 2-quart baking dish.

• • •

Bring 1⅓ cups of cream to a boil in a 1-quart saucepan over medium heat.

• • •

Whisk the egg yolks in the mixing bowl of a stand mixer using the wire whip attachment or a hand-held mixer on low speed to break them up. Add the brown sugar and salt and whisk to blend smoothly. Add the hot cream to the egg yolk mixture, whisking constantly. Add ¼ cup of maple syrup and vanilla and blend thoroughly. Pour the mixture into a 2-cup liquid measuring cup and divide it evenly among the ramekins, filling each almost to the top.

• • •

Carefully pour the boiling water into the baking dish until it reaches partway up the sides of the ramekins. Cover the baking dish tightly with aluminum foil. Bake for 26 to 28 minutes, until the custards are set around the edges but slightly soft in the center.

• • •

Remove the baking dish from the oven. Remove the ramekins from the water bath and cool on a rack. Cover loosely with waxed paper and then tightly wrap with plastic wrap and chill at least 2 hours.

• • •

GARNISH

Whip the remaining ¼ cup of cream in the bowl of an electric stand mixer with the wire whip attachment or in a medium mixing bowl using a hand-held mixer on medium speed until frothy. Add the remaining 1 teaspoon of maple syrup and continue whipping until the cream holds soft peaks.

• • •

Fit a 10- or 12-inch pastry bag with a large open star tip and fill the bag partway with the whipped cream. Pipe a rosette or star in the center of each custard.

• • •

keeping The baked pots de crème, without the whipped cream, will keep up to 2 days, tightly covered with aluminum foil, in the refrigerator. Pipe the whipped cream rosettes or stars on the pots de crème before serving.

adding style Bake the pots de crème in demitasse cups instead of ramekins.

raspberry and lemon cream martinis

I AM NOT A MARTINI DRINKER, BUT I LOVE THE LOOK OF MARTINI GLASSES AND WANTED TO USE THEM TO CREATE AN ELEGANT DESSERT. THESE MINIATURE MARTINIS LOOK SOPHISTICATED, TASTE DELICIOUS, HAVE A SOFT, MOUSSE-LIKE TEXTURE, AND ARE VERY EASY TO MAKE. BE SURE TO MAKE THE LEMON CURD AT LEAST THE DAY BEFORE YOU ASSEMBLE THESE SO IT HAS TIME TO COOL AND THICKEN. ONCE THEY ARE ASSEMBLED, SERVE THE MARTINIS WITHIN 3 HOURS.

MAKES six ¼-cup servings | USE six 2-ounce mini martini glasses

½ cup heavy whipping cream

½ teaspoon pure vanilla extract

½ cup chilled Lemon Curd (page 78)

¾ cup (3½ ounces) fresh raspberries

1 teaspoon finely grated or minced lemon zest

Whip the cream in a chilled bowl of an electric stand mixer with the wire whip attachment or in a chilled large mixing bowl using a hand-held mixer on medium speed until frothy. Add the vanilla and continue to whip until the cream holds soft peaks.

• • •

Stir the lemon curd to make sure there are no lumps. Gently fold the lemon curd into the whipped cream in 2 stages, blending thoroughly.

• • •

Fit a 12- or 14-inch pastry bag with a large open star tip and fill the bag partway with the lemon cream. Pipe the cream into the mini martini glasses, filling them one-third full. Set aside 6 raspberries for garnishing the tops, and arrange 3 or 4 raspberries over the cream in each glass, laying them on their sides. Pipe the remaining lemon cream over the raspberries to fill the glasses.

• • •

GARNISH

Place a raspberry, with the pointed end facing up, on top of the lemon cream in each glass. Scatter lemon zest over the top.

• • •

keeping Refrigerate the martinis, loosely covered with waxed paper and then tightly wrapped with plastic wrap, up to 3 hours before serving.

making a change Replace the raspberries with blueberries or blackberries.

mocha soufflés with cacao nib whipped cream

WHEN YOU SERVE THESE INDIVIDUAL-SIZE SOUFFLÉS, YOUR GUESTS WILL BE DELIGHTED AND VERY IMPRESSED. SOUFFLÉS RISE HIGH IN THE OVEN TO CREATE A VERY DRAMATIC EFFECT, BUT THEY NEED TO BE EATEN AS SOON AS THEY COME OUT OF THE OVEN OR THEY WILL COLLAPSE. THE KEY TO SERVING THESE AT YOUR NEXT DINNER PARTY IS TO PREPARE THEM A DAY IN ADVANCE AND KEEP THEM TIGHTLY COVERED IN THE REFRIGERATOR, THEN JUST BAKE THEM RIGHT BEFORE YOU PLAN TO SERVE THEM. THE CACAO NIB WHIPPED CREAM IS AN INCREDIBLE GARNISH FOR THESE DELECTABLE SOUFFLÉS. THE CACAO NIBS NEED TO STEEP IN THE CREAM OVERNIGHT, SO BEGIN PREPARING THE CREAM THE DAY BEFORE YOU WHIP IT.

MAKES *eight ¼-cup servings* | USE *eight 2½ × 1⅝–inch round ramekins*

½ cup heavy whipping cream

1 tablespoon plus 1 teaspoon (½ ounce) cacao nibs

2 teaspoons plus 1 tablespoon confectioners' sugar

2 teaspoons unsalted butter, softened

2 teaspoons granulated sugar

4 ounces bittersweet chocolate (62 to 72% cacao content), finely chopped

1½ ounces (3 tablespoons) unsalted butter, cut into small pieces

1½ teaspoons instant espresso powder

1 teaspoon pure vanilla extract or vanilla paste

¼ teaspoon kosher or fine-grained sea salt

2 extra-large eggs, at room temperature

1 extra-large egg white, at room temperature

⅛ teaspoon cream of tartar

¼ cup (1½ ounces) superfine sugar

CACAO NIB CREAM

Bring the cream to a boil in a ½-quart saucepan over medium heat. Turn off the heat and add the cacao nibs. Transfer the cream to a bowl and cover tightly. Chill overnight.

• • •

Strain the cream to remove the cacao nibs. Whip the chilled cream in the bowl of an electric stand mixer with the wire whip attachment or in a large mixing bowl using a hand-held mixer on medium speed until frothy. Add 2 teaspoons of confectioners' sugar and whip the cream until it holds soft peaks. Cover the bowl tightly with plastic wrap and chill while preparing the soufflés.

• • •

SOUFFLÉS

Position a rack in the center of the oven and preheat the oven to 375°F. Use a paper towel or your fingertips to coat the inside of the ramekins with 2 teaspoons of softened butter. Sprinkle the inside of each with granulated sugar and tilt the ramekins so the sugar sticks to the butter and coats the insides of the ramekins completely. Turn out any excess sugar. Set the ramekins aside while preparing the soufflé batter.

• • •

Melt the chopped chocolate and remaining 1½ ounces of butter pieces together in the top of a double boiler over hot water. Stir often with a rubber spatula to help melt the chocolate evenly. Or melt them in a microwave-safe bowl on low power for 30-second bursts. Stir with a rubber spatula after each burst. Remove the top pan of the double boiler, if using, and wipe the bottom and sides very dry.

• • •

In a small bowl, dissolve the espresso powder in the vanilla and stir until it is a thick paste. Add this and the salt to the chocolate mixture and stir until well blended. Let the mixture cool, stirring occasionally with a rubber spatula to prevent a skin from forming on top.

• • •

Separate the whole eggs and place the yolks in a ½-quart mixing bowl. Pour about 1 cup of the chocolate mixture into the egg yolks to temper them and bring them up to the temperature of the chocolate. Stir together well. Transfer this mixture back to the remaining chocolate mixture and blend together thoroughly.

• • •

Whip the egg whites from the separated eggs plus 1 more egg white in a grease-free bowl of an electric stand mixer with the wire whip attachment or in a large grease-free mixing bowl using a hand-held mixer on medium-high speed until frothy.

• • •

Add the cream of tartar to the egg whites and continue to whip. When soft peaks form, gradually sprinkle on the superfine sugar and continue to whip until the egg whites hold glossy and firm but not stiff peaks. Fold the whipped egg whites into the chocolate mixture in 3 stages.

• • •

Divide the mixture evenly among the ramekins. Place the ramekins in a 2-quart baking dish. Bake the soufflés for 14 minutes, until they are puffed over the top, look set, and the center wiggles a little. You can also test for doneness with a cake tester inserted into the center of a soufflé. It should come out moist, but not runny.

• • •

Remove the baking dish from the oven, sprinkle the top of each soufflé lightly with the remaining 1 tablespoon of confectioners' sugar, and serve immediately, topped with a dollop of cacao nib whipped cream.

• • •

streamlining The unbaked soufflés will keep up to 2 days, tightly covered with plastic wrap, in the refrigerator.

mascarpone—raspberry parfaits

RICH, CREAMY MASCARPONE CUSTARD IS ALTERNATELY LAYERED IN A MINI PARFAIT GLASS WITH RASPBERRY SAUCE, THEN TOPPED WITH FRESH RASPBERRIES. IN FRANCE, THIS TYPE OF LAYERED DESSERT IS CALLED A VERRINE, REFERRING TO THE GLASS IT IS LAYERED IN, AND IS CURRENTLY THE LATEST TREND. THIS DESSERT IS SO LIGHT AND FRESH THAT IT FEELS LIKE YOU'RE EATING A CLOUD. BOTH THE MASCARPONE CUSTARD AND THE RASPBERRY SAUCE CAN BE MADE A FEW DAYS IN ADVANCE, THEN THE PARFAIT CAN BE ASSEMBLED BEFORE SERVING. THIS RECIPE CONTAINS RAW EGGS, WHICH THE USDA RECOMMENDS NOT TO BE EATEN BY PREGNANT WOMEN, VERY YOUNG CHILDREN, THE ELDERLY, AND PEOPLE WITH COMPROMISED IMMUNE SYSTEMS.

MAKES twelve ¼-cup servings | USE twelve 2-ounce mini parfait or mini martini glasses

½ pound mascarpone, softened

3 extra-large egg yolks, at room temperature

4 tablespoons (1½ ounces) granulated sugar, divided

1 teaspoon pure vanilla paste

¼ teaspoon freshly grated nutmeg

Pinch of kosher or fine-grained sea salt

2 extra-large egg whites, at room temperature

1 cup fresh or defrosted fresh-frozen raspberries

2 tablespoons (¾ ounce) superfine sugar

1 tablespoon framboise, Chambord, kirsch, or Grand Marnier

1 teaspoon freshly squeezed lemon juice

12 fresh raspberries

MASCARPONE CUSTARD

Whisk the mascarpone in a 2-quart mixing bowl until smooth.

• • •

Whip the egg yolks and 2 tablespoons of granulated sugar in the bowl of an electric stand mixer with the wire whip attachment or in a large mixing bowl using a hand-held mixer on medium speed until the mixture holds a slowly dissolving ribbon as the beater is lifted, about 5 minutes.

• • •

Fold the whipped egg yolks into the mascarpone in 3 stages, blending thoroughly. Add the vanilla paste, nutmeg, and salt and mix well.

• • •

Whip the egg whites in a grease-free bowl of an electric stand mixer with a grease-free wire whip attachment or in a grease-free large mixing bowl using a hand-held mixer on medium speed until frothy. Sprinkle on the remaining 2 tablespoons of granulated sugar and whip until the whites hold soft peaks. Fold the whipped whites into the mascarpone mixture in 3 stages, blending thoroughly.

• • •

Tightly cover the bowl with plastic wrap and chill until ready to use.

• • •

RASPBERRY SAUCE

Puree 1 cup of fresh or fresh-frozen raspberries in the work bowl of a food processor fitted with the steel blade. Strain into a 1-quart bowl, pushing through as much of the liquid as possible, eliminating the seeds. Add the superfine sugar, liqueur, and lemon juice and stir together thoroughly.

• • •

ASSEMBLY

Place the mini parfait or mini martini glasses on a serving tray or flat surface. Place 1 teaspoon of raspberry sauce in the bottom of each glass. Cover the raspberry sauce with 2 generous tablespoons of the mascarpone custard. Slightly shake each glass to evenly distribute the custard. Spoon 1 teaspoon of raspberry sauce over the top of the custard. Place one of the remaining raspberries, with the pointed end facing up, on top of the raspberry sauce in each glass.

• • •

Serve immediately.

• • •

keeping The mascarpone custard and the raspberry sauce can be made up to 4 days in advance. Keep them tightly covered, separately, in the refrigerator.

making a change For the sauce, replace the raspberries with blueberries or blackberries, and garnish with the same type of berry.

lemon crème brûlée

CRÈME BRÛLÉE, COLD BAKED CUSTARD WITH A CRISP, CARAMELIZED SUGAR TOPPING, IS A CLASSIC FRENCH DESSERT. THE FLAVOR OF LEMON ADDS A BRIGHT TOUCH TO THIS SUCCULENT, CREAMY CUSTARD. BECAUSE THE CARAMELIZED SUGAR TOPPING BECOMES TOO HARD IF IT SITS IN THE REFRIGERATOR, CARAMELIZE THE TOP OF THE CUSTARDS RIGHT BEFORE SERVING.

MAKES eight ¼-cup servings | USE eight 2½ × 1⅝-inch round ramekins

---

1½ cups heavy whipping cream

Finely grated zest of 1 large lemon

¼ cup (1½ ounces) plus 8 teaspoons (1 ounce) granulated sugar

Pinch of kosher or fine-grained sea salt

3 extra-large egg yolks, at room temperature

1 teaspoon freshly squeezed lemon juice

½ teaspoon pure lemon extract

2 to 3 cups boiling water

1 large lemon

CUSTARD

Position a rack in the center of the oven and preheat the oven to 325°F. Place the ramekins in a 2-quart baking dish.

• • •

Warm the cream, lemon zest, ¼ cup of sugar, and salt in a 2-quart saucepan over medium heat until tiny bubbles form around the edges.

• • •

Whisk the egg yolks in a large mixing bowl to break them up. Add the hot cream mixture slowly, while stirring to blend smoothly.

• • •

Mix together the lemon juice and lemon extract and add to the cream mixture, blending thoroughly. Strain the mixture into a 2-cup liquid measuring cup and divide it evenly among the ramekins, filling each almost to the top.

• • •

Carefully pour the boiling water into the baking dish until it reaches partway up the sides of the ramekins. Bake the cus-tards for 20 minutes, until they are set around the edges but jiggle slightly in the center.

• • •

Remove the baking dish from the oven. Remove the rame-kins from the water bath and cool on a rack. Cover loosely with waxed paper and then tightly wrap with plastic wrap and chill at least 4 hours.

• • •

TOPPING

Sprinkle 1 teaspoon of sugar evenly over the custard in each ramekin. Use a butane kitchen torch to lightly caramelize the sugar on top of the custards.

• • •

Using a citrus peeler, form curls of lemon zest from the other large lemon to decorate the top of each crème brûlée.

• • •

keeping The crème brûlée, without the caramelized sugar topping, will keep up to 2 days, tightly covered with aluminum foil, in the refrigerator.

coconut crème brûlée

LUSCIOUS, RICH COCONUT MILK AND SHREDDED COCONUT GIVE FLAVOR AND TEXTURE TO THIS CLASSIC, CREAMY BAKED CUSTARD. IT'S BEST TO CARAMELIZE THE TOPS OF THE CUSTARDS JUST BEFORE SERVING SO THE TOPPING DOESN'T BECOME TOO HARD. BE SURE TO BAKE THE CUSTARDS AT LEAST A DAY BEFORE SERVING BECAUSE THEY NEED TIME TO COOL AND CHILL.

MAKES eight ¼-cup servings | USE eight 2 ½ × 1⅝–inch round ramekins

⅔ cup heavy whipping cream

¼ cup unsweetened coconut milk

3 extra-large egg yolks, at room temperature

¼ cup (1½ ounces) plus 8 teaspoons (1 ounce) granulated sugar

½ teaspoon pure vanilla extract

Pinch of kosher or fine-grained sea salt

2 tablespoons (¼ ounce) sweetened shredded coconut

2 to 3 cups boiling water

CUSTARD

Position a rack in the center of the oven and preheat the oven to 325°F. Place the ramekins in a 2-quart baking dish.

• • •

Warm the cream and coconut milk in a 2-quart saucepan over medium heat until tiny bubbles form around the edges.

• • •

Whip the egg yolks in the large bowl of an electric stand mixer with the wire whip attachment or in a large mixing bowl using a hand-held mixer on high speed, gradually adding ¼ cup of sugar, until the mixture is very thick and pale colored. Add the vanilla and salt and blend well.

• • •

With the mixer on low speed, slowly add the hot cream mixture to the yolk mixture and blend thoroughly. Stir in the coconut. Transfer the mixture to a 2-cup liquid measuring cup and divide it evenly among the ramekins, filling each almost to the top.

• • •

Carefully pour the boiling water into the baking dish until it reaches partway up the sides of the ramekins. Bake the custards for 20 minutes, until they are set around the edges but jiggle slightly in the center.

• • •

Remove the baking dish from the oven. Remove the ramekins from the water bath and cool on a rack. Cover loosely with waxed paper and then tightly wrap with plastic wrap and chill at least 4 hours.

• • •

TOPPING

Sprinkle 1 teaspoon of sugar evenly over the custard in each ramekin. Use a butane kitchen torch to lightly caramelize the sugar on top of the custards.

• • •

keeping The crème brûlée, without the caramelized sugar topping, will keep up to 2 days, tightly covered with aluminum foil, in the refrigerator.

adding style Serve the crème brûlée on a small plate with a few fresh raspberries.

butterscotch crème brûlée

MY HUSBAND AND I ATE DINNER AT ZIN RESTAURANT IN HEALDSBURG, CALIFORNIA, ON A RECENT TRIP TO THE SONOMA WINE COUNTRY. FOR DESSERT WE HAD AN OUTRAGEOUSLY DELICIOUS BUTTERSCOTCH CRÈME BRÛLÉE SERVED WITH SMALL OATMEAL COOKIES. I LOVED THE DESSERT SO MUCH THAT I WANTED TO RE-CREATE IT AT HOME, AND I THINK I WAS PRETTY SUCCESSFUL. CARAMELIZE THE TOP OF THE CRÈME BRÛLÉE RIGHT BEFORE SERVING SO IT DOESN'T BECOME TOO FIRM. MAKE THE CUSTARDS THE DAY BEFORE YOU PLAN TO SERVE THEM BECAUSE THEY NEED TIME TO COOL AND CHILL.

MAKES twelve ¼-cup servings | USE twelve 2½ × 1⅝–inch round ramekins

1½ cups heavy whipping cream

Pinch of kosher or fine-grained sea salt

1½ ounces (3 tablespoons) unsalted butter, cut into small pieces

½ cup (3½ ounces) firmly packed light brown sugar

3 extra-large egg yolks, at room temperature

½ teaspoon pure vanilla extract

2 to 3 cups boiling water

4 tablespoons (2 ounces) granulated sugar, divided

CUSTARD

Position a rack in the center of the oven and preheat the oven to 325°F. Place the ramekins in a 3-quart baking dish.

• • •

Warm the cream and salt in a 1-quart saucepan over medium heat until tiny bubbles form around the edges.

• • •

Melt the butter in a 2-quart saucepan over medium heat. Add the brown sugar and stir together with a heat-resistant spatula until thoroughly blended. Bring to a boil and stir constantly for 2 minutes. Pour the hot cream into the butter mixture and stir to remove any lumps.

• • •

Whisk together the egg yolks and vanilla in a large mixing bowl. Pour the hot cream mixture into the egg yolk mixture, stirring continuously. Strain the mixture into a 2-cup liquid measuring cup and divide it evenly among the ramekins, filling each almost to the top.

• • •

Carefully pour the boiling water into the baking dish until it reaches partway up the sides of the ramekins. Bake the custards for 20 minutes, until they are set around the edges but jiggle slightly in the center.

• • •

Remove the baking dish from the oven. Remove the ramekins from the water bath and cool on racks. Cover loosely with waxed paper and then tightly wrap with plastic wrap and chill at least 4 hours.

• • •

TOPPING

Sprinkle 1 teaspoon of granulated sugar evenly over the custard in each ramekin. Use a butane kitchen torch to lightly caramelize the sugar on top of the custards.

• • •

keeping The crème brûlée, without the caramelized sugar topping, will keep up to 2 days, tightly covered with aluminum foil, in the refrigerator.

adding style Serve the crème brûlée on a small plate with two Toasty Oatmeal Cookies (page 153).

toasted pecan crème caramel

I'VE UPDATED THIS CLASSIC EGG CUSTARD BY INFUSING THE MILK WITH FINELY CHOPPED TOASTED PECANS, WHICH GIVES THE CUSTARD SUBTLE FLAVOR AND COLOR. AS WITH ALL RECIPES FOR CRÈME CARAMEL, THESE ARE BAKED IN CARAMEL-LINED MOLDS THAT FORM A TOPPING AND SAUCE WHEN THE CUSTARDS ARE TURNED OUT OF THE MOLD. IT'S A GOOD IDEA TO MAKE THESE SEVERAL HOURS TO A DAY AHEAD OF WHEN YOU PLAN TO SERVE THEM SO THEY HAVE TIME TO COOL AND CHILL.

MAKES eight ¼-cup servings | USE eight 2½ × 1⅝-inch round custard cups or shallow bowls

¾ cup (3 ounces) pecan halves

½ cup (3½ ounces) granulated sugar, divided

3 tablespoons water, divided

¼ teaspoon freshly squeezed lemon juice

1¼ cups milk (whole or 2%)

1 tablespoon honey

Pinch of kosher or fine-grained sea salt

2 extra-large eggs, at room temperature

1 extra-large egg yolk, at room temperature

½ teaspoon pure vanilla extract

1 quart boiling water

Position a rack in the center of the oven and preheat the oven to 350°F. Place the custard cups in a 2-quart baking pan.

• • •

Place the pecans in a cake or pie pan and toast in the oven for 12 minutes. Stir twice as they are toasting. Remove the pan from the oven and cool on a rack. Finely chop ¼ cup of the pecans. Reserve the remaining pecan halves for garnish.

• • •

CARAMEL

Combine ¼ cup of sugar and 2 tablespoons of water in a 1-quart saucepan over medium-high heat. Bring the mixture to a boil and stir to dissolve the sugar. Brush around the inside of the pan with a damp pastry brush at the point where the sugar syrup meets the sides of the pan to prevent the sugars from crystallizing. Do this two times. Cook the mixture, without stirring, until it turns a rich golden brown, about 8 minutes.

• • •

Remove the pan from the heat and stir in the remaining 1 tablespoon of water and lemon juice. Be careful because the mixture may bubble and foam up. Return the pan to the heat and stir to dissolve any lumps.

• • •

Divide the caramel evenly among the custard cups. Tilt and rotate each cup so the caramel completely covers the bottom.

• • •

CUSTARD

Warm the milk, honey, salt, and the ¼ cup of chopped toasted pecans in a 2-quart heavy-duty saucepan over medium heat until tiny bubbles form around the edges. Remove the saucepan from the heat, cover it, and let the milk infuse for 15 minutes. Uncover the milk mixture and bring it to a boil over medium heat.

• • •

Whip the eggs, egg yolk, and vanilla in the bowl of an electric stand mixer with the wire whip attachment or in a large mixing bowl using a hand-held mixer on medium speed until frothy. Slowly sprinkle on the remaining ¼ cup of sugar and whisk until well blended. In a steady stream, pour in the hot milk mixture and mix thoroughly.

• • •

Strain the custard into a 2-cup liquid measuring cup to remove the pecans. Pour the custard into the caramel-lined cups, dividing it evenly among them.

• • •

Place the baking pan on the oven rack. Carefully pour the boiling water into the baking pan until it reaches halfway up the sides of the cups or bowls.

• • •

Bake the custard for 20 minutes, until a toothpick or cake tester inserted in the center comes out clean. Remove the baking pan from the oven and transfer the custard cups to a rack to cool. Cover loosely with waxed paper and then tightly wrap with plastic wrap and chill at least 2 hours.

• • •

To unmold the custards, run a thin-bladed knife around the edges of the custard cups. Place a serving plate over the top of a custard cup and invert the custard onto the plate. Repeat with each custard cup.

• • •

Place a toasted pecan half on top of each custard and serve.

• • •

keeping Store the baked custard in the custard cups, tightly covered with a double layer of plastic wrap, in the refrigerator up to 3 days.

adding style Serve each crème caramel with a star or rosette of whipped cream on top and then garnish with the pecan halves.

Omit the pecan halves and sprinkle the whipped cream with toasted, finely chopped pecans instead.

toasted coconut–chocolate pudding

COCONUT AND CHOCOLATE ARE AN IDEAL FLAVOR COMBINATION. TOASTING THE COCONUT ADDS A SURPRISING CRUNCH TO THIS CREAMY STIRRED PUDDING.

MAKES *eight ¼-cup servings* | USE *eight 2½ × 1⅝–inch round ramekins*

⅓ cup plus 1 tablespoon (1 ounce) sweetened shredded coconut

3 ounces bittersweet chocolate (62 to 72% cacao content), finely chopped

¼ cup (1½ ounces) granulated sugar

2 tablespoons (½ ounce) unsweetened cocoa powder (natural or Dutch-processed), sifted

1 tablespoon plus 1½ teaspoons cornstarch, sifted

Pinch of kosher or fine-grained sea salt

2 extra-large egg yolks, at room temperature

1¼ cups milk (whole or 2%), divided

¾ cup heavy whipping cream, divided

1 tablespoon unsalted butter, softened

1½ teaspoons pure vanilla extract

PUDDING

Position a rack in the center of the oven and preheat the oven to 350°F. Place the ramekins in a 2-quart baking dish.

• • •

Toast the coconut in a cake or pie pan for 3 minutes. Stir and toast another 3 minutes, until light golden. Remove the pan from the oven and cool on a rack. Reserve 1 tablespoon for the garnish.

• • •

Melt the chopped chocolate in the top of a double boiler over hot water or in a microwave-safe bowl on the lowest power for 30-second bursts. Stir with a rubber spatula as needed.

• • •

Whisk together the sugar, cocoa powder, cornstarch, and salt in a 2-quart mixing bowl until well combined.

• • •

In a small bowl, use a fork to lightly beat the egg yolks with ¼ cup of milk. Add to the cocoa mixture and whisk together until smooth.

• • •

Bring the remaining 1 cup of milk and ½ cup of cream to a boil in a 2-quart saucepan over medium heat. Remove the saucepan from the heat and slowly add to the cocoa mixture, whisking until smooth. Pour the mixture back into the saucepan and stir constantly over medium heat until the pudding thickens, 3 to 5 minutes.

• • •

Remove the saucepan from the heat and stir in the butter until melted. Add the vanilla and melted chocolate and stir until thoroughly blended. Stir in all but the reserved 1 tablespoon of toasted coconut.

• • •

Divide the pudding evenly among the ramekins, filling each. Cover loosely with waxed paper and cool to room temperature. Tightly cover with plastic wrap and chill in the refrigerator, about 2 hours.

• • •

GARNISH

Whip the remaining ¼ cup of cream until it holds soft peaks.

• • •

Serve each pudding with a scoop of whipped cream and sprinkle the top with the reserved toasted coconut.

• • •

keeping The puddings, without the garnish, will keep up to 4 days, tightly covered with plastic wrap, in the refrigerator.

rice pudding

THIS IS A CREAMY, VERY SATISFYING PUDDING MADE ON THE STOVE TOP. IT'S DELICIOUS EATEN EITHER WARM OR COLD. THIS IS ONE OF MY HUSBAND'S FAVORITE DESSERTS.

MAKES *eight ¼-cup servings* | USE *eight 2½ × 1⅝–inch round ramekins*

1½ cups whole milk

1¼ cups heavy whipping cream, divided

⅓ cup (2½ ounces) short-grain rice

⅛ teaspoon kosher or fine-grained sea salt

2 extra-large egg yolks, at room temperature

¼ cup (1½ ounces) firmly packed light brown sugar

⅓ cup (1¾ ounces) raisins

1 teaspoon pure vanilla extract

¼ teaspoon freshly grated nutmeg

2 teaspoons confectioners' sugar

RICE PUDDING

Bring the milk and 1 cup of cream to a boil in a 2-quart saucepan over medium heat. Add the rice and salt and simmer, stirring frequently, until the rice is cooked, 15 to 20 minutes.

• • •

Whisk the egg yolks in a small mixing bowl to break them up. Add the brown sugar and whisk together to blend smoothly. Stir in about ½ cup of the rice mixture.

• • •

Transfer the egg mixture back to the saucepan with the remaining rice mixture. Stir over low heat until the mixture is thickened but does not boil, 5 to 10 minutes. Remove the saucepan from the heat and stir in the raisins, vanilla, and nutmeg.

• • •

Divide the rice pudding evenly among the ramekins, filling each. Cover loosely with waxed paper and cool to room temperature. Tightly cover with plastic wrap and chill in the refrigerator, about 2 hours.

• • •

GARNISH

Whip the remaining ¼ cup of cream in the bowl of an electric stand mixer with the wire whip attachment or in a large mixing bowl using a hand-held mixer on medium speed until frothy. Add the confectioners' sugar and continue whipping the cream until it holds soft peaks.

• • •

Serve each rice pudding with a scoop of the whipped cream.

• • •

keeping The rice puddings, without the garnish, will keep up to 4 days, tightly covered with plastic wrap, in the refrigerator.

chapter six

COOKIES

walnut fingerprint cookies

BECAUSE A THUMB WOULD MAKE TOO BIG AN INDENTATION IN THE CENTER OF THESE SMALL COOKIES, I'VE DUBBED THEM "FINGERPRINTS" INSTEAD. YOU HAVE THREE CHOICES FOR THE FILLING: RASPBERRY PRESERVES, APRICOT PRESERVES, OR BITTERSWEET CHOCOLATE GANACHE. WHICHEVER YOU CHOOSE, THEY ARE EQUALLY DELECTABLE. THESE COOKIES WILL DISAPPEAR QUICKLY.

MAKES *about 4 dozen 1¼-inch cookies*

1 cup (4½ ounces) lightly toasted walnuts

4 tablespoons (1¾ ounces) granulated sugar, divided

1 cup (4½ ounces) all-purpose flour

½ teaspoon ground cinnamon

¼ teaspoon baking powder

4 ounces (8 tablespoons, 1 stick) unsalted butter, softened

2 tablespoons (1 ounce) light brown sugar

1 extra-large egg, at room temperature

1 teaspoon pure vanilla extract

2 tablespoons (about) raspberry or apricot preserves

2 ounces bittersweet chocolate (62 to 72% cacao content), very finely chopped

3 tablespoons heavy whipping cream

COOKIES

Pulse the walnuts and 1 tablespoon of granulated sugar together in the work bowl of a food processor fitted with the steel blade until the nuts are finely ground, about 1 minute.

• • •

Over a medium-size bowl, sift together the flour, cinnamon, and baking powder.

• • •

Beat the butter in the bowl of an electric stand mixer with the flat beater attachment or in a large bowl using a hand-held mixer on medium speed until fluffy, about 1 minute. Add the brown sugar and remaining 3 tablespoons of granulated sugar and beat together well. Stop occasionally and scrape down the sides and bottom of the bowl with a rubber spatula.

• • •

Separate the egg, then add the yolk to the butter mixture and blend well. Place the egg white in a small bowl, cover tightly with plastic wrap, and keep at room temperature.

• • •

Add the vanilla to the butter mixture and blend thoroughly. Add ⅓ cup of the walnut mixture to the butter mixture, blending well. Place the remaining walnut mixture in a bowl. Add the flour mixture to the butter mixture in 3 stages, blending thoroughly after each addition.

• • •

Gather the dough into a flat disk and cover tightly with plastic wrap. Chill until firm but pliable, at least 2 hours.

• • •

Adjust the oven racks to the upper and lower thirds and preheat the oven to 350°F. Line 2 baking sheets with parchment paper or nonstick liners.

• • •

Pinch off pieces of dough that are 1 scant teaspoonful. Roll each piece between your palms into a ball, coat with the reserved egg white, and roll in the ground walnut mixture, coating completely. Place the balls on the baking sheets, leaving about 1 inch between them. Use your index finger to press an indentation in the center of each, making a well.

• • •

PRESERVE AND JAM FILLING

Fit a 10- or 12-inch pastry bag with a ½-inch round plain pastry tip. Fill the bag partway with the preserves or jam and pipe a small mound into the center of half of the cookies.

• • •

Bake all the cookies for 7 minutes. Remove from the oven and use your index finger to press down the centers of the unfilled cookies to maintain the indentation in each. Switch the baking sheets in the oven so that the baking sheet from the top rack is now on the lower rack. Bake another 6 to 7 minutes, until set and light golden. Remove the baking sheets from the oven and cool the cookies on the baking sheets on racks.

• • •

GANACHE FILLING

Place the chopped chocolate in a small bowl. In a small saucepan over medium heat, bring the cream to a boil. Immediately pour the cream over the chocolate. Let it stand for 30 seconds so the chocolate begins to melt, then blend together with a heat-resistant spatula or a whisk until very smooth and creamy.

• • •

Cover the bowl tightly with plastic wrap to prevent a skin from forming on top and let the mixture cool to room temperature. Chill in the refrigerator until thick but not firm, about 1 hour.

• • •

Fit a 10- to 12-inch pastry bag with a ½-inch round plain pastry tip. Fill the bag partway with the ganache. Pipe a small mound of ganache into the center of each baked unfilled cookie.

• • •

keeping Store the filled cookies in a single layer on a baking sheet, lightly covered with waxed paper and tightly wrapped with aluminum foil, at room temperature up 3 days. The unfilled cookies can be stored up to 5 days.

making a change Replace the walnuts with toasted and skinned hazelnuts or sliced almonds.

Use 3 tablespoons of raspberry preserves or apricot jam to fill all the cookies.

Use about 1 tablespoon of each raspberry preserves and apricot jam to fill two-thirds of the cookies. Fill the remaining cookies with the chocolate ganache, creating an assortment of cookies.

fudgy chocolate-hazelnut bites

CHOCOLATE AND HAZELNUTS ARE A FABULOUS FLAVOR COMBINATION. COCOA POWDER IS WHAT GIVES THESE RICH YET LIGHT COOKIES THEIR DEEP, DENSE CHOCOLATE FLAVOR. MY FAVORITE COCOA POWDER IS PERNIGOTTI BECAUSE IT HAS A TINY BIT OF VANILLA THAT GREATLY ENHANCES THE COCOA FLAVOR. WHEN YOU WANT SOMETHING CHOCOLATY, THESE ARE EXTREMELY SATISFYING.

MAKES *about 4 dozen 1-inch cookies*

½ cup (2¼ ounces) unsweetened cocoa powder (natural or Dutch-processed)

½ cup (3½ ounces) superfine sugar

¼ cup (1 ounce) toasted and finely ground hazelnuts

Pinch of kosher or fine-grained sea salt

3 extra-large egg whites, at room temperature

⅛ teaspoon cream of tartar

1 teaspoon pure vanilla extract

2 teaspoons confectioners' sugar

Adjust the oven racks to the upper and lower thirds and preheat the oven to 300°F. Line 2 baking sheets with aluminum foil, shiny side up.

• • •

Over a 1-quart bowl, sift together the cocoa powder and ¼ cup of superfine sugar. Add the hazelnuts and salt and toss to blend. Set aside briefly.

• • •

Whip the egg whites and cream of tartar in the bowl of an electric stand mixer with a grease-free wire whip attachment or in a grease-free large mixing bowl using a hand-held mixer on medium-high speed until the egg whites hold soft peaks. Very slowly sprinkle on the remaining ¼ cup of superfine sugar while the egg whites continue to whip until they hold firm and glossy but not stiff peaks. Fold in the cocoa and hazelnut mixture in 4 stages. Fold in the vanilla, blending thoroughly.

• • •

Fit a 12- or 14-inch pastry bag with a ½-inch plain round pastry tip and fill the bag partway with the meringue mixture. Pipe out ½- to ¾-inch mounds onto the baking sheets, leaving 1 inch of space between them.

• • •

Bake the cookies for 7 minutes. Switch the baking sheets and bake another 8 to 10 minutes. The tops of the cookies should give slightly when touched. Remove the baking sheets from the oven and cool the cookies on the baking sheets on racks. Peel the cookies off of the foil.

• • •

Lightly dust the tops of the cookies with confectioners' sugar.

• • •

keeping Store the cookies in an airtight plastic container at room temperature up to 1 week. To freeze up to 4 months, wrap the container tightly in several layers of plastic wrap and aluminum foil. Use a large piece of masking tape and an indelible marker to label and date the contents. If frozen, defrost the cookies overnight in the refrigerator and bring to room temperature before serving.

hazelnut and cacao nib madeleines

THESE LITTLE CAKE-LIKE COOKIES TAKE THEIR CLASSIC RIBBED SHELL SHAPE FROM THE PANS THEY ARE BAKED IN. FINELY GROUND CACAO NIBS ADD SUBTLE CHOCOLATE FLAVOR AND CRISP TEXTURE TO THESE TRADITIONAL COOKIES. GROUND HAZELNUTS ALSO ADD THEIR LUSCIOUS FLAVOR, WHICH IS A GREAT COMPLEMENT TO THE CACAO NIBS. THESE ARE PERFECT FOR AFTERNOON COFFEE AND TEA AND AS PART OF AN ASSORTMENT OF SMALL COOKIES.

MAKES 3¼ dozen cookies | USE two 20-cavity (1⅝ × 1⅛–inch) mini madeleine pans

Nonstick baking spray

1 tablespoon (¼ ounce) cacao nibs

3 tablespoons (¾ ounce) toasted and finely ground hazelnuts

2 extra-large eggs, at room temperature

½ cup (3½ ounces) granulated sugar

⅔ cup (3 ounces) all-purpose flour

⅛ teaspoon baking powder

⅛ teaspoon kosher or fine-grained sea salt

2 ounces (4 tablespoons, ½ stick) unsalted butter, melted and cooled

½ teaspoon pure vanilla extract

2 teaspoons confectioners' sugar

Spray the cavities of the madeleine pans with nonstick baking spray, then place the madeleine pans on a baking sheet.

• • •

Finely grind the cacao nibs in a clean coffee grinder. In a small bowl, mix together the ground cacao nibs and the ground hazelnuts.

• • •

Whip the eggs in the bowl of an electric stand mixer with the wire whip attachment or in a large mixing bowl using a hand-held mixer on medium speed until frothy, about 1 minute. Add the granulated sugar and whip together until the mixture is very thick and pale colored and holds a slowly dissolving ribbon as the beater is lifted, about 5 minutes.

• • •

In a medium-size bowl, sift together the flour and baking powder. Add the salt and toss to blend. Fold this mixture into the whipped egg mixture in 3 stages.

• • •

Combine the butter and vanilla in another small bowl and fold into the batter in 2 stages, blending in thoroughly. Fold in the ground hazelnuts and cacao nibs in 3 stages.

• • •

Cover the bowl tightly with plastic wrap and let the batter stand at room temperature for 1 hour so it thickens.

• • •

Position a rack in the center of the oven and preheat the oven to 350°F.

• • •

Fit a 12- or 14-inch pastry bag with a ½-inch plain round pastry tip and fill the bag partway with the batter. Pipe the batter into each cavity of the madeleine pans, filling them.

• • •

Bake the madeleines for 13 minutes, until the tops spring back lightly when touched. Remove the baking sheet from the oven. Holding the madeleine pans upside down over cooling racks, gently shake them to release the madeleines. Cool the madeleines completely on the racks.

• • •

Lightly dust the tops of the madeleines with the confectioners' sugar.

. . .

keeping Store the madeleines between layers of waxed paper in an airtight plastic container at room temperature up to 3 days. To freeze up to 3 months, wrap the container tightly in several layers of plastic wrap and aluminum foil. Use a large piece of masking tape and an indelible marker to label and date the contents. If frozen, defrost the madeleines overnight in the refrigerator. Bring to room temperature to serve.

adding style Drizzle the cooled madeleines with thin lines of bittersweet or semisweet chocolate.

Half-dip the cooled madeleines in melted bittersweet or semisweet chocolate (see page 8).

Make madeleine sandwich cookies by spreading a thin layer of raspberry or apricot jam on the flat side of one cooled madeleine and topping it with the flat side of another cooled cookie.

Make madeleine ganache sandwich cookies by spreading the flat side of one cooled madeleine with soft ganache (see Ganache Filling, page 130) and topping it with the flat side of another cooled cookie.

devilish dark chocolate madeleines

THESE LITTLE CAKE-LIKE COOKIES ARE BAKED IN CLASSIC RIBBED SHELL-SHAPED PANS. TRADITIONAL MADELEINES ARE LIGHT COLORED, BUT THESE WILL QUICKLY BECOME YOUR FAVORITES BECAUSE THEY ARE MADE WITH LUSCIOUS 70 PERCENT CACAO CONTENT BITTERSWEET CHOCOLATE. THESE ARE SO DELICIOUS THAT THEY DISAPPEAR VERY RAPIDLY.

MAKES 3¼ dozen cookies | USE two 20-cavity (1⅝ × 1⅛–inch) mini madeleine pans

Nonstick baking spray

1½ ounces bittersweet chocolate (70 to 72% cacao content), finely chopped

1½ ounces (3 tablespoons) unsalted butter, cut into small pieces

½ teaspoon pure vanilla extract

1 extra-large egg, at room temperature

3 tablespoons (1¼ ounces) superfine sugar

¼ cup (1 ounce) all-purpose flour

⅛ teaspoon kosher or fine-grained sea salt

2 teaspoons confectioners' sugar

Position a rack in the center of the oven and preheat the oven to 350° F. Spray the cavities of the madeleine pans with nonstick baking spray. Place the madeleine pans on a baking sheet.

• • •

Melt the chocolate and butter together in the top of a double boiler over low heat. Stir often with a rubber spatula to help melt evenly. Remove the top pan of the double boiler and wipe the bottom and sides very dry. Stir the melted chocolate mixture with a rubber spatula occasionally to prevent a skin from forming on top. Or place the chocolate and butter in a microwave-safe bowl and melt on low power for 30-second bursts. Stir with a rubber spatula after each burst.

• • •

Add the vanilla to the melted chocolate mixture and blend well.

• • •

Whip the egg in the bowl of an electric stand mixer with the wire whip attachment or in a large mixing bowl using a hand-held mixer on medium speed until frothy, about 1 minute. Add the superfine sugar and whip until the mixture

is very thick and pale colored and holds a slowly dissolving ribbon as the beater is lifted, about 5 minutes.

• • •

Over a medium-size bowl, sift the flour, then add the salt and toss to blend.

• • •

With the mixer speed on low, add the flour mixture in 2 stages, blending well after each addition. Stop and scrape down the sides and bottom of the bowl. The mixture should be smooth. Pour the melted chocolate mixture into the batter and blend in thoroughly.

• • •

Transfer the batter to a 2-cup liquid measuring cup. Pour the batter slowly into each cavity of the madeleine pans, filling them three-fourths full.

• • •

Bake the madeleines for 8 minutes, until the tops spring back lightly when touched. Remove the baking sheet from the oven. Holding the madeleine pans upside down over cooling racks, gently shake them to release the madeleines. Cool the madeleines completely on the racks.

• • •

Lightly dust the tops of the madeleines with the confectioners' sugar.

• • •

keeping Store the madeleines between layers of waxed paper in an airtight plastic container at room temperature up to 3 days. To freeze up to 3 months, wrap the container tightly in several layers of plastic wrap and aluminum foil. Use a large piece of masking tape and an indelible marker to label and date the contents. If frozen, defrost the madeleines overnight in the refrigerator and bring to room temperature to serve.

adding style Drizzle the cooled madeleines with thin lines of bittersweet, semisweet, milk, or white chocolate.

Half-dip the cooled madeleines in melted bittersweet or semisweet chocolate (see page 8).

Make madeleine sandwich cookies by spreading a thin layer of raspberry or apricot jam on the flat side of one cooled madeleine and topping it with the flat side of another cooled cookie.

Make madeleine ganache sandwich cookies by spreading the flat side of one cooled madeleine with soft ganache (see Ganache Filling, page 130) and topping it with the flat side of another cooled cookie.

crackly ginger chips

IF YOU LIKE GINGER, THESE LITTLE BITE-SIZE MORSELS ARE FOR YOU! EVERYONE WHO TASTES THESE IS DELIGHTED AND SURPRISED BY THEIR DEEP, FULL GINGER FLAVOR. THEY ARE CRISP AND CRUNCHY, JUST THE WAY A GINGER COOKIE SHOULD BE. ALTHOUGH THESE ARE GREAT ON THEIR OWN, THEY ARE PERFECT COOKIES TO USE TO MAKE ICE CREAM SANDWICHES.

MAKES *about 8½ dozen 1-inch cookies*

1½ cups (6¾ ounces) cake flour

½ teaspoon baking soda

1 teaspoon ground ginger

½ teaspoon ground cinnamon

⅛ teaspoon ground cloves

⅛ teaspoon kosher or fine-grained sea salt

2 tablespoons (½ ounce) finely minced un-crystallized candied ginger

2½ ounces (5 tablespoons) unsalted butter, softened

⅓ cup (2 ounces) firmly packed light brown sugar

1 extra-large egg yolk, at room temperature

2 tablespoons unsulfured molasses

⅓ cup (2 ounces) granulated sugar

Over a medium-size bowl, sift together the cake flour, baking soda, ground ginger, cinnamon, and cloves. Add the salt and toss to blend. Add the un-crystallized candied ginger and toss to coat completely.

• • •

Beat the butter in the bowl of an electric stand mixer with the flat beater attachment or in a large mixing bowl using a hand-held mixer on medium speed until fluffy, about 1 minute. Add the brown sugar and beat together until completely blended, about 1 minute.

• • •

Use a fork to lightly beat together the egg yolk and molasses in a small bowl and add to the butter mixture. Blend completely, stopping occasionally to scrape down the sides and bottom of the bowl with a rubber spatula. Add the flour mixture in 3 stages, stopping to scrape down the bowl after each addition. Blend thoroughly. Cover the bowl tightly with plastic wrap and chill for 30 minutes.

• • •

Adjust a rack to the upper third of the oven and preheat the oven to 350°F. Line 3 baking sheets with parchment paper or nonstick liners.

• • •

Place the granulated sugar in a bowl. Dampen your hands with cold water. Pinch off ¼-teaspoon-size pieces of the dough and roll each piece into a ball between your palms. Roll the balls in the granulated sugar to coat completely, then place them on the lined baking sheets, leaving at least 1 inch of space between them.

• • •

Keep 2 baking sheets of cookies chilled. Bake 1 sheet of the cookies at a time for 12 minutes, until the tops are cracked and the cookies are firm.

• • •

Remove the baking sheet from the oven and cool the cookies on the baking sheet on a rack. Repeat with the remaining baking sheets.

• • •

keeping Store the cookies in an airtight plastic container at room temperature up to 1 week. To freeze up to 4 months, wrap the container tightly in several layers of plastic wrap and aluminum foil. Use a large piece of masking tape and an indelible marker to label and date the contents. If frozen, defrost the cookies overnight in the refrigerator and bring to room temperature before serving.

peek-a-boo hazelnut sandwich cookies

A DOT OF APRICOT PRESERVES PEEKS THROUGH A HOLE IN THE CENTER OF THESE DELECTABLE
SANDWICH COOKIES. FINELY GROUND TOASTED HAZELNUTS ARE BLENDED INTO A BUTTERY DOUGH
THAT IS ROLLED OUT AND CUT INTO FLUTED-EDGE ROUNDS. THESE ELEGANT LITTLE COOKIES ARE
JUST THE RIGHT SIZE TO SERVE WITH AFTERNOON TEA OR COFFEE OR AS PART OF A COOKIE PLATTER.

MAKES *about 3¼ dozen sandwich cookies*

3 ounces (¾ stick, 6 tablespoons) unsalted butter, softened

⅓ cup (2 ounces) granulated sugar

1 extra-large egg yolk, at room temperature

½ teaspoon pure vanilla extract or vanilla paste

⅔ cup (2½ ounces) finely ground toasted hazelnuts

1 cup (4½ ounces) plus 2 tablespoons (½ ounce) all-purpose flour

¼ teaspoon ground cinnamon

⅛ teaspoon freshly grated nutmeg

Pinch of kosher or fine-grained sea salt

¼ cup apricot preserves

2 tablespoons (about) confectioners' sugar

COOKIES

Beat the butter in the bowl of an electric stand mixer using the flat beater attachment or in a large mixing bowl using a hand-held mixer on medium speed until fluffy, about 1 minute. Add the granulated sugar and beat until completely blended, about 1 minute.

• • •

Use a fork to lightly beat together the egg yolk and vanilla in a small bowl and add to the butter mixture. Blend completely, stopping occasionally to scrape down the sides and bottom of the bowl with a rubber spatula. Add the hazelnuts and blend thoroughly.

• • •

Mix the flour and cinnamon together in a medium-size bowl. Add the nutmeg and salt and toss to blend well. Add this mixture to the hazelnut mixture in 3 stages, blending thoroughly after each addition and mixing until the dough is smooth. Shape the dough into a disk, tightly wrap it in plastic wrap, and chill until firm, about 3 hours.

• • •

Adjust the oven racks to the upper and lower thirds and preheat the oven to 350°F. Line 3 baking sheets with parchment paper or nonstick liners.

• • •

Divide the dough into 2 equal pieces. Roll out each piece between sheets of lightly floured waxed or parchment paper to a thickness of ¼ inch. Remove the top sheet of paper. Use a 1¼-inch round fluted-edge cutter to cut out cookies. Using a ½-inch round plain-edge cutter, cut out the center from half of the rounds. Transfer the cookies to the baking sheets, leaving 1 inch of space between them. Gather the scraps together, knead slightly, roll out, and cut out more cookies.

• • •

Place 2 of the baking sheets in the oven and bake the cookies for 5 minutes. Switch the 2 baking sheets and bake another 4 minutes, until set and very lightly colored. Remove the baking sheets from the oven and cool the cookies on the baking sheets on racks. Repeat with the remaining baking sheet.

• • •

ASSEMBLY AND GARNISH

Place about ½ teaspoon of apricot preserves on the flat side and in the center of the solid cookies. Sift the confectioners' sugar over the tops of the cookies with holes and place them, sugared side up, on top of the preserves on each cookie to make sandwiches.

• • •

keeping Store the assembled cookies in a single layer on a baking sheet, tightly wrapped with aluminum foil, at room temperature up to 2 days.

Store the unassembled cookies between layers of waxed paper in an airtight container at room temperature up to 2 days. To freeze up to 4 months, wrap the container tightly in several layers of plastic wrap and aluminum foil. Use a large piece of masking tape and an indelible marker to label and date the contents. If frozen, defrost the cookies overnight in the refrigerator and bring to room temperature before serving.

making a change Replace the ground hazelnuts with ground almonds.

Replace the apricot preserves with raspberry preserves.

walnut filo triangles

THESE ARE SIMILAR TO PASTRIES FOUND THROUGHOUT NORTH AFRICA AND THE MIDDLE EAST. A FILLING OF GROUND WALNUTS, HONEY, AND CINNAMON IS ENCLOSED WITHIN BUTTERED FILO DOUGH THAT IS FOLDED INTO TRIANGLES. AFTER THE TRIANGLES ARE BAKED, THEY ARE QUICKLY DIPPED INTO HONEY SYRUP, MAKING THEM GLISTEN. THESE TAKE A BIT OF WORK TO ASSEMBLE, BUT THEY ARE WELL WORTH IT.

MAKES 3 dozen 2¼ × 3–inch triangles

1½ cups (6¾ ounces) walnuts

2 tablespoons (¾ ounce) granulated sugar

1 teaspoon finely grated lemon zest

½ teaspoon ground cinnamon

⅓ cup plus ½ cup honey

½ pound 9 × 14–inch sheets frozen filo pastry dough, thawed

4 ounces (8 tablespoons, 1 stick) unsalted butter, melted

½ cup water

¼ cup (1½ ounces) superfine sugar

Finely grated zest of ½ lemon

TRIANGLES

Adjust the oven racks to the upper and lower thirds and preheat the oven to 350°F. Line 2 baking sheets with parchment paper or nonstick liners.

• • •

Pulse together the walnuts, granulated sugar, 1 teaspoon of lemon zest, and cinnamon in the work bowl of a food processor fitted with the steel blade until the nuts are finely ground, about 1 minute. Transfer the mixture to a bowl and add ⅓ cup of honey. Stir until the mixture is thoroughly blended.

• • •

Unroll the filo dough onto a smooth, flat surface. Use a serrated slicing knife to cut the dough into 4 equal strips, measuring 2¼ × 14 inches. Stack the filo dough strips and cover with a damp paper towel to keep the filo from drying out.

• • •

Lay 1 filo dough strip vertically flat on the work surface and brush with butter. Lay another filo dough strip on top and brush with butter. Place 1 teaspoon of the ground walnut mixture at the lower right-hand corner of the buttered filo dough strips. Take the lower right-hand corner of the filo and fold it over to the left side to form a triangle and cover the walnut mixture. Then fold the triangle up to make another triangle on top of the first. Fold that triangle to the right. Keep repeating this folding until you reach the top of the buttered filo dough strips. Brush the triangle all over with butter and place it seam side down on the lined baking sheet.

• • •

Repeat with the remaining filo dough strips, ground walnut mixture, and butter, forming 36 triangles total. Leave about 1 inch of space between the triangles on the baking sheets.

• • •

Bake the triangles for 8 minutes. Switch the pans and bake another 8 to 10 minutes, until golden. In the meantime, prepare the honey syrup.

• • •

HONEY SYRUP

Place the water, superfine sugar, zest from ½ lemon, and the remaining ½ cup of honey in a 1-quart saucepan. Bring to a boil and simmer until the mixture thickens, about 10 minutes.

• • •

Line a baking sheet with waxed or parchment paper and place 1 large or 2 small cooling racks over the paper. While the triangles are hot, dip them into the hot sugar syrup to coat completely. Use a slotted spoon or skimmer to remove the triangles from the sugar syrup and transfer them to the cooling racks.

• • •

Serve the triangles at room temperature.

• • •

keeping Store the triangles on a baking sheet in a single layer covered with waxed paper, then tightly wrapped with aluminum foil, at room temperature up to 2 days.

streamlining The walnut filling can be made up to 4 days in advance and kept in a tightly covered container in the refrigerator.

making a change Replace the ground walnuts with ground almonds or hazelnuts.

Instead of dipping the triangles in the hot sugar syrup, dust them with confectioners' sugar.

almond and mocha macaroon sandwich cookies

THESE ARE A MINIATURE VERSION OF THE VERY POPULAR MACAROONS FOUND IN PASTRY SHOPS THROUGHOUT FRANCE. THEY ARE PERFECT FOR AFTERNOON TEA AND AS PART OF A COOKIE ASSORTMENT. ONE OR TWO OF THESE WILL SATISFY YOUR CRAVING FOR A TREAT.

MAKES *about 3½ dozen 1-inch sandwich cookies*

2 extra-large egg whites (¼ cup), at room temperature

¼ teaspoon cream of tartar

¾ cup (2½ ounces) confectioners' sugar, sifted, divided

⅔ cup (2 ounces) blanched slivered or sliced almonds

½ cup water

1 teaspoon instant espresso powder

1 teaspoon pure vanilla extract

3 ounces bittersweet chocolate (62 to 72% cacao content), very finely chopped

⅓ cup heavy whipping cream

COOKIES

Line 2 jelly-roll pans with aluminum foil with the shiny side up.

• • •

Place about 1 inch of water in a 3-quart saucepan and warm it over medium heat. Place the egg whites in the bowl of an electric stand mixer or in a large mixing bowl. Set the bowl in the saucepan of warm water and stir constantly until the egg whites feel warm to the touch or register 160°F on an instant-read thermometer. Remove the bowl from the water and wipe the sides and bottom dry.

• • •

With a grease-free wire whip attachment of a stand mixer, or in a grease-free large mixing bowl using a hand-held mixer, beat the egg whites on medium speed until frothy. Add the cream of tartar and continue to whip on medium speed until the egg whites hold soft peaks. Slowly sprinkle on ¼ cup of confectioners' sugar and whip the egg whites until they hold firm but not stiff peaks.

• • •

Place the almonds and remaining ½ cup of confectioners' sugar in the work bowl of a food processor fitted with a steel blade. Pulse until the almonds are very finely ground, about 1 minute. Fold this mixture into the whipped egg white mixture in 3 stages. Blend well after each addition.

• • •

Fit a 12- or 14-inch pastry bag with a ½-inch round plain pastry tip. Fill the pastry bag partway with the macaroon mixture. Holding the pastry bag vertically, pipe out mounds that are about ¾ inch in diameter. Leave at least 1 inch of space between them. Pipe out mounds that are uniform in size, so they will be the same size when assembled. If there are any points on top of the macaroons, smooth them with a damp fingertip. Let the macaroons stand at room temperature for 20 minutes so the tops dry slightly and form a light skin before they bake, creating the correct texture.

• • •

Adjust the oven racks to the upper and lower thirds and preheat the oven to 350°F.

• • •

Bake the macaroons for 7 minutes. Switch the pans and bake another 6 minutes, until set. Remove the pans from the oven and immediately lift up a corner of the aluminum foil on each pan. Pour ¼ cup of water under the foil on each pan. This creates steam, which makes it easy to remove the macaroons from the foil. Be careful to pour the water under the foil and not on top. Place each pan on a cooling rack and let the macaroons cool completely on the baking pans. Carefully remove the macaroons from the foil.

• • •

MOCHA GANACHE FILLING

In a small bowl, dissolve the espresso powder in the vanilla.

• • •

Place the chocolate in a 1-quart mixing bowl. In a small saucepan over medium heat, bring the cream to a boil. Immediately pour the cream over the chocolate. Let it stand for 30 seconds so it begins to melt the chocolate, then blend together with a heat-resistant spatula or a whisk until very smooth and creamy. Add the espresso mixture and blend in thoroughly.

• • •

Cover the bowl tightly with plastic wrap to prevent a skin from forming on top and let the mixture cool to room temperature. Chill in the refrigerator until thick, but not firm, about 1 hour.

• • •

Fit a 12- or 14-inch pastry bag with a ½-inch round plain pastry tip. Fill the pastry bag partway with the ganache. Pipe a small mound of ganache on the flat side of 1 macaroon and top it with the flat side of another macaroon. Gently press the cookies together to spread the ganache filling out to the edges. Serve the macaroons at room temperature.

• • •

keeping Store the assembled cookies in a single layer on a baking sheet between sheets of waxed paper, tightly covered with plastic wrap in the refrigerator, up to 2 days. The texture will soften slightly, but this doesn't affect their flavor.

Store the unfilled macaroons between layers of waxed paper on a baking sheet, tightly covered with aluminum foil, in a cool, dry place up to 2 days.

streamlining The ganache filling can be made up to 3 weeks in advance. Store it in an airtight plastic container tightly covered with plastic wrap or a freezer bag in the refrigerator, away from any strong-flavored foods. Bring the ganache to room temperature before using. It should be pliable enough to hold the indentation of your finger, but not so soft that it is liquid.

adding style Dust the tops of the assembled macaroons lightly with 2 teaspoons of confectioners' sugar.

toasted pecan shortbread bites

TOASTED PECANS ADD THEIR RICH, WARM FLAVOR TO THESE CLASSIC BUTTERY SHORTBREAD BITES. THESE ARE BAKED IN TINY FLUTED-EDGE TARTLET MOLDS THAT IMPART THEIR DESIGN TO THE EDGES.

MAKES 2½ dozen cookies | USE thirty 1⅝ × ¾–inch round fluted-edge tartlet pans

Nonstick baking spray

⅓ cup (1¼ ounces) finely chopped pecans

4 ounces (8 tablespoons, 1 stick) unsalted butter, softened

¼ cup (1½ ounces) superfine sugar

1 cup (4½ ounces) all-purpose flour

⅛ teaspoon kosher or fine-grained sea salt

Position a rack in the center of the oven and preheat the oven to 350°F. Coat the inside of the tartlet pans with nonstick baking spray. Place the pans on a baking sheet.

• • •

Place the pecans in a cake or pie pan and toast in the oven for 8 minutes. Remove the pan from the oven and place on a rack to cool. Reduce the oven temperature to 300°F.

• • •

Beat the butter in the bowl of an electric stand mixer with the flat beater attachment or in a large mixing bowl using a hand-held mixer on medium speed until light and fluffy, about 2 minutes. Add the sugar and beat together until thoroughly blended, about 2 minutes.

• • •

In a medium-size bowl, toss the flour and salt together to blend. Add to the butter mixture in 3 stages, blending thoroughly after each addition. Stop and scrape down the sides and bottom of the bowl after each addition to ensure even mixing. Add the toasted pecans and continue to mix until the dough is smooth and soft, about 1 minute.

• • •

Pinch off 1-inch pieces of the dough and roll each into a ball between your palms. Place a ball in a tartlet pan and use your fingers to press it into the sides and bottom of the pan. Don't overfill the pan or the shortbread will expand too much as it bakes. Use your thumb to indent the dough in the center of the mold. Repeat until all the dough is pressed into all of the pans. Chill the shortbread for 30 minutes.

• • • •

Bake the shortbread for 30 minutes, until set and very lightly colored. Remove the baking sheet from the oven and cool the cookies completely on the baking sheet on a rack. Gently tap the tartlet pans against a flat surface to remove the shortbread.

• • • •

keeping Store the shortbread between layers of waxed paper in an airtight plastic container at room temperature up to 1 week.

streamlining The shortbread dough can be made up to 3 days in advance and kept tightly wrapped in a double layer of plastic wrap in the refrigerator. To freeze up to 3 months, wrap it snugly in several layers of plastic wrap and enclose it in a freezer bag. Use a large piece of masking tape and an indelible marker to label and date the contents. If frozen, defrost the dough in the refrigerator.

making a change Replace the toasted pecans with toasted unsweetened shredded coconut.

Replace the toasted pecans with toasted walnuts, hazelnuts, almonds, or macadamia nuts.

lemon–lime–coconut squares

THE TROPICAL FLAVORS OF LEMON, LIME, AND COCONUT COMBINE IN THESE TASTY SQUARES. THE CRISP COCONUT PASTRY CONTRASTS PERFECTLY WITH THE LUSCIOUS CITRUSY CURD THAT BAKES ON TOP. LEMON-LIME JUICE IS MADE FROM EQUAL PARTS LEMON AND LIME JUICE. BE SURE TO SQUEEZE YOUR OWN JUICES HERE FOR A FRESH, VIBRANT FLAVOR.

MAKES 5 dozen 1-inch squares | USE a 7 × 11–inch baking pan

1 tablespoon unsalted butter, softened

2 tablespoons (¾ ounce) plus ¾ cup (1½ ounces) sweetened shredded coconut

1 cup (4½ ounces) plus 2 tablespoons (½ ounce) all-purpose flour

⅓ cup (1¼ ounces) confectioners' sugar

⅛ teaspoon plus 1 pinch kosher or fine-grained sea salt

4 ounces (8 tablespoons, 1 stick) unsalted butter, softened

Finely grated or minced zest of 2 large lemons, divided

2 extra-large eggs, at room temperature

½ cup (3½ ounces) granulated sugar

¼ teaspoon baking powder

⅓ cup freshly squeezed lemon-lime juice

Position a rack in the center of the oven and preheat the oven to 350°F. Line a 7 × 11–inch baking pan with a large piece of aluminum foil that extends over the sides. Press the foil under the sides of the pan. Use a paper towel or your fingers to spread 1 tablespoon of butter evenly over the foil.

• • •

COCONUT PASTRY DOUGH

Place 2 tablespoons of coconut in a cake or pie pan and toast for 6 minutes, until light golden brown, shaking after 3 minutes. Remove the pan from the oven and cool on a rack.

• • •

Pulse together 1 cup of flour, confectioners' sugar, ⅛ teaspoon of salt, and the toasted coconut in the work bowl of a food processor fitted with the steel blade.

• • •

Cut the 4 ounces of butter into small pieces and add it along with the zest from 1 lemon to the flour mixture. Process until the dough wraps itself around the blade, about 30 seconds. Turn the pastry dough into the foil-lined baking pan.

Dust your hands with flour and press the dough evenly over the bottom of the pan.

• • •

Bake the dough for 18 minutes, until light golden on the edges. Remove the baking pan from the oven and cool on a rack while preparing the filling. Reduce the oven temperature to 325°F.

• • •

FILLING

Whip the eggs in the bowl of an electric stand mixer with the wire whip attachment or in a large mixing bowl using a hand-held mixer on medium-high speed until frothy. Slowly sprinkle on the granulated sugar and continue to whip on medium-high speed until the mixture is very thick and pale colored and holds a slowly dissolving ribbon as the beater is lifted, about 5 minutes.

• • •

In a small bowl, combine ½ cup of coconut, the remaining 2 tablespoons of flour, baking powder, and 1 pinch of salt and stir to blend well. Add to the egg mixture and blend together on medium speed. Stop and scrape down the sides and bottom of the bowl with a rubber spatula. Add the lemon-lime juice and the zest from the remaining 1 lemon and blend.

• • •

Pour the filling over the crust in the baking pan, then sprinkle the remaining ¼ cup of coconut evenly over the top.

• • •

Bake the pastry for 30 minutes, until the top is set and light golden. Remove the baking pan from the oven and cool completely on a rack.

• • •

Use the foil to lift the pastry from the baking pan and place it on a cutting board. Peel the foil away from the sides. Use a ruler to mark where to cut, measuring 1-inch squares, then use a sharp chef's knife to cut the squares. Peel the squares off the foil.

• • •

keeping Store the squares in a single layer between pieces of waxed paper in an airtight container at room temperature up to 5 days.

streamlining The pastry dough can be made in advance and kept in the refrigerator, tightly wrapped in a double layer of plastic wrap, up to 4 days. To freeze up to 3 months, wrap it snugly in several layers of plastic wrap and enclose it in a freezer bag. Use a large piece of masking tape and an indelible marker to label and date the contents. If frozen, defrost the dough overnight in the refrigerator before using. If it is too firm to press into the pan, let it stand to warm up to room temperature.

making a change Use all lemons or all limes to make the filling.

cardamom butter cookies

CARDAMOM IS ONE OF THE WORLD'S OLDEST SPICES AND HAS A RICH HISTORY. IT IS WIDELY USED IN BAKING IN THE SCANDINAVIAN AND EASTERN EUROPEAN COUNTRIES AND TO FLAVOR COFFEE IN THE MIDDLE EAST. CARDAMOM HAS A DISTINCTIVE WARM, PUNGENT FLAVOR WITH A HINT OF LEMON. I PREFER TO USE WHOLE CARDAMOM SEEDS AND GRIND THEM RIGHT BEFORE USE TO MAINTAIN THEIR FLAVOR, BUT GROUND CARDAMOM IS FINE TO USE ALSO.

MAKES *about 5 dozen 1-inch cookies*

4 ounces (8 tablespoons, 1 stick) unsalted butter, softened

½ cup (1¾ ounces) confectioners' sugar, sifted, divided

1 extra-large egg yolk, at room temperature

1½ teaspoons pure vanilla extract

1 cup (4½ ounces) all-purpose flour

½ teaspoon baking powder

1 teaspoon finely ground cardamom

½ cup (2¼ ounces) walnuts, finely ground

Adjust the oven racks to the upper and lower thirds and preheat the oven to 350°F. Line 2 baking sheets with parchment paper or nonstick liners.

• • •

Beat the butter in the bowl of an electric stand mixer with the flat beater attachment or in a large mixing bowl using a hand-held mixer on medium speed until fluffy, about 2 minutes. Add ¼ cup of confectioners' sugar and beat together well. Stop occasionally and scrape down the sides and bottom of the bowl with a rubber spatula. Add the egg yolk and vanilla. Stop and scrape down the sides and bottom of the bowl with a rubber spatula to encourage even mixing. The mixture may look curdled at this point, but will smooth out as the flour is added.

• • •

Over a medium-size bowl, sift together the flour and baking powder. Add the cardamom and toss to blend well. Add the flour mixture to the butter mixture in 2 stages, mixing thoroughly after each addition. Stop occasionally and scrape

down the sides and bottom of the bowl with a rubber spatula. Add the ground walnuts and stir to distribute evenly.

• • •

Pinch off teaspoon-size pieces of the dough and roll each between your palms into small balls. Place the balls on the lined baking sheets, leaving at least 1 inch of space between them.

• • •

Bake the cookies for 5 minutes. Switch the baking sheets and bake another 5 to 6 minutes, until the cookies are set and very light golden. Remove the baking sheets from the oven and place them on cooling racks. Dust the cookies with the remaining ¼ cup of confectioners' sugar while they are slightly warm. Leave the cookies to cool completely.

• • •

keeping Store the cookies in confectioners' sugar in an airtight container at room temperature up to 5 days. To freeze up to 3 months, wrap the container tightly in several layers of plastic wrap and aluminum foil. Use a large piece of masking tape and an indelible marker to label and date the contents. If frozen, defrost the cookies overnight in the refrigerator and bring to room temperature before serving.

streamlining The cookie dough can be made and kept tightly covered with a double layer of plastic wrap in the refrigerator up to 3 days before baking.

making a change Replace the ground walnuts with finely ground macadamia nuts or pecans.

pecan-ginger biscotti

BISCOTTI ARE CRISP, TWICE-BAKED COOKIES THAT ARE GREAT FOR DIPPING IN COFFEE, TEA, AND HOT CHOCOLATE. THESE MINIATURE BISCOTTI ARE JUST THE RIGHT SIZE TO SATISFY THE CRAVING FOR A LITTLE SOMETHING SWEET. THE FLAVORS OF PECANS AND GINGER COMPLEMENT EACH OTHER PERFECTLY.

MAKES 3 dozen 1½-inch biscotti

⅔ cup (3 ounces) all-purpose flour

¼ cup (1½ ounces) firmly packed light brown sugar

¼ teaspoon kosher or fine-grained sea salt

⅛ teaspoon baking powder

⅛ teaspoon baking soda

3 tablespoons (¾ ounce) finely chopped pecans

2 tablespoons (½ ounce) finely chopped crystallized ginger

1 extra-large egg, at room temperature

1 teaspoon pure vanilla extract

Position a rack in the center of the oven and preheat the oven to 350°F. Line a baking sheet with parchment paper or a nonstick liner.

• • •

Pulse together the flour, brown sugar, salt, baking powder, and baking soda in the work bowl of a food processor fitted with a steel blade. Add the pecans and ginger and pulse a few times.

• • •

Use a fork to lightly beat together the egg and vanilla in a small bowl. With the food processor running, pour this mixture through the feed tube and process until the dough forms itself into a ball, about 30 seconds.

• • •

Divide the dough into 4 equal pieces and form each into a log about 4 inches long, 1½ inches wide, and ⅝ inch high. Place the logs on the baking sheet, leaving a few inches of space between them.

• • •

Bake the biscotti for 15 to 18 minutes, until they are light golden. Remove the baking sheet from the oven and cool on a rack for 10 minutes. Transfer the logs to a cutting board.

Using a serrated knife, cut each log on the diagonal into ½-inch-thick slices. Place the biscotti cut side down on the baking sheet.

• • •

Bake the biscotti another 8 to 10 minutes, until firm and set. Remove the baking sheet from the oven and cool the biscotti completely on the baking sheet on a rack.

• • •

keeping Store the biscotti between layers of waxed paper in an airtight plastic container at room temperature up to 1 week. To freeze up to 4 months, wrap the container tightly in several layers of plastic wrap and aluminum foil. Use a large piece of masking tape and an indelible marker to label and date the contents. If frozen, defrost the biscotti overnight in the refrigerator and bring to room temperature before serving.

making a change Replace the pecans with walnuts or almonds.

Replace the crystallized ginger with finely chopped dried apricots or dried tart cherries.

cantuccini di prato

CANTUCCINI ARE MINIATURE CLASSIC BISCOTTI THAT COME FROM PRATO, NEAR FLORENCE, ITALY. THEY ARE FIRMER AND CRISPIER THAN REGULAR BISCOTTI AND ARE MADE FOR DIPPING IN VIN SANTO, A SWEET DESSERT WINE. BECAUSE THESE ARE SO HARD, THEY KEEP VERY WELL. HOWEVER YOU SERVE THEM, THEY ARE DELICIOUS.

MAKES 7 dozen 2 x ½–inch biscotti

1 cup (4½ ounces) all-purpose flour

¾ cup (4 ounces) raw unblanched whole almonds

½ cup (3½ ounces) granulated sugar

2 teaspoons anise seed

¾ teaspoon baking powder

Pinch of kosher or fine-grained sea salt

1 extra-large egg, at room temperature

2 extra-large egg yolks, at room temperature

1 tablespoon unsalted butter, melted

1 teaspoon freshly grated orange zest

½ teaspoon pure vanilla extract

Position a rack in the center of the oven and preheat the oven to 350°F. Line a baking sheet with parchment paper or a non-stick liner.

• • •

Pulse together briefly the flour, almonds, sugar, anise seed, baking powder, and salt in the work bowl of a food processor fitted with a steel blade.

• • •

Use a fork to lightly beat together the egg, egg yolks, melted butter, orange zest, and vanilla in a small bowl. With the food processor running, pour this mixture through the feed tube and process until the dough forms itself into a ball, about 30 seconds.

• • •

Divide the dough into 5 equal pieces and roll each into a log about 8 inches long and 1 inch wide. Place the logs on the baking sheet, leaving a few inches of space between them. Press the tops of the logs to flatten until they are about ½ inch thick.

• • •

Bake the cantuccini for 15 to 18 minutes, until they are light golden. Remove the baking sheet from the oven and cool on a rack for 10 minutes. Line another baking sheet with parchment paper or a nonstick liner. Adjust the oven racks to the upper and lower thirds of the oven.

• • •

Transfer the logs to a cutting board. Using a serrated knife, cut the logs on the diagonal into ½-inch-thick slices. Place the cantuccini cut side down on the baking sheets.

• • •

Bake the cantuccini another 12 to 15 minutes, until firm and set. Remove the baking sheets from the oven and cool completely on the baking sheets on racks.

• • •

keeping Store the cantuccini in an airtight plastic container between layers of waxed paper at room temperature up to 1 week. To freeze up to 4 months, wrap the container tightly in several layers of plastic wrap and aluminum foil. Use a large piece of masking tape and an indelible marker to label and date the contents. If frozen, defrost the cantuccini overnight in the refrigerator and bring to room temperature before serving.

making a change Replace the almonds with toasted, coarsely chopped hazelnuts.

toasty oatmeal cookies

I ADD A LITTLE MALT POWDER TO THESE COOKIES TO GIVE THEM A TOASTY UNDERTONE. THEY ARE CRUNCHY AND GO PERFECTLY WITH ICE CREAM OR THE CREAMY-SMOOTH TEXTURE OF BUTTERSCOTCH CRÈME BRÛLÉE (PAGE 120).

MAKES *about 4½ dozen 1-inch cookies*

2 ounces (4 tablespoons, ½ stick) unsalted butter, softened

⅓ cup (2 ounces) firmly packed light brown sugar

1 extra-large egg yolk, at room temperature

1 teaspoon pure vanilla extract

⅓ cup (1½ ounces) all-purpose flour

1 cup (3¼ ounces) old-fashioned rolled oats (not quick-cooking)

1 tablespoon (¼ ounce) malt powder

½ teaspoon baking powder

Pinch of kosher or fine-grained sea salt

½ cup (2¼ ounces) walnuts, finely chopped

Adjust the oven racks to the upper and lower thirds and preheat the oven to 350°F. Line 2 baking sheets with parchment paper or nonstick liners.

• • •

Beat the butter in the bowl of an electric stand mixer with the flat beater attachment or in a large mixing bowl using a hand-held mixer on medium speed until fluffy, about 1 minute. Add the brown sugar and beat together well.

• • •

Use a fork to lightly beat together the egg yolk and vanilla, then add to the butter mixture. Stop and scrape down the sides and bottom of the bowl with a rubber spatula to encourage even mixing. The mixture may look curdled at this point, but will smooth out as the dry ingredients are added.

• • •

In a large mixing bowl, stir together the flour, oats, malt powder, baking powder, and salt. Add this to the butter mixture in 2 stages, mixing thoroughly after each addition. Stop occasionally and scrape down the sides and bottom of the bowl with a rubber spatula. Add the walnuts and stir to mix evenly.

• • •

Use a 1-inch round ice cream scoop to drop small balls of the cookie dough onto the lined baking sheets, leaving about 1 inch of space between them.

• • •

Bake the cookies for 6 minutes. Switch the baking sheets and bake another 4 to 6 minutes, until the cookies are set and light golden. Remove the baking sheets from the oven and cool the cookies completely on the baking sheets on racks.

• • •

keeping Store the cookies in an airtight container at room temperature up to 5 days. To freeze up to 3 months, wrap the container tightly in several layers of plastic wrap and aluminum foil. Use a large piece of masking tape and an indelible marker to label and date the contents. If frozen, defrost the cookies overnight in the refrigerator and bring to room temperature before serving.

streamlining The cookie dough can be made and kept tightly covered with a double layer of plastic wrap in the refrigerator up to 3 days before baking.

making a change Replace the walnuts with pecans or macadamia nuts.

man-in-the-moon cookies

THESE CRISP SUGAR COOKIES ARE FORMED WITH A MOON-SHAPED COOKIE CUTTER AND WARMLY SPICED WITH CINNAMON, GINGER, NUTMEG, AND CLOVES.

MAKES *about 7 dozen cookies* | USE *a 1¾ × 1–inch half-moon–shaped cookie cutter*

¾ cup (3¼ ounces) all-purpose flour

¼ cup (1½ ounces) firmly packed light brown sugar

¼ cup (1½ ounces) superfine sugar

¾ teaspoon baking powder

¼ teaspoon ground cinnamon

⅛ teaspoon freshly grated nutmeg

⅛ teaspoon ground cloves

⅛ teaspoon ground ginger

Pinch of kosher or fine-grained sea salt

2 ounces (4 tablespoons, ½ stick) unsalted butter, chilled

1 extra-large egg yolk, at room temperature

1 teaspoon pure vanilla extract

Pulse together briefly the flour, brown sugar, superfine sugar, baking powder, cinnamon, nutmeg, cloves, ginger, and salt in the work bowl of a food processor fitted with a steel blade.

• • •

Cut the butter into small pieces and add to the flour mixture. Pulse until the butter is cut into very tiny pieces, about 30 seconds.

• • •

Use a fork to lightly beat together the egg yolk and vanilla in a small bowl. With the food processor running, pour this mixture through the feed tube. Process until the dough wraps itself around the blade, about 1 minute.

• • •

Shape the dough into a flat disk, wrap tightly in a double layer of plastic wrap, and chill until firm, about 2 hours. If the dough is too cold and firm after chilling, let it stand at room temperature for 10 to 15 minutes to become more pliable before rolling out.

• • •

Adjust the oven racks to the upper and lower thirds and preheat the oven to 350°F. Line 3 baking sheets with parchment paper or nonstick liners.

• • •

Roll out the dough between sheets of lightly floured waxed or parchment paper to a thickness of ¼ inch. Use a 1¾ × 1–inch half-moon–shaped cookie cutter to cut out the cookies. Transfer the cookies to the baking sheets, leaving about 1 inch of space between them. Gather the scraps together, knead slightly, roll out, and cut out more cookies.

• • •

Bake the cookies for 3 minutes. Switch the baking sheets and bake another 4 minutes, until set and very lightly colored. Remove the baking sheets from the oven and cool the cookies completely on the baking sheets on racks.

• • •

keeping Store the cookies in an airtight container at room temperature up to 4 days.

making a change Replace the blend of spices with a single spice.

adding style Sandwich cookies together using jam or chocolate ganache (see Ganache Filling, page 130).

tuile cookie cups

THESE CRISPY LITTLE ALMOND COOKIE CUPS ARE PERFECT FOR HOLDING TINY SCOOPS OF MOUSSE, ICE CREAM, LEMON CURD, OR PASTRY CREAM TOPPED WITH A FRESH BERRY. I PARTICULARLY LIKE TO SERVE THEM WITH CREAMY CARAMEL MOUSSE (PAGE 103) AND MOCHA MOUSSE (PAGE 104).THE RECIPE CALLS FOR FINELY GROUND ALMONDS, WHICH YOU CAN BUY AS ALMOND FLOUR, OR YOU CAN MAKE YOUR OWN BY GRINDING ALMONDS IN A FOOD PROCESSOR. ADD A TABLESPOON OF SUGAR TO EACH CUP OF ALMONDS TO ABSORB THE NATURAL OIL THEY RELEASE DURING GRINDING. THESE TUILE CUPS ARE GREAT FINGER FOOD BECAUSE THEY ARE EASY TO PICK UP. TRY THEM FOR YOUR NEXT PARTY.

MAKES 2 dozen cups | USE two 12-cavity 2-inch round silicone mini muffin pans

Nonstick baking spray

1 ounce (2 tablespoons, ¼ stick) unsalted butter, softened

¼ cup (1½ ounces) superfine sugar

1 extra-large egg white, at room temperature

¼ teaspoon pure vanilla extract

3 tablespoons (¾ ounce) all-purpose flour

1 teaspoon freshly grated nutmeg

Pinch of kosher or fine-grained sea salt

3 tablespoons (¾ ounce) finely ground almonds

Position a rack in the center of the oven and preheat the oven to 375°F. Line 2 baking sheets with aluminum foil and spray the foil with nonstick baking spray.

• • •

Beat the butter in the bowl of an electric stand mixer with the flat beater attachment or in a large mixing bowl using a hand-held mixer on medium speed until fluffy, about 1 minute. Add the sugar and beat together well. Stop occasionally and scrape down the sides and bottom of the bowl with a rubber spatula. Add the egg white and blend well, stopping to scrape down the sides and bottom of the bowl. The mixture may look curdled but will smooth out as the dry ingredients are added. Add the vanilla and blend well.

• • •

Combine the flour, nutmeg, and salt in a small bowl and add to the butter mixture in 2 stages, blending well after each addition. Add the almonds and blend thoroughly, stopping occasionally to scrape down the sides and bottom of the bowl to help mix evenly.

• • •

Using about 1 teaspoon for each, drop small scoops of the batter onto the baking sheets, leaving at least 2 inches of space between them. Use an offset spatula to spread the scoops into small rounds about 3 inches in diameter.

• • •

Bake 1 sheet of the tuiles at a time for 6 minutes, until the outer edges are light golden brown and the centers are set. Remove the baking sheet from the oven and use the offset spatula to lift the tuiles from the pan. Working quickly, place each tuile into a cavity of the silicone mini muffin pans, forming cups. The edges of the tuiles will form slight pleats. Repeat with the remaining baking sheet of tuiles. Let the tuiles set until cool, then gently lift them from the muffin pans.

• • •

Fill tuile cups as desired and serve immediately.

• • •

keeping Store the unfilled tuile cups, tightly wrapped in aluminum foil, at room temperature up to 4 days.

making a change Replace the almonds with walnuts, hazelnuts, or pecans.

chapter seven

SORBETS AND ICE CREAMS

raspberry sorbet shots

THIS IS THE PERFECT SUMMERTIME TREAT. IT'S LIGHT AND CREAMY, ALTHOUGH IT DOESN'T CONTAIN ANY CREAM, AND IS BURSTING WITH FRESH RASPBERRY FLAVOR.

MAKES *1 pint, 16 servings*

⅔ cup (4 ounces) granulated sugar

⅔ cup water

3 cups (12 ounces) fresh raspberries

2 teaspoons freshly squeezed lemon juice

16 sprigs fresh mint

Place the sugar and water together in a 2-quart heavy-duty saucepan. Bring to a boil over medium-high heat and stir gently with a heat-resistant spatula to dissolve the sugar. Remove from the heat, transfer to a 2-quart bowl, and cool to room temperature.

• • •

Puree the raspberries in the work bowl of a food processor fitted with the steel blade, then strain the puree to remove the seeds.

• • •

Stir together the sugar syrup and raspberry puree. Add the lemon juice and stir to blend thoroughly. Tightly cover the bowl with plastic wrap and refrigerate for 1 hour, until cold.

• • •

Process the sorbet in an ice cream maker, following the manufacturer's instructions. Freeze the sorbet in a tightly covered container for at least 30 minutes.

• • •

Using a 1-inch round ice cream scoop, place small scoops of the sorbet in shot glasses or mini martini glasses. Top each with a sprig of mint.

• • •

keeping Freeze the sorbet in a tightly covered container up to 2 weeks. If it is too firm, soften in the refrigerator for 30 minutes before serving.

streamlining The sugar syrup can be made up to 2 weeks in advance and kept in a tightly covered container in the refrigerator.

cantaloupe sorbet

THE LEMONY FLAVOR OF CORIANDER ACCENTS THE FRESH CANTALOUPE IN THIS REFRESHING SORBET.
BE SURE TO USE RIPE MELON FOR THE BEST FLAVOR.

MAKES 1 pint, 16 servings

1 cup (6½ ounces) granulated sugar

½ cup water

1 medium-size ripe cantaloupe (about 3 pounds)

2 teaspoons freshly squeezed lemon juice

2 teaspoons ground coriander

Zest strips from 1 medium lemon

Place the sugar and water together in a 2-quart heavy-duty saucepan. Bring to a boil over medium-high heat and stir with a heat-resistant spatula to dissolve the sugar. Remove from the heat, transfer to a bowl, and cool to room temperature.

• • •

Cut the cantaloupe in half and remove the seeds. Remove the rind and cut the flesh into thick chunks. Place the melon chunks in the work bowl of a food processor fitted with a steel blade. Add the lemon juice, coriander, and cooled sugar syrup and pulse until the mixture becomes liquid.

• • •

Pour the mixture into a 2-quart bowl, cover tightly with plastic wrap, and refrigerate until cold, about 2 hours.

• • •

Process the sorbet in an ice cream maker, following the manufacturer's instructions. Freeze the sorbet in a tightly covered container for at least 30 minutes.

• • •

Using a 1-inch round ice cream scoop, place small scoops of the sorbet in mini martini glasses, shot glasses, or small bowls. Top each serving with a few strips of lemon zest.

• • •

keeping Freeze the sorbet in a tightly covered container up to 2 weeks. If it is too firm, soften in the refrigerator for 30 minutes before serving.

streamlining The sugar syrup can be made up to 2 weeks in advance and kept in a tightly covered container in the refrigerator.

toasted coconut ice cream

THIS LUSCIOUS ICE CREAM HAS A WONDERFUL CREAMY TEXTURE WITH CRUNCHY BITS OF TOASTED COCONUT THROUGHOUT. IT'S A SUMMERTIME TREAT FOR WHEN YOU'RE IN THE MOOD FOR SOMETHING COLD.

MAKES 1 pint, 16 servings

4 tablespoons (½ ounce) plus ½ cup (1 ounce) sweetened shredded coconut

1 cup heavy whipping cream

1 cup milk (whole or 2%)

1 vanilla bean

⅓ cup (2¼ ounces) granulated sugar

4 extra-large egg yolks, at room temperature

Position a rack in the center of the oven and preheat the oven to 300°F. Place 4 tablespoons of coconut in a pie or cake pan and toast in the oven for 3 minutes. Shake the pan and toast another 2 to 3 minutes, until the coconut is light golden. Remove the pan from the oven and cool completely on a rack.

• • •

Place the cream and milk in a 2-quart heavy-duty saucepan. Split the vanilla bean down the center and scrape out the seeds. Add both the seeds and the pod to the milk mixture. Heat the mixture over medium heat until small bubbles form around the edges. Add the remaining ½ cup of untoasted coconut to the milk mixture. Turn off the heat, cover the saucepan, and let the mixture steep for 30 minutes.

• • •

Whip together the sugar and egg yolks in the bowl of an electric stand mixer with the wire whip attachment or in a large mixing bowl using a hand-held mixer on medium speed until it is very thick and pale yellow and it holds a slowly dissolving ribbon when the beater is lifted.

• • •

Reheat the milk mixture to just below the boiling point. Ladle half of the hot milk mixture into a liquid measuring cup, then slowly pour it into the egg yolk mixture, whisking constantly to blend well. Pour this egg mixture into the remaining milk mixture in the saucepan. Whisk the mixture constantly until it is thick enough to coat a spoon or regis-

ters 185°F on a candy thermometer. Immediately remove the thermometer and pour the ice cream custard into a 2-quart bowl. Remove the vanilla bean.

• • •

Cover the bowl tightly with plastic wrap to prevent a skin from forming on top and cool to room temperature. Refrigerate the ice cream custard for several hours, or until it is cold.

• • •

Process the ice cream custard in an ice cream maker, following the manufacturer's instructions. When the ice cream is half frozen, stir in 3 tablespoons of the toasted coconut. Freeze the ice cream in a tightly covered container for at least 30 minutes.

• • •

Using a 1-inch round ice cream scoop, place small scoops of ice cream in shot glasses, mini martini glasses, or small bowls. Sprinkle the remaining 1 tablespoon of toasted coconut over the ice cream and serve.

• • •

keeping Freeze the ice cream in a tightly covered container up to 2 weeks. If it is too firm, soften in the refrigerator for 45 minutes to 1 hour before serving.

streamlining The ice cream custard can be made up to 3 days in advance and kept tightly covered in a bowl in the refrigerator before freezing in the ice cream maker.

double ginger ice cream

"CREAMY," "SMOOTH," AND "SCRUMPTIOUS" ARE THE BEST WORDS TO DESCRIBE THIS ICE CREAM. IT'S RICH, LUSCIOUS, AND FULL OF SWEET-HOT GINGER FLAVOR, TOO. THIS RECIPE USES CANDIED GINGER PUREE, AVAILABLE FROM THE GINGER PEOPLE. THEIR WEB SITE IS WWW.GINGERPEOPLE.COM.

MAKES 1 pint, 16 servings

1 cup milk (whole or 2%)

½ cup (3½ ounces) granulated sugar

1 extra-large egg yolk, at room temperature

Pinch of kosher or fine-grained sea salt

½ cup (6½ ounces) candied ginger puree

1 cup heavy whipping cream

1 teaspoon pure vanilla extract

¼ cup (1¼ ounces) finely chopped crystallized ginger

32 slivers of crystallized ginger

Warm the milk in a 2-quart heavy-duty saucepan over medium heat until small bubbles form around the edges.

• • •

Whip together the sugar, egg yolk, and salt in the bowl of an electric stand mixer with the wire whip attachment or in a large mixing bowl using a hand-held mixer on medium speed until the mixture is very thick and pale yellow and it holds a slowly dissolving ribbon when the beater is lifted.

• • •

Ladle half of the hot milk into a liquid measuring cup, then slowly pour it into the egg yolk mixture, whisking constantly to blend well. Pour this egg mixture into the remaining milk in the saucepan. Stir in the candied ginger puree. Whisk the mixture constantly until it is thick enough to coat a spoon or registers 185°F on a candy thermometer. Immediately remove the thermometer and pour the ice cream custard into a 2-quart bowl. Add the cream and vanilla and stir to blend thoroughly.

• • •

Cover the bowl tightly with plastic wrap to prevent a skin from forming on top and cool to room temperature. Refrigerate the ice cream custard for several hours, or until it is cold.

• • •

Process the ice cream custard in an ice cream maker, following the manufacturer's instructions. When the ice cream is half frozen, stir in the finely chopped crystallized ginger. Freeze the ice cream in a tightly covered container for at least 30 minutes.

• • •

Using a 1½-inch round ice cream scoop, place small scoops of ice cream in shot glasses, mini martini glasses, or small bowls. Top each serving with a sliver or two of crystallized ginger.

• • •

keeping Freeze the ice cream in a tightly covered container up to 2 weeks. If it is too firm, soften in the refrigerator for 45 minutes to 1 hour before serving.

streamlining The ice cream custard can be made up to 3 days in advance and kept tightly covered in a bowl in the refrigerator before freezing in the ice cream maker.

mocha ice cream

DEEPLY-FLAVORED BITTERSWEET CHOCOLATE COMBINED WITH INSTANT ESPRESSO POWDER MAKE A SUPERB ICE CREAM WITH A VELVETY-SMOOTH TEXTURE.

MAKES 1 pint, 16 servings

1 cup heavy whipping cream

1 cup milk (whole or 2%)

2 teaspoons pure vanilla bean paste

2 tablespoons instant espresso powder

⅓ cup (2 ounces) granulated sugar

4 extra-large egg yolks, at room temperature

6 ounces bittersweet chocolate (70 to 72% cacao content), finely chopped

Chocolate-covered espresso beans

Place the cream, milk, and vanilla paste in a 2-quart heavy-duty saucepan. Warm the mixture over medium heat until small bubbles form around the edges. Stir in the espresso powder. Turn off the heat, cover the saucepan, and let the mixture steep for 20 minutes.

• • •

Whip together the sugar and egg yolks in the bowl of an electric stand mixer with the wire whip attachment or in a large mixing bowl using a hand-held mixer on medium speed until the mixture is very thick and pale yellow and it holds a slowly dissolving ribbon when the beater is lifted.

• • •

Reheat the milk mixture to just below the boiling point. Ladle half of the hot milk mixture into a liquid measuring cup, then slowly pour it into the egg yolk mixture, whisking constantly to blend well. Pour this egg mixture into the remaining milk mixture in the saucepan. Whisk the mixture constantly until it is thick enough to coat a spoon or registers 185°F on a candy thermometer. Immediately remove the thermometer and pour the ice cream custard into a 2-quart bowl. Add the chocolate to the custard and whisk together until it's all melted and completely smooth.

• • •

Cover the bowl tightly with plastic wrap to prevent a skin from forming on top and cool to room temperature. Refrigerate the ice cream custard for several hours, or until it is cold.

• • •

Process the ice cream custard in an ice cream maker, following the manufacturer's instructions. Freeze the ice cream in a tightly covered container for at least 30 minutes.

• • •

Using a 1-inch round ice cream scoop, place small scoops of ice cream in shot glasses, mini martini glasses, or small bowls. Top each scoop with a chocolate-covered espresso bean.

• • •

keeping Freeze the ice cream in a tightly covered container up to 2 weeks. If it is too firm, soften in the refrigerator for 45 minutes to 1 hour before serving.

streamlining The ice cream custard can be made up to 3 days in advance and kept tightly covered in a bowl in the refrigerator before freezing in the ice cream maker.

buttermilk and nutmeg ice cream

A TANGY UNDERTONE FROM BUTTERMILK AND WARM RICHNESS FROM NUTMEG MAKE THIS UNUSUAL ICE CREAM A STANDOUT.

MAKES 1 pint, 16 *servings*

¾ cup heavy whipping cream

½ vanilla bean, cut widthwise

⅓ cup (2 ounces) granulated sugar

3 extra-large egg yolks, at room temperature

¾ cup buttermilk

2½ teaspoons freshly grated nutmeg, divided

Place the cream in a 2-quart heavy-duty saucepan. Split the vanilla bean lengthwise down the center and scrape out the seeds. Add both the seeds and the pod to the cream. Heat the mixture over medium heat until small bubbles form around the edges.

• • •

Whip together the sugar and egg yolks in the bowl of an electric stand mixer with the wire whip attachment or in a large mixing bowl using a hand-held mixer on medium speed until the mixture is very thick and pale yellow and it holds a slowly dissolving ribbon when the beater is lifted.

• • •

Ladle half of the hot cream into a liquid measuring cup and slowly pour it into the egg yolk mixture. Pour this egg mixture into the remaining cream in the saucepan. Whisk the mixture constantly until it is thick enough to coat a spoon or registers 185°F on a candy thermometer. Immediately remove the thermometer and pour the ice cream custard into a 2-quart bowl. Remove the vanilla bean.

• • •

Cover the bowl tightly with plastic wrap to prevent a skin from forming on top and cool to room temperature. Stir the buttermilk and 1½ teaspoons of nutmeg into the ice cream custard. Cover with plastic wrap and refrigerate for several hours, or until it is cold.

• • •

Process the ice cream custard in an ice cream maker, following the manufacturer's instructions. Freeze the ice cream in a tightly covered container for at least 30 minutes.

• • •

Using a 1-inch round ice cream scoop, place small scoops of ice cream in shot glasses, mini martini glasses, or small bowls. Sprinkle the remaining nutmeg over each and serve.

• • •

keeping Freeze the ice cream in a tightly covered container up to 2 weeks. If it is too firm, soften in the refrigerator for 45 minutes to 1 hour before serving.

streamlining The ice cream custard can be made up to 3 days in advance and kept tightly covered in a bowl in the refrigerator before freezing in the ice cream maker.

peanut butter ice cream

IF YOU'RE A PEANUT BUTTER LOVER, YOU'LL BE IN HEAVEN WHEN YOU TASTE THIS ICE CREAM. BROWN SUGAR AND PEANUT BUTTER GIVE THIS ICE CREAM DEEP, RICH, AND DELECTABLE FLAVOR.

MAKES 1 pint, 16 servings

1 cup heavy whipping cream

1 cup milk (whole or 2%)

2 teaspoons pure vanilla bean paste

½ cup (3½ ounces) firmly packed light brown sugar

4 extra-large egg yolks, at room temperature

⅓ cup chunky salted peanut butter

1 to 2 tablespoons toasted salted peanuts

Place the cream, milk, and vanilla paste in a 2-quart heavy-duty saucepan. Warm the mixture over medium heat until small bubbles form around the edges.

• • •

Whip together the brown sugar and egg yolks in the bowl of an electric stand mixer with the wire whip attachment or in a large mixing bowl using a hand-held mixer on medium speed until the mixture is very thick and pale yellow and it holds a slowly dissolving ribbon when the beater is lifted.

• • •

Ladle half of the hot milk mixture into a liquid measuring cup, then slowly pour it into the egg yolk mixture, whisking constantly to blend well. Pour this egg mixture into the remaining milk mixture in the saucepan. Whisk the mixture constantly until it is thick enough to coat a spoon or registers 185°F on a candy thermometer. Immediately remove the thermometer and strain the mixture into a 2-quart bowl. Add the peanut butter and whisk together until completely blended.

• • •

Cover the bowl tightly with plastic wrap to prevent a skin from forming on top and cool to room temperature. Refrigerate the ice cream custard for several hours, or until it is cold.

• • •

Process the ice cream custard in an ice cream maker, following the manufacturer's instructions. Freeze the ice cream in a tightly covered container for at least 30 minutes.

• • •

Using a 1-inch round ice cream scoop, place small scoops of ice cream in shot glasses, mini martini glasses, or small bowls. Top each serving with a few peanuts.

• • •

keeping Freeze the ice cream in a tightly covered container up to 2 weeks. If it is too firm, soften in the refrigerator for 45 minutes to 1 hour before serving.

streamlining The ice cream custard can be made up to 3 days in advance and kept tightly covered in a bowl in the refrigerator before freezing in the ice cream maker.

chocolate and coffee ice cream sandwiches

THIS IS A FUN AND EASY WAY TO EAT ICE CREAM AND COOKIES. TWO CHOCOLATE WAFER COOKIES SURROUND LUSCIOUS COFFEE ICE CREAM. BE SURE TO MAKE THESE SANDWICHES IN ADVANCE SO THEY HAVE TIME TO FREEZE BEFORE YOU SERVE THEM.

MAKES 30 ice cream sandwiches | USE a 1½-inch round plain-edge cutter

1 cup (4½ ounces) plus 1 tablespoon (¼ ounce) all-purpose flour

½ cup (3½ ounces) granulated sugar

3 tablespoons (¾ ounce) unsweetened Dutch-processed cocoa powder

¼ teaspoon baking powder

⅛ teaspoon kosher or fine-grained sea salt

4 ounces (8 tablespoons, 1 stick) unsalted butter, softened

2 ounces bittersweet chocolate (66 to 72% cacao content), finely chopped

1¼ cups (5½ ounces) finely chopped toasted walnuts, divided

1 quart coffee ice cream

CHOCOLATE WAFER COOKIES

Combine the flour, sugar, cocoa powder, baking powder, and salt in the bowl of a food processor fitted with a steel blade. Pulse briefly to blend.

• • •

Cut the butter into small pieces and add to the flour mixture. Pulse until it is cut into tiny pieces, about 1 minute. Add the chocolate and ¼ cup of chopped walnuts and pulse until the dough forms a ball, about 30 seconds.

• • •

Shape the dough into a disk, tightly wrap in plastic, and chill until firm, about 3 hours.

• • •

Adjust the oven racks to the upper and lower thirds and preheat the oven to 350°F. Line 2 baking sheets with parchment paper or nonstick liners.

• • •

On a smooth, flat surface, roll out the dough between sheets of lightly floured waxed or parchment paper to a thickness of ¼ inch. Remove the top piece of paper and use a 1½-inch round plain-edge cutter to cut out the cookies. Transfer them to the baking sheets, leaving 1 inch of space between them.

• • •

Bake the cookies for 5 minutes. Switch the baking sheets and bake another 5 to 6 minutes, until set. Remove the baking sheets from the oven and cool the cookies on the baking sheets on racks. When they are cool, gently peel the cookies off the parchment paper or nonstick liners.

• • •

ASSEMBLY

Line a baking sheet with waxed paper. Soften the ice cream slightly at room temperature. Use a small offset spatula to spread 1 tablespoon of ice cream on the bottom of 1 cookie. Top the ice cream with another cookie. Press the cookies together gently. Use the offset spatula or a spreading knife to smooth the edges. Place the ice cream sandwich on the lined baking sheet. Repeat with the remaining cookies and ice cream. If the ice cream becomes too soft to work with, freeze it for 10 to 15 minutes. If the ice cream in the sandwiches becomes too soft as they are assembled, freeze the sandwiches for 10 to 15 minutes before the next step,

• • •

Place the remaining 1 cup of chopped walnuts on a plate and roll the edges of the ice cream sandwiches in the nuts so they stick. Place the sandwiches back on the lined baking sheet and freeze until firm, about 2 hours.

• • •

keeping Freeze the ice cream sandwiches covered with waxed paper and tightly wrapped in several layers of plastic wrap and aluminum foil up to 2 weeks.

streamlining The cookie dough can be made up to 3 days in advance and kept tightly wrapped in a double layer of plastic wrap in the refrigerator. To freeze up to 3 months, wrap it snugly in several layers of plastic wrap and enclose it in a freezer bag. Use a large piece of masking tape and an indelible marker to label and date the contents. If frozen, defrost the dough in the refrigerator.

The baked cookies can be stored between layers of waxed paper in an airtight container at room temperature up to 4 days.

making a change Replace the toasted walnuts with toasted pecans or almonds.

Replace the coffee ice cream with your favorite ice cream or sorbet.

chapter eight

CANDIES

almond buttercrunch toffee

THIS DIVINE CANDY IS RICH, BUTTERY, AND CRUNCHY—EVERYTHING I LOVE ABOUT TOFFEE. IT'S TOPPED WITH FINELY CHOPPED CHOCOLATE THAT MELTS WHILE THE TOFFEE IS STILL HOT, THEN IT'S SPRINKLED WITH A LAYER OF FINELY CHOPPED TOASTED ALMONDS.

MAKES *about 5 dozen pieces* | USE *a 7 × 11–inch (2-quart) rectangular baking pan*

2 cups (6 ounces) sliced almonds

1 tablespoon canola or safflower oil

8 ounces (2 sticks) unsalted butter, cut into small pieces

¾ cup (5 ounces) granulated sugar

3 tablespoons water

¼ teaspoon kosher or fine-grained sea salt

1 teaspoon pure vanilla extract

¼ teaspoon baking soda

12 ounces bittersweet chocolate (62 to 72% cacao content), finely chopped

Position a rack in the center of the oven and preheat the oven to 350°F.

• • •

Place the almonds in a cake or pie pan and toast in the oven for 12 to 14 minutes, until light golden. Stir the almonds every 5 minutes as they are toasting to ensure they brown evenly. Remove the pan from the oven and cool completely on a rack, then chop the almonds finely.

• • •

Line a 7 × 11–inch (2-quart) rectangular baking pan with aluminum foil so that the foil fits snuggly in the pan and hangs a bit over the edges. Using a paper towel, oil the foil that lines the inside of the pan. Sprinkle ¾ cup of the chopped toasted almonds over the bottom of the pan.

• • •

Melt the butter in a 3-quart heavy-duty saucepan over medium heat. Add the sugar, water, and salt and cook, stirring constantly with a heat-resistant spatula, until the mixture registers 260°F on a candy thermometer. Immediately stir in ½ cup of the chopped almonds and continue cooking the mixture until it becomes golden brown and registers 290°F on the candy thermometer. Immediately stir in the vanilla and baking soda. Be careful as the mixture will bubble and foam.

• • •

Turn the toffee out into the prepared pan and spread it evenly in the pan and to the edges. Immediately sprinkle the top of the toffee evenly with the chocolate. Let it stand for 2 minutes, until the chocolate begins to melt. Use a small offset spatula to spread the chocolate evenly over the top of the toffee. Sprinkle the top of the chocolate evenly with the remaining ¾ cup of chopped toasted almonds. Let the toffee set up at room temperature until firm, about 30 minutes, then refrigerate for 15 minutes to set the chocolate.

• • •

Lift the toffee from the pan by holding the overhanging edges of foil. Peel the foil away from the toffee and break the toffee into small pieces. Serve at room temperature.

• • •

keeping Store the toffee between layers of waxed paper in an airtight container at room temperature up to 1 month.

gianduia truffle cups

GIANDUIA IS A DELECTABLE MIXTURE OF CHOCOLATE AND HAZELNUTS THAT WAS CREATED IN TURIN, ITALY, IN THE MID-NINETEENTH CENTURY. IF A CONFECTION, GELATO, CAKE, OR ANY OTHER DESSERT IS CALLED GIANDUIA, YOU CAN BE CERTAIN IT CONTAINS THIS CLASSIC COMBINATION OF CHOCOLATE AND HAZELNUTS. THESE DELECTABLE CANDIES ARE EASY TO MAKE AND WILL DELIGHT ALL WHO EAT THEM.

MAKES about 3½ dozen | USE forty-two 1-inch firm pleated foil candy cups

---

⅔ cup (3 ounces) toasted and skinned hazelnuts

2 tablespoons unflavored vegetable oil, such as canola or safflower

4 ounces bittersweet chocolate (70 to 72% cacao content), finely chopped

2 ounces dark milk chocolate (38 to 41% cacao content), finely chopped

42 toasted and skinned hazelnuts

Pulse ⅔ cup of the hazelnuts in the work bowl of a food processor fitted with the steel blade until they are finely chopped. Add the vegetable oil and pulse until the mixture becomes a paste, about 1 minute.

• • •

Place the bittersweet and dark milk chocolates in the top of a double boiler set over hot water. Stir often with a rubber spatula to help the chocolates melt evenly. Or place the chocolates in a microwave-safe bowl and melt on low power for 30-second bursts. Stir with a rubber spatula after each burst. Remove the top pan of the double boiler, if using, and wipe the bottom and sides very dry.

• • •

Add the hazelnut paste to the melted chocolates and stir to blend thoroughly. Tightly cover the bowl with plastic wrap and chill for 30 to 40 minutes, until slightly thick but still soft enough to pipe.

• • •

Place the foil candy cups on a baking sheet or in a baking pan. Fit a 12- or 14-inch pastry bag with a ½-inch round plain tip and fill the bag partway with the gianduia truffle mixture. Pipe the mixture into the foil cups until they are three-quarters full. Top each truffle cup with a hazelnut, pointed end up.

• • •

Cover the pan with plastic wrap and let the truffle cups set up at room temperature. Serve them at room temperature.

• • •

keeping Store the truffle cups between layers of waxed paper in an airtight container in the refrigerator up to 1 month. To freeze up to 2 months, wrap the container tightly in several layers of plastic wrap and aluminum foil. Use a large piece of masking tape and an indelible marker to label and date the contents. If frozen, defrost the truffle cups overnight in the refrigerator and bring to room temperature before serving.

salted caramel–bittersweet chocolate truffles

THESE TRUFFLES LITERALLY MELT IN THE MOUTH. THEY ARE RICH WITH A CREAMY, VELVETY TEXTURE. I USE FLEUR DE SEL, A DELICATE FRENCH SEA SALT, TO GIVE THESE TRUFFLES A SLIGHTLY SALTY FLAVOR THAT ENHANCES BOTH THE CARAMEL AND THE CHOCOLATE. I'M TEMPTED TO EAT THEM ALL MYSELF, BUT WILL GLADLY SHARE THEM WITH FAMILY AND FRIENDS.

MAKES 5 dozen 1-inch truffles

18 ounces bittersweet chocolate (62 to 72% cacao content), finely chopped, divided

3 ounces (6 tablespoons) unsalted butter

¾ cup (5 ounces) granulated sugar

¾ cup heavy whipping cream

1 teaspoon pure vanilla extract

2½ teaspoons fleur de sel or other fine-grained sea salt, divided

2 tablespoons unsweetened cocoa powder (natural or Dutch-processed)

Place 8 ounces of the chopped chocolate in a 2-quart bowl and set aside.

• • •

Cut the butter into small pieces and place it in a 2-quart saucepan with the sugar. Cook over medium heat, stirring with a heat-resistant spatula, until the sugar and butter melt. Raise the heat to medium-high and cook until the mixture turns amber colored, about 5 minutes.

• • •

At the same time, bring the cream to a boil in a 1-quart saucepan over medium heat. Stir the cream into the butter mixture until completely smooth. Be careful because the cream will bubble and may splatter when added.

• • •

Remove the saucepan from the heat and stir in the vanilla and 1½ teaspoons of salt until thoroughly blended. Immediately pour the caramel over the chocolate in the bowl. Let it stand for 15 to 30 seconds, then stir together until smooth. Cover the bowl with plastic wrap and cool to room temperature. Chill until thick, about 1 hour.

• • •

TRUFFLES

Line 2 baking sheets with waxed or parchment paper. Use a 1-inch round ice cream scoop to scoop out the truffles and place them on the baking sheet. Chill uncovered for 20 minutes.

• • •

Dust your hands with cocoa powder and roll the truffles into balls.

• • •

Melt 7 ounces of the chocolate in the top of a double boiler over low heat, stirring frequently. Or melt the chocolate in a microwave-safe bowl on low power for 30-second bursts. Stir after each burst to make sure the chocolate is melting evenly.

• • •

Remove the top pan of the double boiler, if using, and wipe it dry. Add the remaining 3 ounces of chocolate in 3 stages, stirring until it's completely melted. This tempers the chocolate so it won't have any streaks.

• • •

Keep the chocolate warm over a pan of water that is 2 degrees warmer than the chocolate. Line a baking sheet with waxed or parchment paper.

• • •

Place a truffle into the melted chocolate and coat completely. Use a truffle dipper or a plastic fork with the two middle tines broken out to lift the truffle from the chocolate. Let the excess chocolate drip off, then place the truffle on the clean lined baking sheet.

• • •

After dipping 5 truffles at a time, sprinkle a few grains of the remaining salt on top of each. Let the truffles set at room temperature or place them in the refrigerator for 15 minutes.

• • •

Serve the truffles at room temperature.

• • •

keeping Store the truffles between layers of waxed paper in an airtight container in the refrigerator up to 1 month. To freeze up to 2 months, wrap the container tightly in several layers of plastic wrap and aluminum foil. Use a large piece of masking tape and an indelible marker to label and date the contents. If frozen, defrost the truffles overnight in the refrigerator and bring to room temperature before serving.

bittersweet chocolate—mint truffle squares

FRESH MINT ADDS A BLAST OF FLAVOR TO BITTERSWEET CHOCOLATE IN THESE BITE-SIZE TRUFFLE SQUARES. THESE ELEGANT CONFECTIONS ARE PERFECT TO ACCOMPANY AFTER-DINNER COFFEE.

MAKES 8¼ dozen ¾-inch squares | USE an 8-inch square baking pan

12 ounces bittersweet chocolate (62 to 72% cacao content), finely chopped

1¼ cups heavy whipping cream

2 cups firmly packed fresh mint leaves, rinsed and patted dry

⅓ cup (1¼ ounces) unsweetened cocoa powder (natural or Dutch-processed)

Line an 8-inch square baking pan with aluminum foil so that it fits snugly in the pan and hangs slightly over the edges.

• • •

Place the chopped chocolate in a 2-quart bowl.

• • •

Place the cream in a 1-quart saucepan and bring to a boil over medium heat. Add the mint leaves, turn off the heat, cover the saucepan, and steep for 15 minutes. Use a slotted spoon or skimmer to remove the mint leaves from the cream.

• • •

Return the cream to a boil over medium heat. Pour the cream over the chocolate. Let the chocolate mixture stand for 30 seconds, then stir together until very smooth.

• • •

Pour the chocolate-mint mixture into the lined pan, making sure it fills in the corners. Shake the pan slightly to eliminate any air bubbles. Cover the pan tightly with plastic wrap and refrigerate until firm but not stiff, about 1 hour.

• • •

Lift the truffle mixture from the pan by holding the overhanging edges of foil. Using a ruler and knife, cut the truffle mixture into ¾-inch squares. If the truffles are soft, cover and chill them again.

• • •

Line a baking sheet with waxed or parchment paper. Sift the cocoa powder into a ½-quart bowl. Separate the truffle squares and coat them in the cocoa completely, maintaining their square shape. Shake off any excess cocoa powder and place the squares on the lined baking sheet.

• • •

Serve the truffle squares at room temperature.

• • •

keeping Store the truffle squares between layers of waxed paper in an airtight container in the refrigerator up to 1 month. To freeze up to 2 months, wrap the container tightly in several layers of plastic wrap and aluminum foil. Use a large piece of masking tape and an indelible marker to label and date the contents. If frozen, defrost overnight in the refrigerator and bring to room temperature before serving.

green tea truffles

WE'VE ALL HEARD THE GOOD NEWS ABOUT THE HEALTH BENEFITS OF TEA AND DARK CHOCOLATE. WHILE I WON'T SAY THESE TRUFFLES ARE HEALTH FOOD, THEY ARE DEFINITELY GOOD FOR YOU BECAUSE THEIR WONDERFUL FLAVOR BRINGS YOU GREAT PLEASURE. ENJOY!

MAKES 5 dozen 1-inch truffles | USE 60 glassine candy cups

12 ounces bittersweet chocolate (62 to 72% cacao content), finely chopped

1 cup heavy whipping cream

2 teaspoons green tea leaves

⅓ cup (1¼ ounces) unsweetened cocoa powder (natural or Dutch-processed)

Place the chopped chocolate in a 2-quart bowl and set aside.

• • •

Place the cream in a 1-quart saucepan and bring to a boil over medium heat. Add the tea, cover the saucepan, turn off the heat, and steep for 15 minutes.

• • •

Return the cream to a boil over medium heat. Strain the cream over the chocolate. Let the chocolate mixture stand for 30 seconds, then stir together until very smooth.

• • •

Cover the mixture tightly with plastic wrap and refrigerate until firm but not stiff, about 1 hour.

• • •

Line a baking sheet with waxed or parchment paper. Use a 1-inch round ice cream scoop to scoop out the truffles and place them on the baking sheet.

• • •

Sift the cocoa powder into a ½-quart bowl. Roll the truffles in the cocoa powder, coating completely. Shake off any excess cocoa powder and place the truffles on the baking sheet.

• • •

Serve the truffles at room temperature in individual glassine candy cups.

• • •

keeping Store the truffles between layers of waxed paper in an airtight container in the refrigerator up to 1 month. To freeze up to 2 months, wrap the container tightly in several layers of plastic wrap and aluminum foil. Use a large piece of masking tape and an indelible marker to label and date the contents. If frozen, defrost the truffles overnight in the refrigerator and bring to room temperature before serving.

making a change Replace the bittersweet chocolate with white chocolate and use ⅔ cup of heavy whipping cream.

white chocolate–coconut mounds

THE CRUNCHY TEXTURE AND FLAVOR OF THE TOASTED COCONUT COMBINES BEAUTIFULLY WITH
WHITE CHOCOLATE IN THESE CANDIES.

MAKES *about 2¾ dozen* | USE *thirty-two 1-inch pleated glassine candy cups*

1 cup (2 ounces) sweetened shredded coconut

6 ounces white chocolate, finely chopped

Position a rack in the center of the oven and preheat the oven to 325°F. Line a baking sheet with waxed or parchment paper.

• • •

Place the coconut in a cake or pie pan. Toast in the oven for 5 to 7 minutes, stirring every 2 minutes, until light golden. Remove the pan from the oven and cool the pan completely on a rack.

• • •

Place 5 ounces of the white chocolate in the top pan of a double boiler set over hot water. Stir often with a rubber spatula to help melt the chocolate evenly. Or place the chocolate in a microwave-safe bowl and melt on low power for 30-second bursts. Stir with a rubber spatula after each burst. Remove the top pan of the double boiler, if using, and wipe the bottom and sides very dry.

• • •

Stir in the remaining 1 ounce of white chocolate in 2 to 3 stages, making sure each batch is melted before adding the next. Stir the toasted coconut into the white chocolate, blending completely.

• • •

Using a 1-inch round ice cream scoop, scoop out mounds and place them onto the baking sheet, rounded side up. Chill the mounds in the refrigerator for 15 minutes to set.

• • •

Serve the mounds in individual glassine candy cups.

• • •

keeping Store the mounds between layers of waxed paper in an airtight container in the refrigerator up to 1 month. To freeze up to 2 months, wrap the container tightly in several layers of plastic wrap and aluminum foil. Use a large piece of masking tape and an indelible marker to label and date the contents. If frozen, defrost the mounds overnight in the refrigerator and bring to room temperature before serving.

making a change Replace the white chocolate with bittersweet chocolate (62 to 72% cacao content) or dark milk chocolate (38 to 42% cacao content).

bittersweet chocolate-peppermint candy bark

CHOPPED PEPPERMINT CANDIES ARE MIXED WITH DEEP, DARK BITTERSWEET CHOCOLATE TO CREATE A VERY REFRESHING AND SATISFYING CANDY. THIS IS GREAT TO SERVE DURING THE HOLIDAY SEASON OR ANYTIME.

MAKES *about 3 dozen 1-inch pieces*

---

1 cup (7 ounces) red-and-white-striped round peppermint candies

8 ounces bittersweet chocolate (62 to 72% cacao content), finely chopped

---

Unwrap the candies and place them in the work bowl of a food processor fitted with a steel blade. Pulse until the candies are finely chopped, about 2 minutes.

• • •

Place 6 ounces of the chocolate in the top pan of a double boiler set over hot water. Stir often with a rubber spatula to help melt the chocolate evenly. Or place the chocolate in a microwave-safe bowl and melt on low power for 30-second bursts. Stir with a rubber spatula after each burst. Remove the top pan of the double boiler, if using, and wipe the bottom and sides very dry.

• • •

Stir in the remaining 2 ounces of chocolate in 2 to 3 stages, making sure each batch is melted before adding the next. Stir in the chopped peppermint candies and coat them thoroughly with chocolate.

• • •

Line a baking sheet with waxed or parchment paper. Pour the chocolate mixture onto the baking sheet and use an offset spatula to spread it to a thickness of about ¼ inch.

• • •

Chill the bark in the refrigerator until set, about 30 minutes. Remove the bark from the refrigerator and gently peel off the paper. Break the bark into 1-inch pieces.

• • •

Serve the bark at room temperature.

• • •

keeping Store the bark between layers of waxed paper in an airtight container in the refrigerator up to 1 month. To freeze up to 2 months, wrap the container tightly in several layers of plastic wrap and aluminum foil. Use a large piece of masking tape and an indelible marker to label and date the contents. If frozen, defrost the bark overnight in the refrigerator and bring to room temperature before serving.

making a change Replace the bittersweet chocolate with white chocolate or dark milk chocolate (38 to 42% cacao content).

Replace the round peppermint candies with peppermint candy canes.

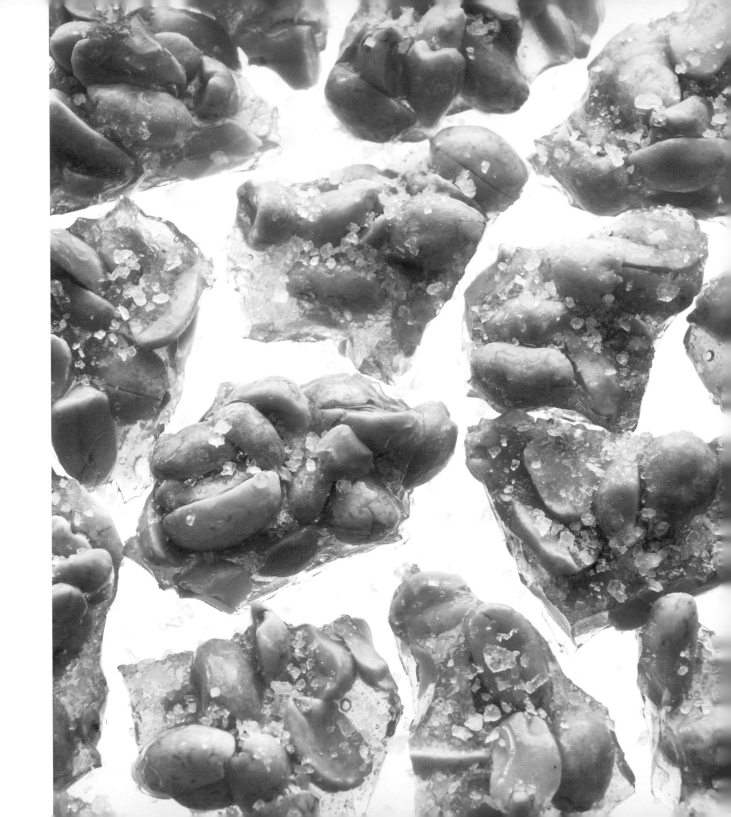

sea salted peanut brittle

FLEUR DE SEL—A PURE AND SMOOTH-TASTING SEA SALT—IS SPRINKLED OVER HOT PEANUT BRITTLE BEFORE IT SETS UP. THE SALT ADDS EXTRA TEXTURE AND FLAVOR TO AN ALREADY DELICIOUS CANDY. I INCLUDE THIS PEANUT BRITTLE EVERY YEAR IN THE CANDY GIFTS I MAKE FOR THE HOLIDAY SEASON, AND IT'S ALWAYS APPRECIATED.

MAKES *about 2 dozen pieces, 10 ounces*

1 tablespoon canola or safflower oil

1 cup (6½ ounces) granulated sugar

¼ cup water

¼ teaspoon cream of tartar

1 cup (5 ounces) toasted salted peanuts

1 to 1½ teaspoons fleur de sel or other fine-grained sea salt

Using a paper towel, oil the back of a baking sheet.

• • •

Combine the sugar, water, and cream of tartar in a 2-quart heavy-duty saucepan and bring to a boil over high heat, without stirring. Place a wet pastry brush at the point where the sugar syrup meets the sides of the pan and sweep it around completely. This helps prevent the sugar from crystallizing. As the mixture cooks, do this one more time. Cook the mixture, without stirring, until it turns light amber colored, about 8 minutes.

• • •

Using a heat-resistant spatula, immediately stir in the peanuts, coating them completely with the caramel. Pour the brittle onto the baking sheet and quickly spread it out thinly. Sprinkle the salt evenly over the top of the hot brittle.

• • •

Let the brittle stand at room temperature until firm, about 30 minutes. Gently lift the peanut brittle off the baking sheet and break it into 1-inch pieces.

• • •

Serve the peanut brittle at room temperature.

• • •

keeping Store the peanut brittle between layers of waxed paper in an airtight container at room temperature up to 1 month.

making a change Replace the peanuts with other nuts, or use a combination of nuts.

malted milk chocolate balls

I LOVE HOW THE TOASTY FLAVOR OF MALT BLENDS SO WELL WITH MILK CHOCOLATE IN THESE SCRUMPTIOUS BALLS. I SERVE THEM IN GLASSINE CANDY CUPS, WHICH DON'T ABSORB ANY LIQUID AND MAKE THE BALLS EASY TO PICK UP AND EAT.

MAKES 4 dozen 1-inch balls | USE 48 individual glassine candy cups

8 ounces dark milk chocolate (38 to 42% cacao content), finely chopped	½ cup heavy whipping cream	⅓ cup (1¼ ounces) unsweetened cocoa powder (natural or Dutch-processed)
	¼ cup (1 ounce) malted milk powder	

Place the chopped chocolate in a 2-quart bowl and set aside.

• • •

Place the cream in a 1-quart saucepan and bring to a boil over medium heat. Add the malted milk powder, cover the saucepan, turn off the heat, and steep for 20 minutes.

• • •

Return the cream to a boil over medium heat. Strain the cream over the chocolate. Let the mixture stand for 30 seconds, then stir together until very smooth. Cover tightly with plastic wrap and refrigerate until firm but not stiff.

• • •

Line a baking sheet with waxed or parchment paper. Use a 1-inch round ice cream scoop to scoop out the balls and place them on the baking sheet.

• • •

Sift the cocoa powder into a ½-quart bowl. Lightly dust your hands with cocoa powder and roll the balls between your palms until smooth and round, then toss the balls in the cocoa, coating completely. Place the balls on the lined baking sheet.

• • •

Serve the balls at room temperature in individual glassine candy cups.

• • •

keeping Store the balls between layers of waxed paper in an airtight container in the refrigerator up to 1 month. To freeze up to 2 months, wrap the container tightly in several layers of plastic wrap and aluminum foil. Use a large piece of masking tape and an indelible marker to label and date the contents. If frozen, defrost the balls overnight in the refrigerator and bring to room temperature before serving.

appendices
sources for ingredients and equipment

A COOK'S WARES
211 37th Street
Beaver Falls, PA 15010
Tel: 800-915-9788; 724-846-9490
Fax: 800-916-2886; 724-846-9562
e-mail: sales@cookswares.com
Web site: www.cookswares.com

This source carries a variety of equipment and utensils as well as some ingredients.

FANCY FLOURS
424 East Main Street, Suite 102 B
Bozeman, MT 59715
Tel: 406-587-0118
Fax: 406-522-0668
e-mail: info@fancyflours.com
Web site: www.fancyflours.com

This store supplies a huge variety of equipment, tools, and some ingredients.

J.B. PRINCE COMPANY
36 East 31st Street
New York, NY 10016-6821
Tel: 800-473-0577; 212-683-3553
Fax: 212-683-4488
e-mail: customerservice@jbprince.com
Web site: www.jbprince.com

J.B. Prince carries a large variety of professional-quality equipment and tools.

**KING ARTHUR FLOUR –
THE BAKER'S CATALOG**
58 Billings Farm Road
White River Junction, VT 05001
Tel: 800-827-6836; 802-299-2240
Fax: 800-343-3002
e-mail: customercare@kingarthurflour.com
Web site: www.kingarthurflour.com

The Baker's Catalog carries a wide variety of equipment and ingredients.

NEW YORK CAKE SUPPLIES
56 West 22nd Street
New York, NY 10010
Tel: 800-942-2539; 212-675-2253
Fax: 212-675-7099
Web site: www.nycake.com

New York Cake Supplies carries a large variety of equipment and ingredients. Although this source has a Web site, all orders must be placed by phone or fax.

PASTRY CHEF CENTRAL, INC.
1355 West Palmetto Park Road, Suite 302
Boca Raton, FL 33486-3303
Tel: 561-999-9483; 888-750-2433 (order status only)
Fax: 561-999-1282
e-mail: customer_service@pastrychef.com
Web site: www.pastrychef.com

This online-only source supplies a large variety of equipment, tools, and ingredients.

SUR LA TABLE
Corporate Headquarters
Seattle Design Center
5701 Sixth Avenue South, Suite 486
Seattle, WA 98108
Tel: 800-243-0852; 866-328-5412
Fax: 206-613-6136; 317-858-5521 (orders only)
e-mail: customerservice@surlatable.com
Web site: www.surlatable.com

Sur La Table carries all kinds of equipment and several types of chocolate and cocoa powder. They have several shops throughout the United States, a catalog, and a Web site.

SURFAS
8777 West Washington Boulevard
Culver City, CA 90232
Tel: 866-799-4770; 310-559-4770
Fax: 310-558-1428
e-mail: customerservice@surfasonline.com
Web site: www.surfasonline.com

Surfas carries a large variety of equipment and ingredients.

SWEET CELEBRATIONS
P.O. Box 39426
Edina, MN 55439-0426
Tel: 800-328-6722; 952-943-1508 (1661)
e-mail: info@sweetc.com
Web site: www.sweetc.com

This source carries a wide variety of equipment and ingredients.

THE SPICE HOUSE
1512 North Wells Street
Chicago, IL 60610
Tel: 312-274-0378   Fax: 312-274-0143
e-mail: spices@thespicehouse.com
Web site: www.thespicehouse.com

This is an excellent source for fresh spices and a variety of spice mills and graters.

WILLIAMS-SONOMA
3250 Van Ness Avenue
San Francisco, CA 94109
Tel: 877-812-6235; 415-421-7900
Tel: 405-717-6131 (outside of the U.S.)
Fax: 702-363-2541
e-mail: Fill out the form on the Web site.
Web site: www.williamssonoma.com

Williams-Sonoma carries a wide variety of equipment and some ingredients. It has stores throughout the United States, as well as a catalog and Web site.

measurement equivalents

U.S. MEASURING SYSTEM	METRIC SYSTEM
capacity	*approximate capacity*
¼ teaspoon	1.25 milliliters
1 teaspoon	5 milliliters
1 tablespoon	15 milliliters
¼ cup	60 milliliters
1 cup (8 fluid ounces)	240 milliliters
2 cups (1 pint; 16 fluid ounces)	470 milliliters
4 cups (1 quart; 32 fluid ounces)	0.95 liter
4 quarts (1 gallon; 64 fluid ounces)	3.8 liters
weight	*approximate weight*
1 dry ounce	15 grams
2 ounces	30 grams
4 ounces (¼ pound)	110 grams
8 ounces (½ pound)	230 grams
16 ounces (1 pound)	454 grams

LIQUID MEASUREMENT

measurement	fluid ounces	ounces by weight	grams
2 tablespoons	1 fluid ounce	½ ounce	14 grams
¼ cup	2 fluid ounces	1¾ ounces	50 grams
⅓ cup	2⅔ fluid ounces	2 ounces	70 grams
½ cup	4 fluid ounces	4 ounces	113 grams
⅔ cup	5⅓ fluid ounces	5 ounces	142 grams
¾ cup	6 fluid ounces	5¼ ounces	177 grams
1 cup	8 fluid ounces	8 ounces	227 grams

measurement	equivalent
¼ cup (2 fluid ounces)	5 tablespoons
⅓ cup (2⅔ fluid ounces)	7 tablespoons
½ cup (4 fluid ounces)	11 tablespoons
⅔ cup (5⅓ fluid ounces)	14 tablespoons
¾ cup (6 fluid ounces)	16 tablespoons
1 cup (8 fluid ounces)	20 tablespoons

DRY MEASUREMENT

measurement	equivalent
3 teaspoons	1 tablespoon
2 tablespoons	⅛ cup
4 tablespoons	¼ cup
5⅓ tablespoons	⅓ cup
8 tablespoons	½ cup
10⅔ tablespoons	⅔ cup
12 tablespoons	¾ cup
16 tablespoons	1 cup

metric conversions

KNOWN FACTOR	MULTIPLY BY	TO FIND
weight		
Ounces	28.35	Grams
Pounds	0.454	Kilograms
Grams	0.035	Ounces
Kilograms	2.2	Pounds
measurement		
Inches	2.5	Centimeters
Millimeters	0.04	Inches
Centimeters	0.4	Inches

KNOWN FACTOR	MULTIPLY BY	TO FIND
Volume		
Teaspoons	4.93	Milliliters
Tablespoons	14.79	Milliliters
Fluid ounces	29.57	Milliliters
Cups	0.237	Liters
Pints	0.47	Liters
Quarts	0.95	Liters
Gallons	3.785	Liters
Milliliters	0.034	Fluid ounces
Liters	2.1	Pints
Liters	1.06	Quarts
Liters	0.26	Gallons

KNOWN FACTOR	DIVIDE BY	TO FIND
Volume		
Milliliters	4.93	Teaspoons
Milliliters	14.79	Tablespoons
Milliliters	236.59	Cups
Milliliters	473.18	Pints
Milliliters	946.36	Quarts
Liters	0.236	Cups
Liters	0.473	Pints
Liters	0.946	Quarts
Liters	3.785	Gallons

index

Page numbers in italics indicate illustrations.

A

All-purpose flour, 3
Almond(s)
  buttercrunch toffee, 170, 171
  in cantuccini di prato, 152
  in cobbler topping, 82
  -cornmeal cakes, 41–42, 42
  in crisp topping, 89
  filling, 76
  grinding, 142
  mocha and macaroon sandwich cookies,
    142–143
  muffins, apricot, and toasted coconut, 58
  pastry dough, 77
  tartlets, lemon and berry, 77–78
  tartlets, Venetian, 74, 75–76
  toasting, 89, 170
  tuile cookie cups, 155–156
Almond paste, 41
Apple-walnut crisps, 92–93
Apricot
  almond, and toasted coconut muffins, 58
  glaze, 98
  -orange loaf cakes, 34–35
  preserves, in peek-a-boo hazelnut
    sandwich cookies, 138–139

B

Baker's Catalog, The, 185
Baking pans, types of, 5
Baking sheets, 5
Bark, bittersweet chocolate–peppermint
    candy, 180, 181

Berry(ies). See also specific berries
  almond, and lemon tartlets, 77–78
  cobblers, mixed, 82–83
  filling, 82, 89
  in pavlovas with passion fruit sauce, 79,
    80, 81
Biscotti
  cantuccini di prato, 152
  pecan-ginger, 150, 151
Biscuit dough topping, 84–85
Bittersweet chocolate, 2
  cupcakes, five-spice, 26–27
  ganache filling, 70, 130
  ganache filling, mocha, 143
  ganache frosting, 20, 22, 23, 24, 25, 27
  ganache tartlets, cacao nib–walnut,
    69–70, 71
  and hazelnut tartlets, 67–68
  ice cream, mocha, 164
  madeleines, devilish dark, 134–135
  mousse, mocha, 104–105, 105
  –peppermint candy bark, 180, 181
  pots de crème, -espresso, 108
  pudding, toasted coconut, 125
  soufflés, mocha, with cacao nib whipped
    cream, 112, 113–114
  in toffee, almond buttercrunch, 170, 171
  in truffle cups, gianduia, 172, 173
  truffles, salted caramel–, 174–175, 175
  truffles, green tea, 178
  truffle squares, –mint, 176, 177
  wafer cookies, 167
Blackberries, in cobblers, mixed berry,
    82–83

Blueberry(ies)
  in cobblers, mixed berry, 82–83
  filling, 94–95
  -raspberry crisps, 89, 90, 91
  shortcakes, lemon-cornmeal, 53–54
  in tartlets, berry, almond, and lemon,
    77–78
  turnovers, 94–95
Brittle, sea salted peanut, 182, 183
Brownie bites, wicked, 28, 29–30
Brown sugar. See also Cobblers; Crisps;
    Galettes
  in biscotti, cantuccini di prato, 152
  in biscotti, pecanginger, 150, 151
  in brownie bites, wicked, 28, 29–30
  bundt cakes, and cornmeal, with honey
    whipped cream, 12–13, 13
  in bundt cakes, mixed spice and walnut,
    14, 15–16
  in bundt cakes, spiced chocolate-pecan,
    17
  in cheesecakes, petite, with raspberry
    sauce, 36–37
  in cookies, man-in-the-moon, 154
  in cookies, oatmeal, toasty, 153
  in cookies, walnut fingerprint, 129
  in crème brûlée, butterscotch, 120, 121
  in gingerbread bites, 31, 32, 33
  light and dark, 4
  in mousse, creamy caramel, 102, 103
  in muffins, apricot, almond, and toasted
    coconut, 58
  in pastry dough, cacao nib, 69

in peanut butter cupcakes with
    bittersweet chocolate ganache
    frosting, 23, 24, 25
in peanut butter ice cream, 166
in pots de crème, cardamom, 106–107,
    107
in pots de crème, maple, 109
in rice pudding, 126
in scones, raisin and walnut, 49–50
in shortcakes, raspberry, ginger, and
    honey, 55, 56, 57
in strudel, caramelized pear and dried
    cherry, 61–62
in tea cakes, maple walnut, 39
in tea cakes, walnut and lemon, 38
Bundt cakes
    brown sugar and cornmeal, with honey
        whipped cream, 12–13, 13
    chocolate-pecan, spiced, 17
    spice, mixed, and walnut, 14, 15–16
Bundt cupcake pans, 5. See also Bundt cakes
    dried cherry, toasted pecan, and sour
        cream pound cakes in, 18–19
Butter
    softening, 2, 8
    unsalted, 2
Butter cookie crust, 36
Butter cookies, cardamom, 148–149, 149
Buttermilk
    in bundt cakes, mixed spice and walnut,
        14, 15–16
    in bundt cakes, spiced chocolate-pecan,
        17
    in cobbler dough, 82
    doughnut holes, spiced, 60
    ice cream, and nutmeg, 165
    in loaf cakes, apricot-orange, 34–35
    in muffins, coconut–macadamia nut, 59
    in scones, raisin and walnut, 49–50
Butterscotch crème brûlée, 120, 121

C

Cacao content of chocolate, 2
Cacao nib(s)
    about, 2, 69
    madeleines, hazelnut and, 132–133, 133
    pastry dough, 69
    –walnut ganache tartlets, 69–70, 71
    whipped cream, 112, 113
Cake flour, 3
Cakes. See also Bundt cakes; Cupcakes; Tea
        cakes
    almond-cornmeal, 41–42, 42
    brownie bites, wicked, 28, 29–30
    cheesecakes, petite, with raspberry sauce,
        36–37
    gingerbread bites, 31, 32, 33
    loaf, apricot-orange, 34–35
    pound, dried cherry, toasted pecan, and
        sour cream, 18–19
    pound, triple lemon, 43–44
Candied ginger. See Ginger, candied
Candies. See also Truffle(s)
    bark, bittersweet chocolate–peppermint
        candy, 180, 181
    malted milk chocolate balls, 184
    peanut brittle, sea salted, 182, 183
    toffee, almond buttercrunch, 170, 171
    white chocolate–coconut mounds, 179
Candy cups, foil, gianduia truffle cups in,
        172, 173
Candy cups, glassine
    green tea truffles in, 184
    malted milk chocolate balls in, 184
    white chocolate–coconut mounds in, 179
Candy thermometer, 5–6
Cantaloupe sorbet, 160
Cantuccini di prato, 152
Caramel
    crème caramel, toasted pecan, 122,
        123–124
    mousse, creamy, 102, 103

salted, –bittersweet chocolate truffles,
        174–175, 175
Caramelized
    pear and dried cherry strudel, 61–62
    sugar topping, 118, 119, 120
    walnut tartlets, 72–73
Cardamom
    butter cookies, 148–149, 149
    pots de crème, 106–107, 107
Cheesecakes, petite, with raspberry sauce,
        36–37
Cherry, dried
    and pear strudel, caramelized, 61–62
    scones, –cornmeal, 46, 47–48
    sour cream pound cakes, and toasted
        pecan, 18–19
Chocolate
    bark, bittersweet chocolate–peppermint
        candy, 180, 181
    brownie bites, wicked, 28, 29–30
    bundt cakes, pecan, spiced, 17
    chopping, 8
    and coffee ice cream sandwiches,
        167–168
    cupcakes, bittersweet chocolate five-
        spice, 26–27
    drizzling, 8
    ganache filling, 70, 130
    ganache filling, mocha, 143
    ganache frosting, bittersweet chocolate,
        20, 22, 23, 24, 25, 27
    ganache tartlets, cocoa nib–walnut,
        69–70, 71
    -hazelnut bites, fudgy, 131
    ice cream, mocha, 164
    madeleines, devilish dark, 134–135
    malted milk balls, 184
    mousse, mocha, 104–105, 105
    piping dot, 73
    pots de crème, -espresso, 108

Chocolate (continued)
  pudding, toasted coconut–, 125
  soufflés, mocha, with cacao nib whipped
    cream, 112, 113–114
  storing, 8
  tartlets, bittersweet chocolate and
    hazelnut, 67–68
  in toffee, almond buttercrunch, 170, 171
  truffle cups, gianduia, 172, 173
  truffles, green tea, 178
  truffle squares, bittersweet chocolate–
    mint, 176, 177
  truffles, salted caramel–bittersweet
    chocolate, 174–175, 175
  types of, 2
  wafer cookies, 167
  white chocolate–coconut mounds, 179
Cinnamon
  –cocoa powder garnish, 22
  –sour cream cupcakes, 20, 21–22
Cobbler dough topping, 82
  biscuit, 84–85
  ginger, 86, 88
Cobblers
  berry, mixed, 82–83
  peachy, 84–85
  pear and triple ginger, 86, 87, 88
Cocoa butter, 2
Cocoa powder
  in brownie bites, wicked, 29
  in bundt cakes, spiced chocolate pecan,
    17
  in chocolate hazelnut bites, fudgy, 131
  cinnamon garnish, 22
  in cookies, chocolate wafer, 167
  in cupcakes, bittersweet chocolate five-
    spice, 26–27
  in malted milk chocolate balls, 184
  in pudding, toasted coconut–chocolate,
    125
  in truffles, green tea, 178

in truffle squares, bittersweet chocolate–
    mint, 177
in truffles, salted caramel–bittersweet
    chocolate, 174–175
types of, 2, 131
Coconut
  chocolate pudding, toasted coconut–,
    125
  crème brûlée, 119
  ice cream, toasted coconut, 161
  -lemon-lime squares, 146–147
  mounds, white chocolate–, 179
  muffins, apricot, almond, and toasted
    coconut, 58
  muffins, –macadamia nut, 59
  pastry dough, 146
  scones, macadamia nut and toasted
    coconut, 51–52, 52
  toasting, 9, 51, 58, 135, 161, 179
Coconut milk, in crème brûlée, coconut,
    119
Coffee. See Espresso
Coffee ice cream and chocolate sandwiches,
    167–168
Confectioners' sugar, 4
Cookie crust, butter, 36
Cookie cups, tuile, 155–156
  creamy caramel mousse in, 102, 103
Cookie cutters, 6
Cookie dough, storing, 149, 153, 168
Cookies
  biscotti, pecan-ginger, 150, 151
  cantuccini di prato, 152
  cardamom butter, 148–149, 149
  chocolate-hazelnut bites, fudgy, 131
  chocolate wafer, 167
  dipping in chocolate, 8
  filo triangles, walnut, 140–141, 141
  ginger chips, crackly, 136–137, 137
  madeleines, devilish dark chocolate,
    134–135

madeleines, hazelnut and cacao nib,
    132–133, 133
man-in-the-moon, 154
oatmeal, toasty, 153
sandwich
  chocolate and coffee ice cream,
    167–168
  hazelnut, peek-a-boo, 138–139
  macaroon, almond and mocha,
    142–143
  madeleine, 133, 135
  madeleine, ganache, 133, 135
  shortbread bites, toasted pecan, 144, 145
  squares, lemon-lime-coconut, 146–147
  storing, 130, 131, 137, 139, 143, 148, 153,
    154, 156
  walnut fingerprint, 128, 129–130
Cook's Wares, A, 185
Coriander, in cantaloupe sorbet, 160
Cornmeal
  -almond cakes, 41–42, 42
  and brown sugar bundt cakes with
    honey whipped cream, 12–13, 13
  scones, –dried cherry, 46, 47–48
  shortcakes, lemon-, 53–54
Crackly ginger chips, 136–137, 137
Cream. See also Custard; Whipped cream
  in biscuit dough topping, 84–85
  cacao nib, 113
  in ganache frosting, bittersweet
    chocolate, 23, 25
  lemon, with lemon-cornmeal
    shortcakes, 53–54
  lemon, and raspberry martinis, 110, 111
  in malted milk chocolate balls, 184
  mousse, creamy caramel, 102, 103
  mousse, mocha, 104–105, 105
  in muffins, apricot, almond, and toasted
    coconut, 58
  in pudding, rice,126
  in pudding, toasted coconut–chocolate,
    125

in scones, cornmeal–dried cherry, 46,
47–48
in scones, macadamia nut and toasted
coconut, 51–52, 52
in truffles, green tea, 178
in truffle squares, bittersweet chocolate–
mint, 176, 177
in truffles, salted caramel bittersweet
chocolate, 174–175, 175
in walnut filling, caramelized, 72–73
whipping, 9, 33
Cream cheese
in cheesecakes, petite, 36–37
pastry dough, 94
Creamy caramel mousse, 102, 103
Crème brûlée
butterscotch, 120, 121
coconut, 119
lemon, 118
Crème caramel, toasted pecan, 122, 123–124
Crisps
apple-walnut, 92–93
raspberry-blueberry, 89, 90, 91
Cupcakes
bittersweet chocolate five-spice, 26–27
cinnamon–sour cream, 20, 21–22
peanut butter, with bittersweet chocolate
ganache frosting, 23, 24, 25
Custard. See also Ice cream
crème brûlée, butterscotch, 120, 121
crème brûlée, coconut, 119
crème brûlée, lemon, 118
crème caramel, toasted pecan, 122,
123–124
mascarpone raspberry parfaits, 115–116,
117
pots de crème, cardamom, 106–107, 107
pots de crème, chocolate-espresso, 108
pots de crème, maple, 109
storing, 108, 109, 116, 118, 119, 120, 124

D

Demerara sugar, 4
topping, 49, 57, 95
Devilish dark chocolate madeleines, 134–135
Double ginger ice cream, 162, 163
Double lemon meringue tartlets, 64, 65–66
Dough, rolling out, 9
Doughnut holes, buttermilk, spiced, 60
Dried cherry, toasted pecan, and sour
cream pound cakes, 18–19
Dry measures, 188

E

Egg(s). See also Custard; Meringue(s)
functions in desserts, 2–3
raw, 115
soufflés, mocha, with cacao nib whipped
cream, 112, 113–114
wash, 95
whipping, 9
Egg whites, whipping, 9, 79, 131, 142
Electric mixer, 6–7
Equipment, 5
sources for, 185
Espresso
ganache filling, mocha, 143
ice cream, mocha, 164
mousse, mocha, 104–105, 105
pots de crème, chocolate-, 108
soufflés, mocha, with cacao nib whipped
cream, 112, 113–114
Espresso cups, mocha mousse in, 104–105,
105

F

Fancy Flours, 185
Fillings. See also Lemon curd
almond, 76
apple, 92
berry, 82, 89
blueberry, 94–95
chocolate and hazelnut, 68
ganache, 70, 130
ganache, mocha, 143
jam, 130
nectarine, 97
peach, 84
pear, 86, 99
pecan, 99–100
walnut, 98
walnut, caramelized, 72–73
whipped cream, 81
whipped cream, honey, 55, 56, 57
Filo (dough)
in strudel, caramelized pear and dried
cherry, 61–62
triangles, walnut, 140–141, 141
Fingerprint cookies, walnut, 128, 129–130
Fleur de sel, 174
Flour, 3
Food processor, 6
chopping and grinding nuts in, 9
Frosting, bittersweet chocolate ganache, 20,
22, 23, 24, 25, 27
Fudgy chocolate-hazelnut bites, 131

G

Galettes
nectarine and walnut, 96, 97–98
pear and pecan, 99–100
Ganache
filling, 70, 130
filling, mocha, 143

Ganache (continued)
 frosting, bittersweet chocolate, 20, 22, 23,
  24, 25, 27
 madeleine sandwich cookies, 133
 storing, 27, 143
 tartlets, cacao nib–walnut, 69–70, 71
Gianduia truffle cups, 172, 173
Ginger
 chips, crackly, 136–137, 137
 dough, 86, 88
 forms of, 3
 gingerbread bites, 31, 32, 33
 and pear cobblers, triple ginger, 86,
  87, 88
 whipped cream, 33
Ginger, candied, 3
 in gingerbread bites, 31, 32, 33
 in ginger chips, crackly, 136–137, 137
 ice cream, double ginger, 162, 163
Ginger, crystallized, 3
 ice cream, double ginger, 162, 163
 in pear cobblers, and triple ginger, 86,
  87, 88
 -pecan biscotti, 150, 151
 raspberry, and honey shortcakes, 55, 56, 57
Ginger People, The, 163
Gingerbread bites, 31, 32, 33
Glaze, apricot, 98
Green tea truffles, 178

H

Hazelnut(s)
 and bittersweet chocolate tartlets, 67–68
 and cacao nib madeleines, 132–133, 133
 -chocolate bites, fudgy, 131
 chopping and grinding, 9
 gianduia truffle cups, 172, 173
 paste, 173
 sandwich cookies, peek-a-boo, 138–139
 toasting, 68

Honey
 in caramel mousse, creamy, 102, 103
 in crème caramel, toasted pecan, 122,
  123–124
 raspberry, and ginger shortcakes, 55,
  56, 57
 syrup, 140–141
 in walnut filling, caramelized, 72–73
 whipped cream, 12–13, 57

I

Ice cream
 buttermilk and nutmeg, 165
 coconut, toasted, 161
 ginger, double, 162, 163
 mocha, 164
 peanut butter, 166
 sandwiches, chocolate and coffee ice
  cream, 167–168
Ice cream scoops, 6
Ingredients, 2–4
 sources for, 185

J

Jam filling, in fingerprint cookies, 130

K

King Arthur Flour, 185
Kosher salt, 3

L

Lemon
 cream, with lemon–cornmeal
  shortcakes, 53–54

cream and raspberry martinis, 110, 111
 crème brûlée, 118
 in lemon-lime-coconut squares, 146–147
 meringue tartlets, double lemon, 64,
  65–66
 pastry dough, 65
 pound cakes, triple lemon, 43–44
 shortcakes, -cornmeal, 53–54
 syrup, 44
 tea cakes, walnut, 38
Lemon curd, 78
 in almond, lemon, and berry tartlets,
  77–78
 in lemon cream, 53–54, 110
 -lime coconut, 146–147
 in meringue tartlets, double lemon,
  65, 66
 in shortcakes, lemon-cornmeal, 53–54
 storing, 66, 78
Lemon zest
 garnish, 13, 110, 118
 grating/chopping, 78
Lime-lemon-coconut squares, 146–147
Liquid measures, 187
Loaf cakes, apricot-orange, 34–35
Loaf pans, mini, 5
 loaf cakes, apricot-orange, 34–35
 pound cake, triple lemon, 43–44

M

Macadamia nut(s)
 chopping and grinding, 9
 muffins, –coconut, 59
 scones, and toasted coconut, 51–52, 52
Macaroon, almond and mocha sandwich
  cookies, 142–143
Madeleine(s)
 devilish dark chocolate, 134–135
 hazelnut and cacao nib, 132–133, 133

sandwich cookies, 133, 135
sandwich cookies, ganache, 133, 135
Madeleine pans, 5
Malted milk chocolate balls, 184
Malt powder, in toasty oatmeal cookies, 153
Man-in-the-moon cookies, 154
Maple walnut tea cakes, 39
Martini glasses, mini
   creamy caramel mousse in, 103
   mascarpone raspberry parfaits in,
      115–116, 117
   mocha mousse in, 104–105, 105
   raspberry and lemon cream in, 110, 111
Mascarpone raspberry parfaits, 115–116, 117
Measurement
   dry, 188
   equivalents, 186
   liquid, 187
   metric conversions, 188–189
Measuring cups and spoons, 6
Meringue(s)
   browning, 66
   lemon tartlets, double lemon, 64, 65, 66
   pavlovas with passion fruit sauce, 79,
      80, 81
   shells, 79
   storing, 81
Metric measuring system
   equivalents, 186
   liquid, 187
   U.S. conversions, 188–189
Microplane graters, 6
Microwave, melting chocolate in, 8, 73
Milk chocolate, dark, 2
Mini pistachio tea cakes, 40
Mini processor, 6
Mint–bittersweet chocolate truffle squares,
   176, 177
Mixed berry cobblers, 82–83
Mixed spice and walnut bundt cakes, 14,
   15–16

Mixers, 6–7
Mocha
   and almond macaroon sandwich
      cookies, 142–143
   ganache filling, 143
   ice cream, 164
   mousse, 104–105, 105
   soufflés with cacao nib whipped cream,
      112, 113–114
Mounds, white chocolate coconut, 179
Mousse
   caramel, creamy, 102, 103
   mocha, 104–105, 105
Muffin pans, mini, 5. See also Muffins
   almond-cornmeal cakes, 41–42, 42
   brownie bites, wicked, 28, 29–30
   cheesecakes, petite, 36–37
   cupcakes, bittersweet chocolate five-
      spice, 26–27
   cupcakes, cinnamon–sour cream, 20,
      21–22
   cupcakes, peanut butter, with bittersweet
      chocolate ganache frosting, 23,
      24, 25
   gingerbread bites, 31, 32, 33
   tea cakes, maple walnut, 39
   tea cakes, pistachio, mini, 40
   tea cakes, walnut and lemon, 38
   tuile cookie cups, 155–156
Muffins
   apricot, almond, and toasted coconut, 58
   coconut–macadamia nut, 59

Nectarine and walnut galettes, 96, 97–98
New York Cake Supplies, 185
Nutmeg
   and buttermilk ice cream, 165
   grated, 3

Nuts. See also specific nuts
   chopping and grinding, 9
   storing, 10
   substituting, 3
   toasting, 10

O

Oatmeal
   cookies, toasty, 153
   in crisp topping, 89
Offset spatula, 7
Orange-apricot loaf cakes, 34–35

P

Parchment paper pastry bag, 7, 8, 73
Parfaits, mascarpone-raspberry, 115–116, 117
Passion fruit sauce, pavlovas with, 79, 80, 81
Pastry(ies). See also Pastry dough; Tartlets
   filo triangles, walnut, 140–141, 141
   galettes, nectarine and walnut, 96, 97–98
   galettes, pear and pecan, 99–100
   strudel, caramelized pear and dried
      cherry, 61–62
   turnovers, blueberry, 94–95
Pastry bag, 7
   chocolate dot, 73
   ganache, 27, 130
   lemon cream, 110
   macaroons, 142
   madeleine batter, 132
   melted chocolate, drizzling, 8
   meringue rosettes, 66
   meringue shells, 79
   whipped cream, 33, 81, 103, 104, 107, 108,
      109
Pastry brushes, 7
Pastry Chef Central, Inc., 185

Pastry dough, 67–68, 75
  almond, 77
  cacao nib, 69
  coconut, 146
  cream cheese, 94, 95
  filo, in strudel, caramelized pear and
    dried cherry, 61–62
  filo triangles, walnut, 140–141, 141
  lemon, 65
  pecan, 99
  rolling out, 9
  storing, 66, 68, 70, 73, 76, 78, 98, 100, 147
  walnut, 72, 97
Pastry tips, sizes and shapes, 7
Pavlovas with passion fruit sauce, 79, 80, 81
Peachy cobblers, 84–85
Peanut brittle, sea salted, 182, 183
Peanut butter
  cupcakes with bittersweet chocolate
    ganache frosting, 23, 24, 25
  ice cream, 166
Pear
  cobblers, and triple ginger, 86, 87, 88
  filling, 86, 99
  galettes, and pecan, 99–100
  strudel, and dried cherry, caramelized,
    61–62
Pecan(s)
  biscotti, ginger, 150, 151
  -chocolate bundt cakes, spiced, 17
  crème caramel, toasted pecan, 122,
    123–124
  dried cherry, and sour cream pound
    cakes, toasted pecan, 18–19
  filling, 99–100
  pastry dough, 99
  and pear galettes, 99–100
  shortbread bites, toasted pecan, 144, 145
  in strudel, caramelized pear and dried
    cherry, 61–62
  toasting, 123, 145

Peek-a-boo hazelnut sandwich cookies,
  138–139
Peppermint candy–bittersweet chocolate
  bark, 180, 181
Perfect Purée of Napa Valley, 79
Petite cheesecakes with raspberry sauce,
  36–37
Pistachio paste, 40
Pistachio tea cakes, mini, 40
Pots de crème
  cardamom, 106–107, 107
  chocolate-espresso, 108
  maple, 109
Pound cakes
  dried cherry, toasted pecan, and sour
    cream, 18–19
  lemon, triple, 43-44
Prince (J.B.) Company, 185
Pudding(s)
  toasted coconut–chocolate, 125
  rice, 126

R

Raisin(s)
  in rice pudding, 126
  and walnut scones, 49–50
Ramekins
  cobblers, berry, mixed, 82–83
  cobblers, peachy, 84–85
  cobblers, pear and triple ginger, 86, 87,
    88
  crème brûlée, butterscotch, 120, 121
  crème brûlée, coconut, 119
  crème brûlée, lemon, 118
  crisps, apple-walnut, 92–93
  crisps, raspberry-blueberry, 89, 90, 91
  pots de crème, cardamom, 106–107, 107
  pots de crème, chocolate espresso, 108
  pots de crème, maple, 109

pudding, toasted coconut–chocolate, 125
pudding, rice, 126
sizes and shapes, 5
soufflés, mocha, with cacao nib whipped
  cream, 112, 113–114
Raspberry(ies)
  -blueberry crisps, 89, 90, 91
  in cobblers, mixed berry, 82–83
  and lemon cream martinis, 110, 111
  -mascarpone parfaits, 115–116, 117
  sauce, 115, 116
  sauce, petite cheesecakes with, 36–37
  shortcakes, ginger, honey, and, 55, 56, 57
  sorbet shots, 158, 159
  in tartlets, berry, almond, and lemon,
    77–78
Rice pudding, 126
Rolling dough, 9
Rolling pins, 7

S

Salt(ed)
  caramel–bittersweet chocolate truffles,
    174–175, 175
  sea, 3, 174
  sea, peanut brittle, 182, 183
  types of, 3
Sandwich cookies. See Cookies, sandwich
Sauce(s)
  caramel, 103
  passion fruit, pavlovas with, 79, 80, 81
  raspberry, 115, 116
  raspberry, petite cheesecakes with, 36–37
  strawberry, 41
Scones
  cornmeal–dried cherry, 46, 47–48
  macadamia nut and toasted coconut,
    51–52, 52
  raisin and walnut, 49–50

Sea salt, 3, 174
Sea salted peanut brittle, 182, 183
Shortbread bites, toasted pecan, 144, 145
Shortcakes
    lemon-cornmeal, 53–54
    raspberry, ginger, and honey, 55, 56, 57
Sorbet
    cantaloupe, 160
    raspberry, shots, 158, 159
Soufflés, mocha, with cacao nib whipped
        cream, 112, 113–114
Sour cream
    in bundt cakes, spiced chocolate-pecan, 17
    –cinnamon cupcakes, 20, 21–22
    in ganache frosting, bittersweet
        chocolate, 22
    pound cakes, dried cherry, toasted
        pecan, and, 18–19
    in tea cakes, maple walnut, 39
Spatulas, 7
Spice(s), spiced
    bundt cakes, mixed spice and walnut,
        14, 15–16
    bundt cakes, chocolate-pecan, 17
    cookies, man-in-the-moon, 154
    cupcakes, five-spice bittersweet
        chocolate, 26–27
    doughnut holes, buttermilk, 60
    substituting, 3
Spice House, The, 185
Squares
    lemon-lime-coconut, 146–147
    truffle, bittersweet chocolate–mint, 176,
        177
Storage
    almond-cornmeal cakes, 42
    biscotti, 151, 152
    bundt cakes, 13, 16, 17, 19
    candies, 170, 179, 180, 183, 184
    cheesecakes, 37
    chocolate, 8

cobbler dough, 85, 88
cobblers, 83, 85, 88
cookie dough, 149, 153, 168
cookies, 130, 131, 137, 139, 143, 148, 153,
    154, 156
crisps, 91, 93
cupcakes, 22, 25, 27
custards, 108, 109, 116, 118, 119, 120, 124
doughnut holes, 60
filo triangles, 141
galettes, 98, 100
ganache, 27, 143
gingerbread bites, 33
ice cream, 161, 163, 164, 165, 166, 168
lemon curd, 66, 78
loaf cakes, 35
madeleines, 133, 135
meringues, 81
mousse, 105
muffins, 58, 59
nuts, 10
pastry dough, 66, 68, 70, 73, 76, 78, 98,
    100, 147
pavlovas, 81
pound cakes, 44
puddings, 125
scones, 48, 50, 52
shortbread/shortbread dough, 145
shortcakes, 54, 57
sorbet, 158
strudel, 62
tartlets, 68, 70, 73, 76, 78
tartlet shells, 66, 70, 78
tea cakes, 38, 39, 40
truffles, 173, 175, 177, 178
turnovers, 95
Strawberry sauce, 41
Strudel, caramelized pear and dried cherry,
    61–62

Sugar
    caramelized, toppings, 118, 119, 120
    Demerara/turbinado garnish, 49, 57, 95
    types of, 4
Sugar thermometer, 5–6
Superfine sugar, 4
Surfas, 185
Sur La Table, 185
Sweet Celebrations, 185
Syrup
    honey, 140–141
    lemon, 44

T

Tartlet pans, fluted, 5. See also Tartlets
Tartlets. See also Galettes
    almond, lemon, and berry, 77–78
    almond, Venetian, 74, 75–76
    bittersweet chocolate and hazelnut,
        67–68
    cacao nib–walnut ganache, 69–70, 71
    lemon meringue, double lemon, 64,
        65–66
    storing, 68, 70, 73, 76, 78
    walnut, caramelized, 72–73
Tartlet shells
    baked, with filling, 68, 73, 76
    baked, without filling, 66, 69–70, 77–78
    pastry dough, 67–68
    pastry dough, lemon, 65
    storing, 66, 70, 78
Tea, in green tea truffles, 178
Tea cakes
    maple walnut, 39
    pistachio, mini, 40
    walnut and lemon, 38
Techniques, 8–9
Thermometer, candy (sugar), 5–6
Timers, 7

Toasted coconut–chocolate pudding, 125
Toasted coconut ice cream, 161
Toasted pecan crème caramel, 122, 123–124
Toasted pecan shortbread bites, 144, 145
Toasty oatmeal cookies, 153
Toffee, almond buttercrunch, 170, 171
Toppings
    biscuit dough, 84–85
    for crisps, 89, 92
    frosting, bittersweet chocolate ganache,
        20, 22, 23, 24, 25, 27
    ginger dough, 86, 88
    lemon zest, 13, 110, 118
    sugar, 49, 57, 95
    sugar, caramelized, 118, 119, 120
    whipped cream, 33, 83, 85, 91, 92–93, 103,
        104, 109, 124, 125, 126
Triple lemon pound cakes, 43–44
Truffle(s)
    bittersweet chocolate–mint squares,
        176, 177
    caramel, salted, –bittersweet chocolate,
        174–175, 175
    cups, gianduia, 172, 173
    green tea, 178
Tuile cookie cups, 155–156
    creamy caramel mousse in, 102, 103

Turbinado sugar, 4
    topping, 49, 95
Turnovers, blueberry, 94–95

U

Unsweetened chocolate, 2
U.S. measuring system. *See* Measurement

V

Vanilla extract, 3
Vanilla paste, 3
Venetian almond tartlets, 74, 75–76
Verrine, 115

W

Walnut(s)
    -apple crisps, 92–93
    in brownie bites, wicked, 28, 29–30
    bundt cakes, mixed spice and, 14, 15–16
    in butter cookies, cardamom, 148–149,
        149

    –cacao nib ganache tartlets, 69–70, 71
    filling, 98
    filo triangles, 140–141, 141
    fingerprint cookies, 128, 129–130
    grinding, 129, 140
    and lemon tea cakes, 38
    in loaf cakes, apricot-orange, 34–35
    maple tea cakes, 39
    and nectarine galettes, 96, 97–98
    in oatmeal cookies, toasty, 153
    pastry dough, 72, 97
    scones, raisin and, 49–50
    tartlets, caramelized, 72–73
    toasting, 92
Whipped cream
    cacao nib, 112, 113
    filling, 81
    filling, honey, 12-13, 57
    garnish, 33, 83, 85, 91, 92–93, 103, 104, 109,
        124, 125, 126
    ginger, 33
    storing, 9
White chocolate, 2
    –coconut mounds, 179
Wicked brownie bites, 28, 29–30
Williams-Sonoma, 185

9/09   641.86
BLOOM